THE TOMMIES' MANUAL
1916

THE TOMMIES'
MANUAL

ABOUT THE EDITOR

Hannah Holman is the author of the Amberley bestseller *Titanic Voices* ('Heartstopping accounts' *Juliet Gardiner, BBC History Magazine*) and editor of *Life as a Battle of Britain Spitfire Pilot* by Pilot Officer Arthur Donahue ('Thrusts the reader straight into the cockpit ... powerful and emotive' *All About History*). She is currently editing *The Trench Cook Book 1917: Western Front Recipes from Bully Beef Pie to Trench Tea*, also for Amberley. She studied English Literature at the University of Birmingham and works for a City firm managing public sector assets. Married with four children, she lives in Bath.

THE TOMMIES' MANUAL

1916

Edited by Hannah Holman

AMBERLEY

LIST OF PRELIMINARY ILLUSTRATIONS:

First published 2016

Amberley Publishing
The Hill, Stroud
Gloucestershire, GL5 4EP

www.amberley-books.com

British Library Cataloguing in Publication Data.
A catalogue record for this book is available from the British Library.

ISBN 978-1-4456-3822-5 (paperback)
ISBN 978-1-4456-3837-9 (ebook)

Typesetting and Origination by Amberley Publishing.
Printed in Great Britain.

CONTENTS

Fig. 10.—ATTACKING ROUND A LEFT TRAVERSE. (Back view.)

NOTES

FOR

INFANTRY OFFICERS

ON

TRENCH WARFARE.

Compiled by the General Staff.

WAR OFFICE,
March, 1916.

LONDON:
PRINTED FOR HIS MAJESTY'S STATIONERY OFFICE,
By HARRISON AND SONS, ST. MARTIN'S LANE,
PRINTERS IN ORDINARY TO HIS MAJESTY.

1. Front cover of War Office manual *Notes for Infantry Officers on Trench Warfare* printed by the Army Printing and Stationary Services and published in March 1916, see part 1. Courtesy of Jonathan Reeve b607p1.

⊙THE⊙

WIPERS TIMES.

OR

SALIENT NEWS.

No 1. Vol. I'.   Saturday, 12th February, 1916.   PRICE 20 FRANCS

Editorial.

Having managed to pick up a printing outfit (slightly soiled) at a reasonable price, we have decided to produce a paper. There is much that we would like to say in it, but the shadow of censorship enveloping us causes us to refer to the war, which we hear is taking place in Europe, in a cautious manner. We must apologise to our subscribers for the delay in going to press. This has been due to the fact that we have had many unwelcome visitors near our printing works during the last few days, also to the difficulty of obtaining an overdraft at the local bank. Any little short-comings in production must be excused on the grounds of inexperience and the fact that pieces of metal of various sizes had punctured our press. We hope to publish the "Times" weekly, but should our effort come to an untimely end by any adverse criticism or attentions by our local rival, Messrs. Hun and Co., we shall consider it an unfriendly act, and take steps accordingly. We take this opportunity of stating that we accept no responsibility for the statements in our advertisements. In conclusion we must thank those outside our salaried staff who have contributed to this, our first issue, and offer our condolences to those who have paid 20 francs for a copy. The latter will at least have the comfort of knowing that proceeds have gone to a worthy cause.

The EDITOR.

The Editor takes no responsibility for the views expressed, or the thirst for information on the part of our subscribers.

2. Editorial of the first issue of the *Wipers Times*, began in January 1916 by Captain Roberts after he discovered the remains of a shell-shattered old printing works just off the main square in Ypres, Belgium. A fellow member of his regiment, who was a printer in civilian life, repaired the machine, and brought a sample of his work to Roberts who then started publishing the *Wipers Times* as his own divisional magazine. The title was a jokey Anglicized pronunciation of Ypres.

The first edition of twelve pages was published on Saturday 12 February, with a print run of 100 copies, and priced at 20 francs. It was an immediate success with the troops. Courtesy of Jonathan Reeve b60612feb16.

INTRODUCTION

The First World War is commonly viewed as a futile war, characterised by a criminal waste of young men's lives. The 'lions' were sent over the top by 'donkeys', the generals. This impression of events assumes that the generals sent their soldiers to their deaths with barely a thought, treating men as mere cannon fodder. It is true that Britain's military leaders believed the war would be one of attrition of men and

3. Front cover of *Guide for the 303in Vickers machine Gun: Its Mechanism & Drill with Questions & Answers* published in June 1915 by commercial publisher Gale & Polden Ltd. Courtesy of Jonathan Reeve b613pcvr.

machines, but it is wrong to believe that tactics and strategy were not at the very heart of their orders, however disastrous or murderous the outcome.

This book provides a sampler of some of the hundreds of military manuals issued to British soldiers which, if nothing else, proves that every conceivable aspect of trench warfare was studied and codified, with best practise disseminated as widely as possible. From how to plan a scouting trip across no-man's-land, build latrines, bury the dead, care for the standard issue Lee-Enfield rifle or fire the mighty 18-pounder artillery piece, the Army Printing and Stationary Services published a manual on it.

The manuals were a mix of 'how to' handbooks to pieces of military kit, such as *Handbook of the 18-PR QF Gun - Land Service* (the 18-pounder field gun), training manuals on how to give specific instruction and assessment such as part 3's *Infantry Machine-Gun Company Training*, and finally doctrinal manuals that laid down new military thinking such as part 7's *Training of Platoons for Offensive Action*.

The Army Printing and Stationary Services

The Army Printing and Stationary Services (AP&SS) originated in July 1915 when the British Expeditionary Force established a Base Stationary Unit at Le Havre. It was commanded by Captain S. G. Partridge. Military manuals had originally been printed in London for the War Office Central Distribution Section (early

4. The British 18-pounder artillery gun in its pit at the remains of Zonnebeke, Belgium, October 1917. This was the single most widely deployed gun on the Western Front by the British. All the other types of artillery pieces together just about equalled the number of 18-pounders used. Courtesy of Jonathan Reeve B119pic23.

manuals bare the code letters CDS). Partridge's department began by merely distributing and sometimes reprinting these manuals but it wasn't long before they were originating their own manuals and were thus accorded their own coding, 'SS'. The majority of manuals bore the instructions 'For official use only' or 'Not to be carried into action or front-line trenches'.

Later in the war the AP&SS's role was extended to printing orders, telephone directories, field service postcards and translations of captured German documents. Captain Partridge was a skilled bureaucrat who had spent eight years in the War Office Secretariat and remained in post at the AP&SS throughout the war, making him the British Army's publisher in chief.

Commercial Book Publishers

The First World War offered to many commercial firms the possibility of profit. Book publishers were no exception. Hundreds of titles were issued aimed at soldiers or their families who would often post them out to the front. Almost every British

5. Trench in 'Sausage Valley', near Contalmaison on the Somme, 30 June 1916. Signallers keep a sharp look out on the eve of the 'big push'. Courtesy of Jonathan Reeve 3d47.

household knew someone close to them fighting on one of the battlefronts. Aldershot-based company Gale & Polden were the market leader, with titles as diverse as *Tips for the Front: What to DO and What to AVOID on Active Service*, *Notes on First Aid for NCOs and Men* and *Handbook for the Maxim Gun*.

Read or Ignored?

It is, however, unknown as to how much notice was paid to the flood of manuals that flowed from AP&SS's printing presses 'A' based at Boulogne, 'B' at Abbeville and 'C' at Le Havre, or for that matter the commercial presses based back in 'Blightly'. Clearly the instructional handbooks on how to operate the machinery of war needed to be referred to from time to time, and dutiful officers needed to be on top of the latest developments in order to organise their troops, but the common soldier probably spent more time reading the unofficial, satirical news sheet *The Wipers Times* ...

Illustrations from the War Office Manuals

Many, although not all, of the manuals produced were illustrated with line art drawings and black and white photographs. The following gives some idea of the range and type of illustration deployed – some are highly technical whereas others are mini sketches, with the British 'Tommy' appearing prominently.

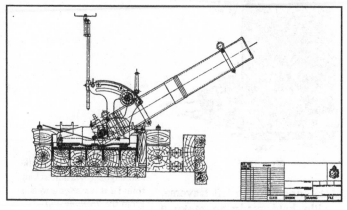

6. A trench mortar, from the *Handbook of the 9.45-Inch Trench Mortar Material with Instructions for its Care and Use*, front elevation. Courtesy of Jonathan Reeve b608plate14.

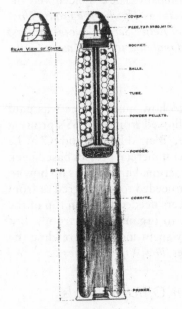

CARTRIDGE, Q.F. 18 Pᴿ SHRAPNEL, MARK I.
SCALE - ½.

REAR VIEW OF COVER.

COVER.
FUZE, T&P. Nº80, Mᴷ IV.
SOCKET.
BALLS.
TUBE.
POWDER PELLETS.
POWDER.
CORDITE.
PRIMER.

7. One of the most commonly fired British artillery shells of the First World War, the shrapnel Mark I for the 18-pounder. From the *Handbook of the 18-PR QF Gun - Land Service*. Courtesy of Jonathan Reeve b609plate16.

Fig. 12.

Attacking round a left traverse, rifle held ready to make a downward point with the bayonet.

8. Method of using the rifle and bayonet when attacking round a traverse of a trench. From the *Training and Employment of Bombers*, September 1916. Courtesy of Jonathan Reeve b610p48.

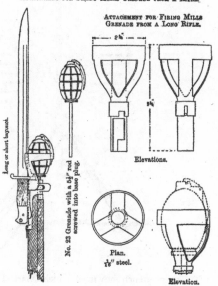

ATTACHMENT FOR·FIRING MILLS GRENADE FROM A LONG RIFLE.

Long or short bayonet.

No. 23 Grenade with a 6⅜" rod screwed into base plug.

Elevations.

Plan.
1/16" steel.

Elevation.

9. Attachment for firing Mills Grenade from a rifle. From the *Training and Employment of Bombers*, September 1916. Courtesy of Jonathan Reeve b610p93.

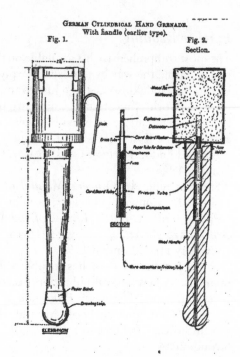

GERMAN CYLINDRICAL HAND GRENADE.
With handle (earlier type).

Fig. 1.

Fig. 2.
Section.

SECTION

ELEVATION

10. The German cylindrical hand grenade. From the *Training and Employment of Bombers*, September 1916. Courtesy of Jonathan Reeve b610p98.

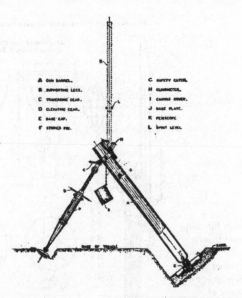

11. A Stokes trench howitzer 3-inch Mark I. From the *Stokes Trench Howitzer 3-inch Mark I*, 1917. Courtesy of Jonathan Reeve b612p5.

Further Reading

The most comprehensive list available on the military manuals issued during the war by the British Army has been compiled by Peter E. Hodgkinson, Simon Justice and Tony Ball at Centre for First World War Studies, University of Birmingham, and the document can be accessed by typing into your preferred search engine 'List-of-SS-Pamphlets.doc'

Edward Budd, *A Printer Goes To War*, H. Baker Publishers, London 1975

Stephen Bull, *An Officer's Manual of the Western Front 1914-1918*, Conway Publishers, London 2008

Paddy Griffith, *Battle Tactics of the Western Front: The British Army's Art of Attack, 1916-18*, (Chapter 10), Yale University Press, London 1994

Naval & Military Press has republished over 40 individual manuals, see www.naval-military-press.com.

Peter T. Scott, *The Army Printing and Stationary Services 1914-1918*, Antiquarian Books Monthly Review, March 1979

Neil Storey, *The Tommy's Handbook*, The History Press, Stroud, 2014

1

NOTES FOR INFANTRY OFFICERS ON TRENCH WARFARE

This was very much the 'bible' for the infantry officer on the Western Front, first issued in March 1916, and a critically important manual. It covers a wide range of subjects, many of which became the subject of entire manuals all of their own later in the war. This book therefore met a need of giving the basic essentials of trench warfare. From care of a soldier's feet, to barbed wire entanglement plans, through the differences between the Lewis and Vickers machine guns and how to build a trench system, *Notes for Infantry Officers* had it covered.

NOTES FOR INFANTRY OFFICERS ON TRENCH WARFARE.

CHAPTER I.

SPECIAL CHARACTERISTICS OF TRENCH WARFARE.

1. *Trench Fighting only a Phase of Warfare.*

The importance assumed by trench warfare and the progress made in the application of field fortification and in the science of the attack and defence of elaborate systems of trenches, have rendered necessary special instruction in the details of trench construction and trench fighting. It must, nevertheless, be clearly understood that trench fighting is only a phase of operations, and that instruction in this subject, essential as it is, is only one branch of the training of troops. To gain a decisive success the enemy must be driven out of his defences and his armies crushed in the open.

The aim of trench fighting is, therefore, to create a favourable situation for field operations, which the troops must be capable of turning to account.

2. *Considerations affecting Design of Defences.*

1. Three facts in particular give to modern trench fighting under present conditions most of its special characteristics. These are—

    (a) The continual proximity of the opposing forces ;
    (b) The length of time for which they have generally occupied the same ground ;
    (c) The fact that neither side has a flank so long as it remains on the defensive, so that every attack must be frontal.

2. As a result of the length of time the opposing forces have been in close proximity on practically the same ground, the original trenches dug at the end of a period of manœuvre operations have grown into a complicated system of entrenchments. The design and organization of these have been influenced by the nature of

the artillery, up to calibres far heavier than could be utilised in ordinary field operations, which the stationary nature of the fighting has made it possible to bring up. Arrangements have been made by a carefully thought out system of inter-communication for the maximum co-operation between artillery and infantry, both in attack and defence, and artillery has had time to register on all targets within range. Thus either side has it in its power to concentrate heavy fire at very short notice upon any selected target, and to maintain that fire for a length of time which difficulties of ammunition supply would put out of the question in manœuvre operations. Consequently, the rapidity with which artillery can form a barrage to meet attack makes it necessary that the moment of the assault should come as a surprise, and the trenches from which an attack is to be made should therefore be within close assaulting distance of the opposing front line.

3. A system of trenches must therefore be designed which facilitates the preparation and launching of an unexpected assault, and at the same time is adapted to meet a sudden attack by the enemy. The organization of a trench system to facilitate attack is an important point, which is frequently neglected. If additional trenches have to be hastily made when an attack is intended, the intention to attack will be obvious to the enemy by aerial reconnaissance, and surprise will be out of the question.

4. Modern field fortifications owe their elaborate form to the means employed in attack and defence respectively. A general idea of what those means are is therefore necessary.

The aim of the first stages of attack is to obtain a footing in the enemy's defences and to consolidate and extend the gain thus made. Penetration is effected by means of an infantry assault, which, as has been said, must unavoidably be frontal and depends for success on a certain measure of surprise.

The infantry attack may be assisted by any or all of the following methods :—

(a) The previous destruction, by bombardment or explosion of mines or a combination of both, of the enemy's material defences, including obstacles ;

(b) The shaking of the moral and destruction of the *personnel* of the defending force by bombardment or by the employment of one of the new agents of war, such as asphyxiating gas or jets of liquid fire, prior to assault ;

(c) Keeping down hostile fire over the area to be crossed by the attacking infantry long enough to enable the assaulting troops to reach the cover of the enemy's defences ;

(d) The isolation, by artillery barrages, of the area to be assaulted, so as to prevent the arrival of reinforcements ;

(e) The dispersal or destruction of troops collecting for counter-attack.

5. To meet these measures the defence employs the following means :—

(a) Constant close observation, with a view to the detection of any signs of impending attack ;*

(b) Concentration of fire on any detected assembly which might be the prelude to assault ;

(c) Concentration of fire of artillery, machine guns, and rifles, from as wide a front as possible, over any part of the zone lying between the two lines, so as to prevent the penetration of the defence ;

(d) Obstacles to delay the assaulting troops as long as possible under this fire ;

(e) Barrages of fire to prevent the reinforcement of, or the sending up of materials, ammunition, or supplies to, any body of troops that has succeeded in penetrating the defence ;

(f) Disposition of works so as to localise and confine the effect of penetration at any point ;†

(g) Destruction by artillery fire of any enemy troops that have penetrated ;

(h) Immediate counter-attack, to drive out the attackers before they can have recovered from the confusion of the assault and have established themselves securely in the captured area.

3. *Nature of Field Defences.*

A consideration of the above shows that there are certain features which are essential in a system of trenches. They must be strong, to resist heavy bombardment ; they must be sited and designed to favour, by the utilization of oblique and enfilade fire of rifles and, above all, of machine guns, the development of the maximum volume of fire over any part of their front ; they must be protected by a strong and well hidden wire entanglement, in order to retain attacking infantry under this fire ; they must provide protection for the garrison against weather and against the effect of artillery fire. Fire and shelter trenches must be numerous in order to accommodate the additional troops to be placed in them previous to an attack on the enemy's line, and also, in the defence, to induce dispersion of hostile artillery fire, to permit the temporary withdrawal of the garrison from a heavily shelled zone, and to accommodate troops for local counter-attack in close proximity to the points where they may be required. Communications must be ample, to admit of the rapid re-occupation of temporarily evacuated trenches, to minimise the interference of hostile fire with reinforcement and supply, and to facilitate local counter-attack. Close observation of the enemy must be provided for by listening posts in advance of the front line and by observing stations in or behind it. Finally, the system of trenches must admit of immediate

---

* *E.g.,* instalment of gas apparatus, advance of saps, passages cut in enemy's wire to facilitate egress.

† See Sections 14, 15.

readjustment of the front, so that the effect of penetration at any point may be localised and need not weaken the hold of the defence on adjacent trenches.

4. *The Offensive Spirit in Trench Warfare.*

The attack on such a system of defences as has been described demands in all ranks dash and gallantry of a very high order, and in the subordinate leader, down to the lowest grades, a quick perception, rapid decision, and intelligent initiative. It is more than ever the case that success depends upon qualities of leadership in subordinate commanders, upon rapid appreciation and readiness to accept responsibility on the part of the man on the spot. Much can be done in peace training to foster these qualities and to impress on even the most subordinate leaders the necessity for acting, in cases of urgency, on their own responsibility. At the same time, the state of comparative inactivity, which is the normal condition of life in the trenches, is very unfavourable to the development of these qualities in officers and men. There is an insidious tendency to lapse into a passive and lethargic attitude, against which officers of all ranks have to be on their guard, and the fostering of the offensive spirit, under such unfavourable conditions, calls for incessant attention. Minor local enterprises and constant occupation during the tour of duty in the trenches furnish the best means of maintaining the efficiency of the troops. The repair, maintenance, and improvement of the trenches furnish ample work to afford employment to the troops, who must be made to understand that this work reacts in their own favour in the shape of increased security and comfort and conditions more favourable to health. Constant activity in harassing the enemy may lead to reprisals at first, and for this reason is sometimes neglected, but, if persevered in, it always results in an ultimate mastery, it gives the troops a healthy interest and wholesome topics of conversation, and it achieves the double purpose of raising the moral of our own troops whilst lowering that of the enemy's. Every effort should be made to obtain the mastery over the enemy's snipers.

5. *Training in Night-work.*

The proximity of the opposing lines, the progress of aerial reconnaissance, and the close and continuous watch which either side maintains over the other, have increased the importance of night-work. Many of the daily operations incidental to trench warfare can only be carried out under cover of darkness. The construction of new trenches in sight of the enemy, and much of their maintenance and repair, the construction, repair, and improvement of obstacles, and in many cases the bringing up of materials and stores and the relief of the garrison, cannot be carried out by daylight. The assembly of troops and many of the final stages of preparation for an attack, as, for instance, the removal of our own obstacles, can only be kept from the enemy's knowledge by carrying them out at night. The close reconnaissance of the enemy's front line and his obstacles and of the ground to be crossed by an assault is the work of night patrols, and much of the identification of the troops opposed to us—a very important duty—can only be effected by small enterprises carried out by night against the enemy's patrols or listening posts, or sometimes against a small section of his trenches. Training in all these branches of night-work is an important part of the instruction of troops before leaving for the front.

6. *Discipline.*

The hardships, discomfort, and dangers of life in the trenches make great demands upon the endurance of the troops ; the frontal attack on an enemy in a position strengthened and defended by every device that ingenuity and forethought can conceive calls for exceptional resolution and determination, and the defence of trenches against an attack, preluded generally by a protracted and severe bombardment, and often by the employment of some entirely new and unforeseen agency, requires the utmost steadfastness and devotion. No infantry will possess those qualities to the requisite degree that has not a very high standard of discipline. The first and greatest aim of all training should therefore be the establishment of the strictest discipline. To attain this there is no other method than constant and precise drill, strict enforcement of march discipline, insistence on a rigid exactness in the performance of even the dullest details of camp and barrack routine, and unceasing attention to apparently trifling detail in time of training. Without such previous preparation the silent and thorough execution of work and performance of duties, in darkness and in danger, in the presence of the enemy, and often without direct supervision of a superior, which distinguish good from bad troops and spell success, are impossible of attainment.

7. *Training of Specialists.*

The present type of warfare in the trenches has involved the training of a proportion of men in infantry units in duties of a special nature, *e.g.*, grenade-throwing, pioneer work, sniping, &c.

A word of warning is necessary as regards the training of these men. They must be made to realise that their training in these special duties is *in addition to* their ordinary training as infantry soldiers and must not be allowed to interfere with their performance of the ordinary duties of infantry soldiers, except when they are required for the special duties in which they have been trained.

CHAPTER II.

8. *Deliberate Siting of Trenches.*

1. The problem of selecting the position of fire trenches varies according to the circumstances under which the choice has to be made and the work carried out. The siting and construction of a trench line in the presence of the enemy and under fire is influenced by factors which are absent in the deliberate and undisturbed choice such as can be made when preparing a rear line. It is important to recognise that the two problems are distinct, and that their solution calls for different methods.

2. The first step in the case of a line which is to be constructed free from interference by the enemy, and under circumstances which make time a factor of minor importance, is a deliberate reconnaissance of the ground. This reconnaissance will usually consist of two stages. The first deals with the problem on broad lines, compares the merits of alternative general solutions, determines the general line to be taken up, and lays down certain points or localities as having special importance and calling for special treatment. Following on this, a second, more detailed, reconnaisance is made, in which are considered the form of the works to be constructed for the defence of the tactical features and localities laid down in the general scheme, and the method of treating the intervals between these strong points or localities. As a result of this detailed reconnaissance, large scale plans are produced showing the exact siting and constructional detail of the essential works. The decision as to the general line to be taken up is the business of the General Staff of the formation (division, corps or army) concerned. The Chief Engineer Officer will advise as to the constructional details of the line selected. In both stages of the reconnaissance due weight should be given to the questions of facilities for attack, and of securing good observation for ourselves and denying it to the enemy, cohesion in defence by mutual support of adjoining works, drainage and concealment ; the final decision arrived at is a balance between the often conflicting requirements of these different considerations. The order of importance of the works is another point decided in the two stages of the reconnaissance. Not until the reconnaissance has been completed should any work be begun, and, although the close study of the ground during the execution of the works will probably suggest improvements in detail—in fact, a good deal of the detail should be left to be elaborated at this stage—it will seldom be necessary or advisable to alter any of the essential

features, determined by the reconnaissance, during the construction of the defences.

3. Unless the ground is almost absolutely flat, the most important question in siting trenches is whether to occupy the tops of the hills, establishing the front line trenches on either the crest or the forward slope, or to withdraw the main front line to the reverse slope, taking up what is known as the " back " or " retired " position. The chief argument advanced in favour of this latter position is that it affords greater security against hostile artillery fire. Now it must be borne in mind that the question of protection from artillery fire, so far as it is affected by siting, is almost entirely one of security from observation. Any target can be heavily and accurately engaged if fire on it can be effectively observed from a point in the occupation of the force which is carrying out the bombardment. The position of the observer relative to the gun is immaterial, that of the target to the gun position almost equally so. If either side is in occupation of the hill-tops, and can establish an artillery officer with a telescope and a telephone on the high ground, its facilities for observation of fire are greater than those of its opponent, situated lower down the slopes. That being the case, the " back position " loses the advantage of protection from artillery fire claimed for it, unless we can deny to the enemy's observers the use of the high ground. Experience has shown that, except in the case of isolated features of small extent, when a concentration of fire may effect the desired purpose, the only effective way to deny ground to the enemy is to occupy it oneself.

Front line trenches on the crest or forward slope are certainly exposed to view and therefore to bombardment, though this is not so much the case as it would be if the enemy were looking down on them, and the disadvantage can be diminished by adequate provision of material protection for the garrison. On the other hand, the occupation of the high ground gives a feeling of superiority which reacts favourably on the moral of the troops. Only those who have experienced it can appreciate the depressing effect produced by the feeling of discomfort and inferiority of position under which troops suffer, who have to occupy for some time trenches looked down upon by those of the enemy. The forward position has the further advantage, if the front line is not dug too far down the forward slope, that supporting trenches. communications, and the works in which a large proportion of the garrison live, enjoy a comparative immunity from observation. In offensive action the forward position offers greater facilities for observation, on which the effectiveness of the previous preparation by bombardment largely depends, and for the assembly of troops for the assault, close to the front line and unobserved.

4. Special conditions may justify the deliberate choice of the " retired " position. If it is adopted, arrangements must be made to deny the enemy access to the crest of the hill, and to secure it for ourselves. The front trench line must not be too far below

the crest line—50 to 100 yards will usually be far enough and is a sufficient field of fire if machine guns are well sited—and there must be an ample number of saps forward to the top to allow of continuous observation of the forward slope. With these precautions, and readiness to deliver an immediate and vigorous counter-attack on the enemy if he appears on the crest, the back position may sometimes be taken up when conditions impose a temporarily defensive attitude and the local superiority in artillery is with the enemy. But if the two lines remain facing one another on the same ground for a protracted period it will be impossible to prevent the enemy indefinitely from establishing himself on the crest unless it is included in our line.

5. In deciding on both the general and the detailed trace of the line a common tendency, which is to be avoided, is towards making it too straight. An irregular line, with frequent salients and re-entrants, gives greater facilities for concentration of fire over any desired area and for the most effective employment of machine guns. It will expose short lengths of trench to enfilade fire, but suitable construction will minimise the effect of this. In any case the effect is generally reciprocal ; from a salient in our line some part of the enemy's line pushed forward into the adjoining re-entrant will be exposed to our enfilade fire. These remarks apply with almost equal force to a large salient, constructed to include an important tactical point, and to minor irregularities in the trace of trenches. The latter should be made as a matter of invariable principle. The former should be used boldly where circumstances demand them. The determining considerations in their case are two :—

    (a) Whether the possession of the point in question by us would facilitate future offensive action without unduly weakening our line ;

    (b) Whether its possession by the enemy would seriously threaten the security of our trenches.

9. *Siting of Trenches in the Presence of the Enemy.*

1. The presence of the enemy will frequently make it impossible to select the position of fire trenches entirely on the merits of the ground. Their site will often be decided by the chance and accident of close fighting, and their general position will coincide roughly with the high-water mark reached for the moment by the attack. Troops who are unable to make any further advance will either occupy a hostile trench which has been captured in the course of the attack or start at once to procure for themselves what cover they can with the tools at their disposal, generally, for the most part, only the entrenching tool. Much can be done by officers at this stage in the way of small adjustments of position and of the distribution of their men with a view to the future development of the hasty cover constructed into the best line that circumstances will admit. Unless this is done, much of the work

may be found afterwards to be useless, valuable time and effort will have been wasted, and troops may either have to try and hold an unfavourable position or be exposed again in the construction of a fresh one. Serious work will generally be impossible before dusk, unless arrangements can be made for a heavy covering fire, and after dusk it is difficult to avoid mistakes in the choice and siting of a line. Every officer, then, who finds his command unable to make further progress, should take advantage of the daylight to study the ground as far as circumstances permit, and should make up his mind exactly what line he will take up if forced to dig himself in.

2. The main problem that arises in this case is whether any of the ground won should be abandoned in order to secure a more suitable line of defence. Generally, if the check is merely temporary and it is intended to resume the advance at the earliest opportunity, all ground gained should be held except for very minor adjustments, unless some portion is clearly untenable against counter-attack; if, however, strategical or tactical considerations require a temporary abandonment of the forward movement and the construction of a defensive line to be held for some time, the decision will be governed to a great extent by the same considerations as already discussed in taking up a line deliberately, and it may be advisable to give up ground on some parts of the front.

3. The satisfactory siting of a trench line constructed in these circumstances will largely depend on the power possessed by the officers on the spot to recognise during the various stages of a battle the minor features of real tactical importance. The ability to recognise these is only acquired by previous training, and is a quality which every officer must study to possess.

10. Concealment.

The development of aerial reconnaissance has made concealment of a *position* impossible, but isolated works and gun emplacements can be hidden, and trenches in a wood may remain undetected if clearing is not overdone. But aerial observers can not only invariably locate trenches in open country but can obtain photographs showing every trench and every traverse. Good aeroplane photographs show even the wire entanglements. This is not to be interpreted as meaning that no attention need be paid to the question of concealment. Anything that tends to make a trench less conspicuous and increases the difficulty of observing fire on it for an observer on the ground is of value. If natural cover is turned to account, the existence of a trench at a particular spot may not be detected at once and it may escape the attentions of the enemy's artillery at the stage when it is most vulnerable. In siting trenches with a view to concealment the hiding of the wire entanglements and supervision and communication trenches must not be overlooked. Tracks and much trampled ground show up

24

very clearly from the air, and may draw attention to an otherwise well hidden work. Work done to buildings themselves is easily concealed from aerial reconnaissance, but the existence of trenches round or leading into a building gives a clear indication of its occupation.

The fact that trenches cannot be concealed from aerial observation makes it most important that every system of trenches should be so designed that an attack can be made from them without the necessity of constructing fresh trenches at the last moment, which would give away the fact that an attack was intended. Airmen cannot see whether a trench is occupied or not without coming down dangerously low.

11. *Buildings.*

It will frequently happen that substantial buildings are found close to the selected line of defence. The question then arises whether to occupy them or to demolish them. The decision will depend generally upon two points, whether they have cellars which can be improved into good cover, and whether it is possible to demolish them. Buildings in or near the front line invariably draw a lot of fire from artillery, and unless good cover can be contructed in connection with them are nothing but shell traps. Solid blocks of buildings, on the other hand, with cellars which can be improved to give good cover against bombardment have on many occasions proved very difficult to take. Buildings of this nature had better be included in the line if possible, as they can be converted into strong points, and if left to be occupied by the enemy might prove both a thorn in the flesh to the defence and an obstacle to attack. A building which has no cellars may be left out of the line if it can be effectively demolished so as to afford no cover to the enemy. Effective demolition is a technical job which requires the co-operation of the R.E. and demands a certain amount of time. Where it is neither possible to carry out an effective demolition, nor desirable to distort the line so as to include a building or a group of buildings, these may sometimes be held as an advanced post to prevent their occupation by the enemy. In this case they must be connected up with the main line by communication trenches and special measures to deal at the shortest possible notice with a sudden enterprise must be arranged.

12. *Woods.*

1. A position in a wood affords a certain amount of concealment from observation. It is easy to conceal the wire entanglement so that accurate artillery fire cannot be brought to bear on it. If the position of the line taken up is such that the enemy can establish himself inside the wood he will enjoy similar advantages. Therefore, where there is freedom of choice, the best line to take up is one which secures cover from observation for ourselves, whilst denying the edge of the wood to the enemy. The exact distance

inside the wood of this position cannot be definitely laid down, but experience has shown that 30 to 50 yards from the front edge usually provides ample concealment from observation. Under no circumstances should the front edge itself be occupied, as hostile artillery can obtain the range of it with accuracy. Breastworks with a parados are generally more suitable in a wood than trenches ; in either case the space between parapet and parados should be made as narrow as possible to keep down casualties from splinters of shell bursting in the trees. Otherwise the siting and design of trenches in a wood do not call for any special observations.

2. If a wood cannot be included in the line and has to be left unoccupied in close proximity to it, special arrangements must be made for the concentration of fire on the near edge of the wood and on the ground between it and the front line trench, to deal with an attack by enemy who could assemble unseen under cover of the wood.

13. *General Description of a Line of Trenches.*[*]

The front system of trenches comprises the front line and its support and reserve trenches. In front of the front line is an obstacle continuous except for narrow inconspicuous passages at intervals to serve as exits for reconnoitring patrols. The trenches may be constructed completely below ground, they may consist of a combination of trench and parapet, or the necessary cover may be provided entirely above ground level by the construction of breastworks. The first type is very seldom met with, while the use of breastworks is practically confined to positions where water makes them necessary and where time admits of their construction. The combination of trench and parapet is that most commonly met with, the depth of the trench being generally determined by the wetness of the site and facilities for drainage. The front line generally consists of two parts, the fire trench and the command or supervision trench. The fire trench may either be a continuous trench (though in no case should it be an absolutely straight one), traversed at suitable intervals to give protection from enfilade fire and to localise the effect of shell bursts, or may consist of fire bays, T-shaped or L-shaped in plan, jutting forward from the supervision trench. The latter is a continuous trench affording easy lateral communication close behind the fire bays or fire trench, and connected with them at frequent intervals. In the case of fire bays there must be a communication trench forward from the supervision trench to each bay. In the case of a continuous fire trench the best position for these communication trenches to come into the fire trench is behind a traverse, and there should be one such communication trench behind about every second traverse. (See figs. 2, 3, and 4.)

2. Emplacements for machine guns are constructed in the front

---

* See fig. 1.

line so that the whole front of the line can be swept with machine gun fire, which for the maximum effect should be from a flank across the front covered. It is, therefore, essential that the trace of a trench should not be straight. Machine guns can also often be effectively employed behind the front line in small inconspicuous emplacements, where they may escape detection and consequent bombardment prior to an attack. The question of machine gun emplacements must always receive most careful attention. (See Section 20.)

3. The support trenches (see Section 17 (7)) accommodate the first support to the garrison of the front trench, ready for immediate reinforcement or local counter-attack ; they also furnish cover to which the bulk of the garrison of the front trench can be temporarily withdrawn during bombardment.* The support line should always be constructed as a second line of resistance, if the first line is lost, and should be protected by an obstacle. The line of support trenches may or may not be continuous, it is preferable that it should be ; in any case it is connected to the front line by frequent communication trenches. In order that support trenches may not suffer from the bombardment of the front line they should not be nearer than 50 yards behind it, and the most favourable position is from 70 to 100 yards behind.

4. Behind the support trenches, and also connected with them by communication trenches, lies the reserve line, which may consist of a line of trenches but more usually of dug-outs, often formed by improving the cover afforded by some natural feature. The reserve trenches or dug-outs are to accommodate the battalion reserve, whose purpose is the local counter-attack. The reserve line may be from 400 to 600 yards in rear of the front line.

5. To the above are often added trenches made for a special purpose, e.g., a "bombing trench" (which is a trench dug behind the front line within easy grenade throwing distance of it, its purpose being to enable an enemy who has captured the front line to be driven out by grenades) or so-called "slit" trenches dug off the communication trenches for the accommodation of men during a bombardment. (See Section 19 (8) and fig. 3.)

6. A system of trenches is also usually provided with a series of works prepared for all round defence, and surrounded with a continuous obstacle, known variously as "keeps," " supporting points," "strong points," or "reduits." Their object is to break up a hostile attack which has penetrated the front line and prevent its further development and thus to facilitate counter-attack. Their garrison must hold out to the last, whatever

---

* Under favourable circumstances the bulk of the garrison of the front line may normally be accommodated during the day in the support trenches, leaving the front line to be garrisoned by groups of sentries only. The question of the distribution of men in the trenches is discussed later in Chapter IV. The question of the provision and position of shelter against the weather and bombardment for the garrison of the fire and support trenches is discussed later in this chapter.

happens to the rest of the line. They must come as a surprise to the enemy, and, therefore, be carefully concealed. No definite rules can be laid down as to their number on a given frontage or their relative position with regard to the front line ; this will usually depend on the facilities offered by the ground for their concealment. Adjacent works of this kind should, if possible, afford mutual support to one another.

7. Latrines are provided in all trenches, and must be in positions easy of access and protected from fire. They are usually made in T-heads at the end of short trenches leading off from the super-vision trench.

Communication trenches are made to the front system from points on roads which can be reached without too much exposure to view.

14. *Strong Points and Defended Localities.*

1. In every line there will be a certain number of points of which the loss, or their occupation by the enemy, would seriously endanger the security of the rest of the line, or would weaken the defender's hold on it. There will also probably be other points which are particularly favourable for defence. Such points should receive special treatment so as to develop to the utmost their capabilities for defence, and to enable the troops to hold on to them even after the neighbouring portions of the line have been lost. In addition, if the intervals between them are great, there should be small intermediate works. The important thing about all these works is that they should be designed so as to be able to offer a protracted resistance, unsupported if necessary, to hostile attacks from any direction, flank and rear as well as frontal. The importance of the point to be strengthened, its position, and its nature generally determine the area to be embraced within the perimeter of the work. Speaking generally, large defended localities offer a less concentrated target to the enemy's guns, and are, therefore, less vulnerable, but they absorb large garrisons.

2. The small strong point referred to in last section is generally in the nature of an enclosed infantry redoubt with a continuous parapet round its whole perimeter, designed to be held by a garrison which may be anything from a section to half a company. The garrison should be kept as small as possible, and the defence provided by machine guns as far as possible. This type of work must be carefully concealed and strongly constructed, or it will become a "shell-trap." Good bomb-proof protection for its garrison should be provided within the perimeter of the work. (See fig. 5.)

3. The more important points are better defended by a system of trenches covering a more extended area, and forming what is better described as a defended locality. The perimeter of such a defended locality should be provided with defences against an attack from any direction, these defences consisting either of a

(B 11870)   B continuous fire trench, or of isolated lengths of fire trench sited to cover every possible line of approach, and connected with one another and with the works in the interior of the locality by communication trenches. Small self-contained works such as have been described in the last paragraph might quite well form an element in the defences of the perimeter or in the interior defences of a locality. Within the defended perimeter should be the dug-outs for the garrison and a series of cover and support trenches and communication trenches, many of them prepared for occupation as fire trenches. In this way the interior is cut up into compartments, and the scheme of defence is so organized that, even if the enemy succeeds in establishing a footing at some point in the perimeter, an unbroken front can still be presented to him, and the defender's hold on the locality is practically unaffected. Machine guns play an important part in the defence, and alternative emplacements should be numerous. The sitings of the emplacements should be very carefully considered, and will largely govern the general design of the defences. A defended locality of this nature has the advantage that it does not offer a concentrated artillery target, and that its reduction by bombardment would be a difficult and lengthy operation, entailing a large expenditure of ammunition.

4. Villages placed in a state of defence make the best kind of supporting point. If the defence is properly organized, their capture has usually proved a long and costly operation. Cellars, with their roofs shored up and reinforced, form excellent shelters, and good communications entirely underground can be made by breaking through from cellar to cellar. The organization of the defence will be similar to that already outlined for defended localities. The field of fire from interior lines of resistance must be improved wherever necessary by the thorough demolition of buildings and removal of spreading of the *debris*.

5. These strong points or localities should, as has been already stated, be provided with a good obstacle all round them. In addition, any interior trench which may, under the scheme of defence, at any time become a line of resistance, should also be covered by a wire entanglement.

6. Unity of command is an important thing in the defence of one of these works, and they should, with this in view, be designed for a garrison of a complete unit, as far as possible.

15. *Defences in Rear of the Front System.*

The defences in rear of the front system should consist of a zone 4 or 5 miles deep, in which all points of tactical importance are fortified on the principles laid down in Section 14. The intention is by the occupation of these points to break up the attack of any hostile force which has penetrated the front system, delay any further advance, and facilitate counter-attack. In addition to this primary role, these strong points furnish a framework on which, by digging trenches in the intervals, a new line within the zone can be rapidly constructed to meet any eventuality.

A second similar zone may be prepared in rear of the first.

16. *Procedure when Constructing Trenches in the Presence of the Enemy.*

1. The procedure in the case of constructing a line when hostile interference has not to be reckoned with has already been described. In the construction of a line in the presence of an enemy the first object is to get some sort of cover, as quickly as possible, for the firing line. Normally what happens is that individual men start to dig pits for themselves where they were when the advance stopped. As soon as possible these pits are joined up with one another to form a continuous fire trench. This trench may ultimately form the front fire trench, a continuous trench for purposes of lateral communication being subsequently dug behind it, or it may become the supervision trench, fresh fire trenches being pushed out at intervals from it to the front. In either case, but more especially in the former, much subsequent labour will be saved if the question of traverses in the final trench is taken into account, both in the spacing of the first constructed pits and in the joining of them up to form a trench (see details regarding traverses in Section 17). If it is decided to use the trench first formed as a supervision trench, the next stage, after it is completed, is that T-heads are pushed forward from it to form the firing bays. The work of digging the individual pits will be begun by the infantry with any tools they have, generally, as has been said, mostly with infantry entrenching tools. Troops must, therefore, be well practised in digging themselves in by night or day with these tools. But heavier tools must be got up to the firing line as soon as possible, and every plan for an advance should provide for a certain number of digging tools, other than the entrenching tool, accompanying the attack,* and for this number being supplemented as early as possible with every available pick and shovel. It may be necessary to wait for dark before a large quantity of tools can be brought up and serious work attempted, but it is sometimes possible, under covering fire from the artillery, to dig a continuous trench by day. In any case, every effort must be made to get good trenches dug as soon as possible. One of the first requirements is to get some wire in front of the trench, as this gives a greater feeling of security to the men digging (see Appendix B). During the first two or three days it may be expected that the new line will be subjected to heavy bombardment alternating with repeated counter-attacks. If the front

---

* See Chapter V.

trench is constructed in the first instance very close to the enemy's position it is particularly vulnerable to counter-attack and if the enemy succeeds in breaking through the line at a time when there are no defences prepared behind it, he may force a retirement on a large front. The construction of a supporting line 70 to 100 yards in rear of the front line and of a reserve line should, therefore, be proceeded with simultaneously.

2. The following procedure, adopted in at least one instance by the Germans, may commend itself when the offensive has to be temporarily given up, and the enemy is found established in a prepared line. A line is constructed in the first instance at a considerable distance, say 500 to 600 yards, or even more, from the the enemy's front trench, the exact distance depending on the ground and facilities in the form of cover. This line is made fairly strong and complete before any further advance is attempted. Then, under cover of night, and possibly of a heavy bombardment of the enemy's front line, a new front line is constructed at a distance of 200 to 300 yards from the enemy. From this point further advance would usually be by sap. The advantage of this method is that, before any attempt is made to dig a line within easy reach of small counter-attacks, there is a completed line ready behind the new line, to stop further progress by the enemy if the new line is counter-attacked and broken.

17. *Constructional Details of Trenches.*

1. *Fire Trenches.*—There is no sealed pattern of fire trench. Various types which have been found useful are shown in figs. 6 to 8, but the type used varies according to local conditions. Any fire trench, however, must fulfil the following essential conditions :—

(a) The parapet must be bullet-proof ;
(b) Every man must be able to fire *over* the parapet with proper effect (*i.e.*, so that he can hit the bottom of his own wire) ;
(c) Traverses must be adequate ;
(d) A parados must be provided to give protection against the back-blast of high explosive ;
(e) The trace of the trench should be irregular, to provide flanking fire ;

and, if the trench is to be held for any length of time :—

(f) The sides must be revetted ;
(g) The bottom of the trench must be floored.

The narrower a trench is the better the cover which it affords. However, a trench which may have to be occupied for some time must allow freedom of movement. The result is that a fire trench is usually made broad enough to allow of movement behind the line of men manning the parapet. Every man must be able to use his rifle over the parapet ; on the other hand people moving along the trench do not want to have to stoop down low in order to get their heads under the cover of the parapet. Therefore the trench usually has a firing step about 18 inches broad and 4 feet 6 inches below the crest of the parapet, and behind this a deeper portion from 18 inches to 2 feet 6 inches broad at the bottom and from 6 feet to 7 feet below the crest line of the parapet (see figs. 7, 8). The firing step must have a level surface and give a firm foothold. It may either consist of an earth step strongly revetted with planks held up by well driven pickets, or of stout planks laid on low timber trestles. Sandbags are sometimes used but are not suitable, as such a firing step gets very slippery in wet weather and usually takes a slope to the rear, so that it gives a very insecure foothold. Height from firing step to crest to be frequently tested. The only test is whether the individual man can use his rifle effectively over the top.

2. *Traverses.*—Traverses are strong buttresses of earth jutting out from the front or the rear face of the trench so as to split it into a series of compartments. Their object is to decrease the exposure of the garrison to enfilade fire and to localise the effect of a shell bursting in the trench. For both these purposes they must be strong and solid. They should be made from 9 to 12 feet thick, should overlap the width of the trench by 2 feet at least, and must be strongly revetted. A traverse is described as a "forward" traverse or a "rear" traverse according as it juts out from the back or the front face of the trench respectively. Rear traverses are generally accepted as the best for normal use, but an occasional forward traverse is useful to provide fire to a flank. Traverses add to the length of trench necessary to accommodate a given number of rifles, and, if they are too frequent, add to the difficulty of supervision and control. From 18 feet to 30 feet is the normal length of bay between two adjacent traverses. Traverses in a trench facilitate bombing attacks along its length, as grenades can be thrown from under cover of a traverse, generally into the next bay but one. As a protection against this there should be, at intervals in the line, spaces without traverses, long enough to prevent bombing from behind the traverse

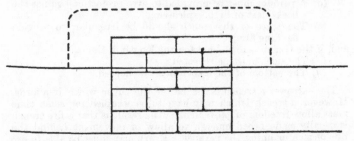

at one end of the space to beyond the traverse at the other end. This length of trench should be straight and the traverses on either side of it should be loopholed for fire inwards. Bombing trenches or pits behind the front line (see figs. 3 and 9) are also useful to stop an attack of this sort.

Traverses will often have to be made in a completed trench which is insufficiently traversed. To do this cut into the face of the trench opposite that from which the traverse is to jut out a recess broad enough and deep enough for the end of the traverse and the passage round it, and with the earth from this recess, supplemented if necessary by more from elsewhere, build up a wall of sandbags or of earth revetted with sandbags or other material 9 feet to 12 feet thick right across the old trench and projecting not less than 2 feet into the recess. (See figure, p. 21.)

3. The sides of trenches which have to be occupied for a long time, and particularly in wet weather in a damp site, must be revetted. Hurdles or rabbit netting held up by stout stakes at frequent intervals, well driven and with their upper ends securely wired to short pickets firmly anchored in the parapet or parados, form a useful type of revetment for this purpose. Sandbags are not so suitable. High revetments in Flanders clay require an intermediate anchorage between the bottom of the revetment stake and the anchorage to its top, unless revetment stakes of 4 to 5 inches diameter are used. The placing of this in the solid ground forming the side of a trench is a difficult operation demanding the assistance of skilled labour. In the winter in Flanders some really solid form of revetment, such as planks or timber, or expanded metal sheets, is necessary.

The fire trench should be provided with frequent exits for the use of patrols. These exits should be in the form of tunnels leading under the parapet, whether the line be trench or breastwork, and communicating with saps.

The top of the parapet should always be irregular, as this helps to conceal men observing or firing over the parapet. Still better concealment is provided if the parados is higher than the parapet and is also irregular, as heads do not then show up against a skyline.

A useful accessory in a trench line is what is known as a "bombing trench" or "bombing pits." The latter are small recesses about 5 feet square dug behind the front line and within easy grenade throwing range of it (see fig. 9). The former is a continuous trench for the same purpose.

A tendency to be guarded against is that towards gradually increasing the width of trenches. Wide trenches are undoubtedly more comfortable to live in but they afford nothing like such good protection as narrower trenches. In repairing a trench of which the side has fallen in men are apt merely to throw the earth out which has fallen in. This should never be allowed; the débris should be cleared away, a strong revetment (hurdles, expanded metal or rabbit-netting) put up against the new face, and a sandbag wall built outside this revetment. The sandbags then support the revetment.

The question of loopholes, drainage, latrines, is dealt with later.

4. *Breastworks.*—Breastworks afford very good cover, but their construction involves much time and very heavy labour. They are therefore usually made only when the state of the ground compels it.

Breastworks are more conspicuous than trenches, but earth breastworks, if well built, do not suffer more heavily than a trench under artillery fire, and are more easily repaired, whilst being very much more comfortable to live in.

Earth breastworks must be at least 10 feet thick at top, and have a very gentle exterior slope. The ditch excavation can be used as an obstacle, and can be filled with wire. When constructing a breastwork one of the most important points to look to is that the near edge of the borrow pit in front of the parapet is far enough from the foot of the interior slope. There is a tendency on the part of the diggers to save themselves labour by digging in towards the parapet. This must be guarded against by marking with a tape a line beyond which there must be no digging, and by constant supervision to see that it is observed. To ascertain the position of this line, find by drawing the minimum width of base necessary to secure a thickness of 10 feet at top, and add at least 2 feet to provide for a berm at the foot of the exterior slope. It will save much time if wooden stretchers are made to carry the earth, and plank gangways are made for the carriers. If no planks or brushwood are available, wire netting laid on the ground will serve to provide a pathway. Work once begun on a breastwork must be completed as quickly as possible, because a new work is likely to prove a tempting target for artillery fire, to which in the early stages it is very vulnerable, and also because it is important to get the work through if possible in the dry. In the kind of site which demands a breastwork, the borrow pit very easily fills with water, and under this condition work becomes very slow and arduous, and may even become impossible. The interior slopes of parapet and parados must be strongly revetted ; hurdlework or some substitute, firmly anchored, forms the best form of revetment ; sandbags do not stand the weather so well. Once the revetment has been put up, digging close to the foot of it must on no account be allowed.

The best method of constructing a breastwork is as follows :—
Put up two revetments of gabions or hurdles—or if using sandbags build two sandbag walls—10 feet apart ; fill in between with earth ; build up a bursting course in front ; finally make a very gentle slope to the front.

Breastworks constructed wholly or mainly of sandbags are much more vulnerable to artillery fire than earth breastworks, and are expensive of material. They are to be avoided except for minor works, such as blocking a trench leading towards the enemy, barricading a road, &c. They are, however, often found in the front line, when breastworks have had to be constructed in the

presence of the enemy, because they can be made more silently.*
They are either formed by gradually raising the parapet of a
trench that has become waterlogged, or they may be made by a
process of sapping to join up two existing trenches or breastworks. The great fault usually in making these breastworks is
to make their sides too straight and steep. The base of such a
breastwork must be broader than the top or the whole wall of
sandbags will collapse in wet weather.

Breastworks must be constructed with traverses in the same
manner as fire trenches, and must have a firing step, to allow of
every man using his rifle over the top. The necessary amount of
cover for free movement along the line, 6 feet 6 inches as a
minimum, can be obtained either by building up the parapet to
this height, when a raised firing step will be required, or by
having the firing step at ground level and digging a narrow
shallow trench immediately behind it and round the ends of
traverses. A parados must be constructed to protect the garrison
from the back-blast of high explosive shell which burst behind
the line. This parados should be about 2 feet 6 inches to 3 feet
thick at its base, strongly revetted on both faces. It should be
as high or slightly higher than the parapet and as close to it as
is compatible with free movement along the line. A path paved
with brick or with floor-board gratings just behind the parados
is a great convenience ; it should communicate with the fire bays
by openings through the parados behind at least every other
traverse. The space between the breastwork and parados should
be floored, and steps taken to allow for drainage from that space.

In a breastwork line, filled sandbags should be stacked close
behind the parados at frequent intervals, to be available for

---

* In building parapets, breastworks or revetments with sandbags, the
following rules must always be observed :—

    (a) Sandbags should be filled only ¾ full and well beaten into the shape
        of a brick ;

    (b) Sandbags must not be built vertically on one another. A slope of
        3/1 is advisable ;

    (c) Breaking joint and the use of frequent headers are necessary ;

    (d) Each layer of sandbags must be at right angles to the face of the
        parapet, not horizontal :—

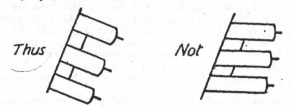

    (e) Sandbags should not be filled with brick rubble ; it is dangerous
        owing to the interstices left between lumps of brick.

building up a gap formed by artillery fire, as a speedy temporary repair.

5. *Loopholes.*—All firing by night, and to meet an attack whether by day or by night, must be over the top of the parapet. In all fire trenches, however, a certain number of loopholes are necessary for the use of snipers to inflict casualties on the enemy whenever opportunity offers, to annoy him, interfere with his work, keep him under cover, and keep down the fire of his snipers. Usually one or two loopholes are made in each bay of the fire trenches.

Various types of loophole have been designed, and are in use. It is not intended to describe them in this pamphlet,* but only to lay down the conditions that a satisfactory loophole must fulfil. The most important of these is concealment from the front ; for this reason, and to obtain if possible enfilade fire, loopholes should be placed obliquely in the parapet. The maximum amount of cover should be provided for the firer, and the steel loophole plates with a metal flap to close the loophole make probably the best form of loophole. Loopholes should have a curtain (sandbag or some form of cloth) hung on the firer's side, to be used in the same way as a photographer uses a black cloth.

Observing stations and look-out posts behind the lines should be provided with inconspicuous loopholes, but loopholes are not, as a rule, much used for looking out from the trench, except where special loopholes for observation with telescopes are made. Periscopes and small pieces of mirror set up at an angle on the parados give a better view with less exposure.

Loopholes have usually to be made in a parapet at night. The alignment must be carefully sited and marked by day.

6. *Overhead Cover.*—Overhead cover is never used in any trench which is to be occupied as a fire trench. Overhead cover for shelters and dug-outs is dealt with in the paragraph on that subject. Beyond this the only case in which overhead protection is likely to be required is, in rare instances, over very exposed lengths of communication trench and in the form of traverse known as a " bridge " traverse.

7. *Support Trenches.* — Support trenches should be designed as traversed fire trenches, but the supervision trench is usually omitted. Protection against shell fire in the form of deep dug-outs can be made in the support line behind the parados, whereas their use in the front trench interferes with the rapid manning of the trench and is inadmissible. The support line should be connected by numerous communication trenches to the front line, and if there is an obstacle in front of the support line it must be so arranged as not to interfere with the rapid reinforcement of the front line trenches.

8. *Communication Trenches.*—To afford protection from enfilade

---

* Descriptions of various types of loophole will be found in notes that are circulated among the troops from time to time.

fire and to minimise exposure to shrapnel in them, communication trenches must be well bent or traversed. The best type is the winding one, but the curves must be sufficiently pronounced to give real protection against enfilade fire. If traverses are made, the best pattern is an island traverse with the trench going round it on both sides. The corners of traverses should be rounded and not square, as they are easier to pass for a man with a load or for a stretcher,* and are easier to revet. The necessary protection can also be obtained by making the trenches zig-zagged in plan, and this makes revetting easier.

Except in such soil as solid chalk, communication trenches which are required to remain serviceable for a long time or to stand wet weather must be revetted. Experience in Flanders has shown that even if the sides are given as flat a slope as 1/1 they will fall in. A berm of 18 inches should be left between the edge of the trench and the parapet. The minimum width at the bottom should be 2 feet 6 inches, and 3 feet is better. Increasing the width reduces the protection afforded, and the width of 3 feet at the bottom should seldom be exceeded. The revetted sides must be given a slope from 4/1 to 3/1, not cut nearly vertical. The depth of the trench from top of parapet to bottom of trench or floorboard should be 7 feet, if possible; what proportion of this depth is trench and what parapet depends on the site and facilities for drainage. The question of drainage must always receive particular attention in the siting and construction of communication trenches, and they should be boarded, with a drain under the boards, as soon as possible after construction. Passing places and, in a long trench, occasional sidings should be arranged, and sign-posts should always be placed at the entrance to communication trenches, and at any branches off them, to show where they lead.

Special arrangements must be made to afford protection against the enemy's bombers working down a communication trench to attack one of the lines behind. For this purpose the enemy's bombers must be kept at a distance of not less than 40 yards from the trench to be protected. This can be done by making the last 40 yards of any communication trench, entering a support or cover or back-line trench from the front, straight and providing for machine gun or rifle fire down the straight portion (see fig. 11). A dog-leg trench will do if proper arrangements can be made for enfilading both reaches of it (see fig. 12). Provision must be made for blocking this last 40 yards of the trench at both ends. *Chevaux de frise* ("knife rests") or other wire obstacles, placed in a recess at the point where the block is to be made, so that the last man to retire can quickly pull them down into position as he passes will do as a temporary expedient for this purpose (see fig. 11).

---

* The minimum curve in winding communication trenches, so that a stretcher can be carried round it by bearers, is 16 foot radius in a trench 3 feet wide.

Communication trenches, if prepared for use as fire trenches, are frequently of the utmost value for flank defence, when the enemy has succeeded in penetrating the front line. The best way of preparing a communication trench for fire is to dig T-heads off the trench so as to form fire bays facing in the required direction, or to cut fire trenches across a re-entrant angle in the trench (see fig. 10). A communication trench prepared for use as a fire trench should be protected on both sides by a good wire entanglement.

18. Obstacles.*

Front trenches and all trenches which may have to be occupied as fire trenches must be protected by an efficient obstacle. Some form of barbed wire entanglement is the most efficient obstacle and is that universally used. A wire entanglement must be broad enough not to be easily bridged or quickly cut through, must be under the close fire of the defence, and near enough to be effectively watched by night. The near edge of the entanglement should be about 20 yards from the trench, and it should be at least 10 yards broad. A height of 2 feet 6 inches is sufficient, a greater height only increases its liability to damage by our own fire. Every effort must be made to conceal and protect the entanglement; this is best done by sinking it in hollows or trenches. Where trenches are made they should be of the form shown in fig. 13, i.e., sloping with the maximum depth furthest from the fire trench, so as to minimise the cover which they might afford to the enemy; further, wire sunk in this manner should be carefully sited so that every portion of it is enfiladed from some point or another in the fire trench. Sunk wire is less visible, less vulnerable to artillery, and less liable to damage by our own fire.

When entanglements are at some distance from the enemy, it may sometimes be useful to construct a second belt of wire beyond the first, with its outer edge some 40 or 50 yards from the trench, to keep hostile bombers at a distance.

Good strong wire entanglements, of the pattern in fig. 14, fixed to well-driven posts, should be constructed wherever it is possible. With proper training, infantry should be able to make entanglements of this nature as close as 100 yards from the enemy on a dark night. The iron posts now issued, which screw into the ground, can be placed in position without noise and strengthen the entanglement. Only when the opposing lines are too close, or as a temporary means of providing some sort of obstacle quickly, recourse may be had to portable obstacles. The best of these is that known as the "knife rest" (see fig. 15, which sufficiently explains their construction). Two or three rows of these knife rests, placed to break joint and wired together, form a fair obstacle which can be quickly and quietly placed in position. Hollow barbed wire spheres are easily made up in the front trench and

---

* See also Appendix B.

thrown out, and, if plentifully used, are better than no obstacle at all.

The maintenance of the wire obstacle calls for constant care. It must be inspected every night, and a few men should be told off in each company as a permanent wiring party for the repair and improvement of the obstacle.

19. *Protection from Shell Fire.*

1. Protection against loss by shell fire is afforded by details in the design of the trenches themselves, already referred to, *e.g.*, traverses, and keeping trenches as narrow as possible, and is supplemented by the provision of shelters or dug-outs. Shelters may be classified as bomb-proof or splinter-proof, according as they are designed to afford protection against shells hitting them direct and bursting on impact, or against the splinters of shells burst over or near them. It is important to distinguish between the two.

2. The first instinct of the men is to improve the protection afforded by the trench by burrowing out for themselves hollows in the front face, under the parapet ("undercutting"). This practice must be absolutely prohibited. Unless these hollows are very carefully shored up they always result, sooner or later, in the parapet falling in, and, even if the shoring up is efficiently done, the existence of these shelters under the parapet weakens its resistance to the burst of a high-explosive shell.

3. Bomb-proof shelters to ensure protection against heavy high-explosive shells have to be dug deep and entered by a narrow opening and steps. This means that it takes an appreciable time to get men out of them, and as in a well-planned attack the assault will be sudden and unexpected, and the fire of the artillery will not be lifted from the front trench until the leading infantry of the assaulting line is almost into it, they are usually inadmissible in the front line, except for the protection of machine guns and their detachments, and for company head-quarters. Deep dug-outs are, moreover, dangerous in an attack by gas.

A certain amount of splinter-proof cover should be provided in the front line, which will also serve as protection against weather. The best position, in the case of a trench, is in the front face of the supervision trench.

4. In the case of strongly constructed breastworks, dug-outs giving good protection against even direct hits by the lighter natures of high-explosive shell can be made under the parapet, and are not so open to the objections which apply to dug-outs in a front fire trench. The parapet over the dug-out must be supported by well-made strong frames and props (see fig. 16).

5. Splinter-proof cover can also be placed behind the parados. In this case protection against black-blast of shells bursting beyond the parados must not be overlooked.

6. No dug-outs must ever be allowed in a trench which interfere with the use of the rifle or free passage along the trench.

7. The use of shelters proof against heavy high-explosive shell in the first system of trenches should therefore generally be confined to the position of the battalion reserves and to " strong points " or " keeps," which may form part of the front system. It is not intended to prohibit their use elsewhere, if the soil or natural features are favourable to their construction, and arrangements can be made to get men out of them quickly, but to point out the dangers that attend their use.

8. Very good protection from a hostile bombardment is afforded by "slit" trenches. These are trenches 1 foot to 2 feet wide and 7 feet deep, dug at right angles to and on either side of the communication trenches. They must be strutted at the top, or they will easily collapse. Each " slit" should be long enough to hold 10 to 12 men (see fig. 3). When they are in use an N.C.O. should be at the end nearest the communication trench. Control is easier when men are sheltered in these "slits" than when in dug-outs. Similar provision can be made further back along the communication trenches for cover for reserves brought up to support a counter-attack.

9. A few notes on the construction of dug-outs are appended. For the construction of deep bomb-proof dug-outs, R.E. advice and assistance will usually be available.

(a) Every deep dug-out must have two or more separate exits to facilitate rapid egress and in case one gets blocked.

(b) Roof timbers must always be made three or four times stronger than is necessary to support merely the load due to the thickness of roof for which they are designed. This is necessary to allow, not only for the shock of the burst of a shell, but also for the possibility that a fresh garrison may take it into their heads to put another 2 or 3 feet of earth on top of the existing roof.

(c) A rectangular timber will support more weight if it stood on its edge, i.e., resting on its shorter side, than when lying flat on its longer side.

(d) The ends of roof timbers should never be supported on sandbag walls or even direct on solid ground. A strong timber frame should always be used on two opposite sides of the shelter to support the ends of roof timbers (see fig. 16).

(e) A "burster" layer, of 6 inches to 1 foot of brick or stone, should always be provided near the top surface of the roof. Over this "burster" layer should be a layer of not less than 6 inches of earth to decrease danger from the scattering of the stone or brick by the burst of the shell. As the object of the " burster " is to explode the shell near the surface, it will be to a large extent defeated if the layer of earth above it is made more than 12 inches thick.

(*f*) Arrangements must be made for ventilating dug-outs. It may occasionally be possible to combine the ventilating pipe with a periscope for look-out purposes.

(*g*) Splinter-proof cover is afforded by a layer of logs or beams, 6 inches or upwards in depth, covered over with a layer of not less than 1 foot of earth. The following forms a roof proof against a 6-inch high explosive shell : A layer of rails or beams, 18 inches of earth, a layer of brick, 2½ feet of earth, another layer of brick 6 inches to 1 foot thick, and over all, 6 inches of earth. The rails or beams must have a good margin of strength over that necessary to support the load above them, so as to stand the shock of the explosion. It will be seen that this roof is fully 6 feet thick. Hence the dug-out will require to be at least 10 feet deep if its position is not to be made too conspicuous.

Fig. 17 shows a typical concreted dug-out.

20. *Machine Gun Emplacements.*   (See figs. 18 to 22.)

In view of the great value of machine guns to the defence the siting and construction of emplacements for them requires very special attention and care. Machine guns should be so sited in each line that there is no part of the ground in front of it which is not under their fire. They should be arranged so as to bring a cross fire to bear in front of the trenches which they protect. In this way their power is more fully developed and also concealment is easier. It is important that machine gun emplacements should be constructed so as to be as inconspicuous as possible. Both sides are constantly on the look out to try and locate the enemy's machine gun emplacements, and any suspected spot is certain, sooner or later, to be made the target for bombardment. For this reason, too, and also to protect them from damage by a chance shell in a general bombardment of the line, emplacements should be made as strong as possible. The ideal arrangement is that each gun should be in a bomb-proof shelter, with overhead cover, and in advance of and to a flank of the part of the line it is to cover. Machine guns in an enclosed emplacement may either be mounted for fire on a fixed line, or so as to have a certain amount of traverse. In the latter case some form of improvised platform mounting, allowing of the gun traversing about its muzzle and not about its centre, enables the size of the loophole to be kept down to a minimum, and is, for this reason, valuable. Machine gun loopholes, at any rate those for use by day, should be as low down in the parapet as possible. Several alternative emplacements should be prepared, some of which may be for using the gun over the top of the parapet. In particular there should be an alternative emplacement, for firing over the top, in connection with each enclosed emplacement and situated close to it. In connection with each of the covered machine gun emplacements there should be provided a good bomb-proof shelter, preferably of the deep dug-out type, to which the crew can temporarily withdraw during a bombardment. This dug-out should communicate direct with the emplacement.

Concrete emplacements can generally be constructed in the reserve trenches.

21. *Latrines.*

The health of the troops demands very careful sanitary arrangements and scrupulous cleanliness in trenches, which may have to be occupied for a considerable length of time. Latrine accommodation must be ample and easy of access; seats should be provided on the scale of at least 2 per cent. of the troops using them. Urine tins should be provided on the same scale. The best place for latrines and urinals for the front line is behind the supervision trench in T-heads at the end of short branches off it. Latrines must be provided for all trenches and shelters which have to be occupied, even for short periods, by troops. The most sanitary system of latrines in trenches is the bucket system, buckets being removed and emptied at night.

A supply of chlorate of lime should be kept in all trenches.

22. *Drainage and Flooring.*

Drainage and precautions for keeping trenches dry and clean, whether they are fire, living, or communication trenches, are questions of great importance, not only from the point of view of preserving the trenches, but also for the health of the troops.

In the case of lines dug deliberately, not in the presence of the enemy, the question of drainage can be carefully studied, and it will often pay to dig drainage trenches of ample capacity before any work on trenches is commenced. Labour spent in this way will be more than repaid. In any case work on drains should keep pace with the progress of the trenches, as trouble is sure to occur if water is allowed to accumulate. For the same reason, care must be taken that the work on each section of trenches is left at an even depth each day when work ceases. Drains should be given a good fall. It will usually pay to revet the sides of an open ditch drain. A good pattern of drain is the box drain, a rectangular channel lined and covered over with planking, laid in the bottom of a trench, which is then covered in again.

In the case of trenches dug in the presence of the enemy the above methods cannot be applied. Drainage is a very difficult problem in these circumstances, even when the ground is not practically flat. Trenches on a forward slope cannot be drained except to the front, and it will seldom be practicable to dig drains leading forward from the trench. Practically all that remains possible as a means of getting rid of the water and keeping trenches reasonably dry and clean is constant pumping and putting down some sort of paving or flooring. Sump-pits, *i.e.*, good deep holes, should be made at intervals to one side of the trench.

They should be revetted and strutted and bridged over with plank covers. From these the water should be pumped out as often as may be necessary over the parapet or the parados, according to which way the ground slopes. If the ground falls to the rear, channels can be cut to lead off into the natural drains of the country and the water pumped into these channels. A channel along the side of the trench or down the centre of it should lead the water into the sump-pits, and it must be constantly cleared. If the channel is cut down the centre of the trench it can be bridged over by special flooring boards, which must be frequently taken up and cleaned. If the level of the water in the ground rises above the level of the floor of the trench, obviously no amount of pumping or digging of sump-pits will keep the trench dry. The only remedy then is to raise the floor of the trench by planks supported on short pile-trestles, and then to raise the parapet accordingly. A most important point is to get some kind of flooring or paving down as soon as possible in any new trench. If this can be done before the mud has been churned up, a great deal of trouble and discomfort will be saved. Floor gratings about 6 feet long and 18 inches to 2 feet wide, made of cross pieces of ¾-inch by 4-inch plank, nailed to two longitudinal pieces of timber about 4 inches by 3 inches, on edge, are easily made up, and are a very good form of flooring for trenches.

23. *Defence of Buildings.*

It will often happen that it is considered advisable to include substantial buildings in the front line. Experience has proved that it is extremely hard to dislodge a determined defender from a properly organized building. On the other hand, buildings in or near the front line invariably draw a great deal of artillery fire. For this reason, a building should not normally be occupied by day, unless it either has cellars which can be improved to provide good bomb-proof cover, or similar cover can be made quite close to the house, and connected with it by communication trenches. Otherwise, if the building has been put into a state of defence, a garrison should be detailed who will only occupy it at the last moment in case of attack. A building is strongest for defence when it has been knocked about a bit. The defensive arrangements should be concentrated on the ground floor and cellars; time spent on work on upper stories is sure to be wasted. In the building itself the work to be done is :—

(a) Reinforce the cellar roof, if possible, with concrete ; it must be well shored up to enable it to carry the extra protection, and also the *débris* which subsequent shelling will bring down on it.

(b) Loophole the walls for rifle or machine gun fire ; the nearer the loopholes are to the ground the better the protection afforded ; but there is a risk of falling *débris* blocking them up.

(c) Thicken walls up to the height of the loopholes. This thickening may be done by throwing earth up against the outside of the building, or making a wall of gabions filled with earth or of earth between hurdles, 3 feet clear of the wall of the building, to serve as a burster, but building up inside with brick rubble or earth in sandbags is better, as loopholes near ground level and cellar windows for machine guns can then be used.

(d) Block up and loophole ground floor windows and doors.

(e) Erect overhead cover over fire positions. This should be in the form of a false roof, preferably of concrete, otherwise of heavy rails or very stout timbers carried on very substantial timber supports, or on rails or girders. This roof will protect the firers from falling *débris*, and the more the house is knocked about the stronger will the cover become.

(f) Improve internal communications by gapping internal walls where necessary.

In connection with the defence of the building there may also be fire trenches in front of it and to either flank communicating by trenches with one another and with the building, the whole forming practically a small strong point of which the house is the keep. "Slit trenches," such as have already been described, situated close behind the house and connected with it by a communication trench, form a useful adjunct to the defensive arrangements.

24. *Training in Digging, &c.*

Infantry must be capable of the construction, repair, and maintenance, without R.E. assistance, of all forms of trenches, shelters (except deep bomb-proof dug-outs), and barbed wire entanglements. Constant practice in digging and making entanglements at night is necessary. Officers and men must be well trained in the method of marking out works to be dug at night and in extending a party silently on a task in darkness. Troops should be trained to dig, &c., fully equipped (except for their packs).

It will be found useful to have a certain number of men in each company specially trained under R.E. supervision in the construction of barbed-wire entanglements, loopholes, revetting, drainage, &c.

(B 11870)

CHAPTER III.

Occupation and Relief of Trenches and General Trench Routine.

25. *System of Relief of Trenches.*

It is absolutely essential that in every unit a thoroughly sound system of carrying out reliefs is established. If the proper arrangements are made and the necessary precautions observed, the relief of trenches can be accomplished, with a little experience, safely and expeditiously. Carelessly conducted reliefs, on the other hand, involve not only great and unnecessary danger to the security of the trench line but avoidable loss of life and discomfort to the men.

The first essential is a careful preliminary reconnaissance. Whenever a unit is about to take over a new line of trenches, parties from it will visit the trenches previously, by day if possible. In the case of a battalion, the party should consist of the C.O., adjutant and machine gun officer, and at least one officer and one N.C.O. from each company. It will often be advisable, especially when taking over a new line and in the case of inexperienced troops, that one officer and N.C.O. from each company should remain a complete 24 hours in the trenches previous to the arrival of the battalion. The snipers of the relieving unit should be in the trenches for 24 hours before the relief takes place.

Detailed information from the unit to be relieved must be obtained on the following points :—*

(*a*) Condition of wire entanglement, parapet, &c.
(*b*) Work in progress.
(*c*) Position of hostile machine guns, snipers, &c., as far as known..
(*d*) Danger points, *e.g.*, where saps run out, portions of trench especially subject to enfilade fire, &c.
(*e*) Position of listening posts.
(*f*) Position of S.A.A. reserve, bomb stores and trench stores.
(*g*) List of trench stores.†
(*h*) Method of communication with supporting artillery.

---

* A Trench " Log Book " kept up daily by each unit in the trenches and handed over to the relieving unit, is a convenient method of recording changes in the trench line and all other information of value regarding the trenches. Such a record is of great assistance to ensure continuity of work.

† Trench stores are the articles which remain permanently in the trenches and are handed over from one unit to another. They include S.A.A., grenades, tools, pumps, loophole plates, braziers, &c.

(i) Arrangements : if heavily shelled ; to meet an attack ; for counter-attack.

(j) Any arrangements for visual signalling or communication by rockets.

(k) Sanitary arrangements.

(l) Water supply.

(m) Arrangements for cooking and supplying hot meals.

(n) Route by which first line transport brings up rations at night and where rations are dumped.

A map of the trench line should also be obtained.

26. *Description of Method of Carrying out a Relief.*

1. The following summary of the steps to be taken in the case of the relief of one brigade by another in the trench line is given as a guide to the normal procedure :—

(a) On receiving orders to take over some portion of the line, the Brigade Staff obtain from the brigade to be relieved all available information regarding the line, work in progress, ammunition and stores available, &c., make what reconnaissance of the line the Brigadier considers necessary, and arrange with the other brigade the details of the relief. It is important that the O.C. Brigade Machine Gun Company should make a thorough reconnaissance of the line.

(b) When the Brigade Staff have arranged how the line is to be held they make the necessary arrangements to enable battalions to carry out their reconnaissance of the line as detailed in Section 25.

It must be remembered that units of an ingoing brigade may not be of the same strength as the units to be relieved. A battalion may not, therefore, take over exactly the same frontage as is held by a battalion in the line, but may take over trenches from two battalions. This case necessitates careful arrangements as regards guides and the handing and taking over.

(c) Reliefs, except in very favourable circumstances, have usually to be carried out under cover of darkness. The time of commencement of relief will depend on local circumstances and conditions, but it is generally advisable to begin reliefs as early as possible. In order to prevent the enemy from detecting our system of reliefs the intervals between reliefs and the hours at which they are carried out should be varied from time to time.

2. The brigade marches off from its billets by battalions, with an interval of about half an hour between battalions on the same road.* Transport accompanying units must be kept down to a minimum and a point must be fixed beyond which it is not allowed to proceed. It is usually at this point that guides from the unit

---

* If relief takes place by day, at least two hours interval must be left between times of starting for different battalions. Relieving battalions then move up by platoons to the meeting place for guides.

to be relieved meet the battalions. Any stores, &c., to be carried up to the trenches,* which may so far have been carried for convenience on the transport, are distributed amongst the men at this point, and the relief then usually proceeds by companies or smaller parties, each with its set of guides provided by the unit to be relieved.

It is usual to provide a guide from each platoon as well as guides for battalion headquarters, and for machine guns. Every guide must be in the possession of a paper showing the number or name of his trench, and the number of men in it.

3. The following notes on equipment for the trenches may be useful :—

Packs are taken to the trenches, except in the case of units going to the trenches to make an attack. Men take waterproof ground sheets, but blankets should not be taken. Every man should carry two sandbags tucked into his belt.

All officers should have electric torches, and a long pole is very useful. Waterproof waders or overalls to the knee are very useful in wet weather.

27. *Precautions and Arrangements necessary during a Relief.*

The following are notes on some of the points to be observed in carrying out reliefs. It is advisable to embody some instructions on these points in Standing Orders for Trench Warfare.

(*a*) All units should be formed up before dark in the order in which and under the commander with whom they will go into the trenches.

(*b*) All parties must be kept closed up while moving to and from the trenches ; the pace in front must be *very* slow. An officer should always be in rear. On dark nights it is often advisable for each man of a party to hold the bayonet scabbard of the man in front. Nothing causes confusion, unnecessary fatigue, and loss of moral so much as men getting lost from their parties while moving up to the trenches.

(*c*) Reliefs will be carried out as quietly as possible ; no lights or smoking are allowed after reaching a point to be decided on by the battalion commander.

(*d*) Before commencing a relief every party must receive orders as to what action is to be taken by them in the event of an attack or alarm taking place while reliefs are in progress. Any retirement of troops should be avoided on principle. As a general rule, parties caught in the open during a relief should occupy the nearest trench or cover available and get into touch at once with the nearest body of troops holding the trench line.

As far as circumstances permit, and especially whenever there is a probability of attack, reliefs should be carried out gradually, so that too many men are not moving in the open at the same time.

---

* Rations for 48 hours and 150 rounds S.A.A. are usually carried on the man, when going into the trenches.

(e) No trench or post should ever be evacuated by the troops to be relieved until the relieving troops have actually occupied it. The method of carrying out the actual relief of a trench must vary according to the nature of the trenches. The following is a usual method :—

The platoon being relieved gets on the firing step. The relieving platoon files in behind and halts. On the word " Pass," which will be given quietly, being passed along, the relieved and relieving platoons change places. The new sentries, who will have been told off prior to the new platoon coming into the trenches, will take over from the old sentries, and the relieved platoon will file out. Where the trenches are too narrow to permit of above, the relieving troops must lie down behind the parados of the fire trench whilst the relief of sentries is carried out. Before dismissing the relieving platoon, the platoon commander will satisfy himself that all sentries have been properly posted and that every man can aim at the bottom of his own wire from the position allotted him.

(f) On taking over any trench the officer in charge will obtain all the information available, will take over the stores and tools in the trench, have the men told off in sentry groups and the first reliefs posted. He will ascertain at once the position of the trenches on his flanks and of the nearest supports, sending out patrols to get into touch with them and act as guides. He will ensure that he has a sufficient number of guides who know the way to company and battalion headquarters.

(g) The completion of a relief must be reported at once—by the company commander to battalion headquarters when the relief of the company is complete, by the battalion commander to brigade headquarters when the relief of the battalion is complete, and by brigade headquarters to divisional headquarters when the relief of the brigade is complete. Both relieved and relieving units must make these reports. The battalion and brigade staffs of units relieved must remain till the relief of all the troops under them has been completed.

28. *Handing over Trenches.*

Officers handing over trenches are responsible that all available information and trench maps of the locality are given to the relieving unit, and that all tools and trench stores are collected and handed over in the most convenient way and place.

A supply of Very lights and other consumable stores sufficient for at least 24 hours should be handed over to the relieving unit.

Lists of stores and reports on trenches, giving all available information, must, whenever possible, be prepared and handed over to relieving units on the day previous to relief taking place.

29. *Duties in Trenches.*

The following precautions for the safety of the trench line must invariably be observed :—

(a) By night, at least one man in every four, and by day at least one in every ten, will be on the look-out in each trench.*

(b) All men in the fire trench, and a proportion of men in the support trench, will always wear their equipment (except packs). Equipment may be taken off by order of a company commander in the case of working parties, when it will be kept close at hand. Every man will be told off to a particular post in case of attack ; he will not leave the proximity of his post without the permission of his immediate commander, nor leave the trench without the permission of an officer. Bayonets will always be fixed in the fire trench during the hours of darkness, during a snow storm or thick mist, or whenever the proximity of the enemy renders this course advisable.

All sentries are posted and relieved by a N.C.O. told off by each platoon for that purpose. One officer per company should be always on duty, and these N.C.O.'s report to him hourly. The officer on duty should be continually moving up and down to see that all is correct.

(c) Where enemy's lines are more than 100 or 150 yards away, a listening post should be established by each platoon, in a sap communicating with the front trench, and at a distance of approximately one-third of the distance to enemy's trench. These posts usually consist of three men and one N.C.O., and are posted at dusk and relieved every four hours. *All* the men of the post are awake for the four hours they are on duty. The officer on duty should visit listening posts twice each night.

(d) Machine guns will be in position and ready loaded by night, by day they may for purposes of concealment be removed, provided they can be immediately placed in position in the event of an attack ; one man must always be on the look-out at each machine gun, and the detachment must remain in close proximity to their gun.

(e) In every trench some form of alarm must be arranged to signal the approach of gas. Whistles should not be used for this purpose. The precautions against attacks by gas are dealt with in special instructions issued to the troops.

(f) Officers in a trench should be divided up along the trench, and must not all be together, especially at night. All the officers of a company must not live in one dug-out, as one shell might knock them all out.

Attacks prepared by artillery fire are most usually made at dawn, as soon as it is light enough for the artillery to observe, or about one hour before dusk. The former is usually the case in attacks on a large scale, or when a prolonged artillery bombardment precedes the attack, the latter when an attack on a small

---

* A good system is to work in groups of six men under a N.C.O. By night, two men of each group are on sentry. By day, only one man of each group is on sentry and the number of groups may be reduced. The number of groups must depend on proximity of enemy's trenches, nature of ground, &c.

scale is to be prepared and carried out before dusk, and the position won then consolidated under cover of darkness.

Units (including reserves) should stand to arms about one hour before dawn and before dusk.

30. *Usual Routine in Trenches.*

1. Rifles must be inspected twice daily, morning and evening, and every precaution must be taken to keep them and all other equipment in good order.* Men should be required to produce their oil bottles at rifle inspection.

2. The chief problem to be faced in the ordinary routine of trench work is to ensure that the maximum amount of work is done daily towards the subjection and annoyance of the enemy and the improvement of the trenches, consistent with the necessity for every man to get a proper amount of rest and sleep. This can only be done by a good system, a definite programme and time table of work being arranged and adhered to as far as possible. Some notes on the system of work in trenches are given in the next section.

3. Rations for 48 hours should be taken into the trenches on the man whenever possible, in order to save the labour of bringing up and distributing rations to the trenches every night. A quantity of sandbags and other stores and material have usually to be carried up to the trenches every night, and the arrangements for carrying parties require careful organization and forethought. The principle to be followed is that parties are detailed from behind to carry up rations or stores to troops in front, so as to avoid troops in front line having to send back parties and thus weaken their line. Thus the battalion reserve supplies carrying parties up to the front line trenches, and the brigade reserve may have to find carrying parties up to the battalion reserve or to the front trenches. Usually it will be possible to bring stores as far as the battalion reserve on pack animals or improvised handcarts. Ration parties and carrying parties must always be armed, wearing the rifle slung.

4. The system by which a unit in the trenches obtains the material required for the construction and repair of the trenches is as follows. In every brigade a "brigade workshop" is usually formed, the necessary personnel (from 12 to 20 men) being found from men in the battalions who are carpenters and artificers by trade. The "brigade workshop" is administered by the Staff Captain of the brigade, with a reliable N.C.O. in charge. It is established as near the trench line as possible, consistent with the men being able to

---

* Every care must be taken to prevent loss of equipment, &c., of which a great and usually avoidable waste may occur through lack of supervision, especially by junior officers. All rifles, ammunition (including fired cases), equipment, tools, trench stores, &c., found lying about within the area held by a unit must invariably be collected, at a pre-arranged dumping ground, special parties being detailed by units for this purpose, if necessary. A list of articles so collected by any unit should be sent to Brigade Headquarters, who will issue instructions as to their disposal.

work in reasonable safety. Its functions are to make up the material obtained from the R.E. into shapes and sizes suitable for carrying up to the trenches, to construct any simple device required for use in the trenches, and to carry out the distribution of the material. The brigade workshop makes up, for instance, barbed wire "knife rests," box loopholes, rifle rests, floor gratings, grenade boxes, signboards for communication trenches, &c.

Each unit in the trenches sends in daily to brigade headquarters, as early in the morning as possible, a request for the material required to be brought up that night. The Staff Captain arranges for its preparation in the brigade workshop and for sending it up to battalion headquarters, who arrange for its further distribution to companies.

31. *Work in Trenches.*

1. The importance of working on a definite system and with a definite programme has already been emphasised. The essential requirements for a fire trench are given in Section 17, and must always receive first attention—the barbed wire entanglement must be at least 10 yards wide, and concealed as far as possible.

The following points come next in order of importance :—

(*a*) The provision of good loopholes for snipers, at least one per section of men in the trench.

(*b*) The construction or improvement of communication trenches ; there should be one per platoon from the support line to the fire trench, if possible. From the support line to the reserve line, two per battalion will suffice.

(*c*) Listening posts, one per platoon, pushed well forward.

(*d*) The construction of bomb-proof or splinter-proof shelter. (See Section 19.)

(*e*) The provision of S.A.A. and grenade stores should be two S.A.A. reserve stores,* and one grenade store per platoon. Both S.A.A. and grenades should be stored in depth, *i e.*, a proportion should be stored in the support and reserve lines as well as in the front line. Suitable positions for these stores are at the points where communication trenches run into the various lines.

(*f*) An inspection trench (behind parados) and bombing pits or trenches (see page 22) may be made if required.

2. When sandbags are to be filled for any work in the trenches, they must not be filled by taking earth from holes made indiscriminately in the ground behind the trenches, as this practice makes this ground difficult to walk over and often interferes with the construction of fresh trenches. A trench which will serve some useful purpose should be made when earth for filling sandbags is required. When filled sandbags have to be carried for any distance, it is preferable to have separate parties for filling and carrying.

---

* In addition to the S.A.A. carried by the men (150 rounds), a supply equivalent to 120 rounds per man should be kept in the trenches and a reserve of 10 to 20 boxes at battalion headquarters.

3. It will be found convenient to have in every company a proportion of men specially trained under R.E. supervision in making loopholes, laying out barbed wire, revetting, &c. All men must, of course, be practised in these duties, but a specially trained squad for the more technical work will be found a great assistance.

4. As a rough guide to the number of men available for work in the trenches, it may be assumed that a company in the trenches will number about 160, leaving out signallers, machine gunners, orderlies, &c. Of these there will be by day about 16 to 20 men engaged in observation and sniping, and another 16 to 20 ready to relieve them. This will leave about 120 available for work, and it should be possible to arrange for them to do two hours' work in the morning and two in the afternoon. By night 40 sentries will be required, and the next relief of 40 must not be required to work before going on duty. The number of sentries by night may be reduced, if parties are working out in front of the trench.

5. The above notes are to be taken as a guide only. Local conditions vary the order of importance in which work should be undertaken. In some trenches it is impossible to do much work to the trenches by day.

The infantry must always be prepared to assist any R.E. and miners working in their section of the line.

32. *Observation and Sniping.*

1. A good system of sniping and observation is of the utmost importance in trench warfare. Usually every battalion has a special detachment of trained snipers working under a selected officer or N.C.O. Their duties are to keep the enemy's lines under constant observation, note any changes in the line and any new work undertaken by the enemy, keep the enemy's snipers in check, and to inflict casualties on the enemy whenever opportunity offers.

2. The following are the chief essentials for a successful sniping organization :—

    (*a*) Careful selection and training of snipers ;
    (*b*) Well-chosen and well-concealed posts or loopholes ;
    (*c*) A good system which will ensure all parts of the enemy's line being kept under constant observation ;
    (*d*) Good discipline, which will prevent posts being given away by carelessness ;
    (*e*) Care of equipment ;
    (*f*) Individual ingenuity in using disguises, masks, dummies, and other devices.

3. The following notes on the above points may be found of use :—

(a) *Selection and Training of Snipers.*—Men selected must be intelligent and well educated, besides being good shots. Observation and the ability to describe what he has seen are most important qualifications in a sniper.

The following are the chief points in which he should receive training :—

Shooting at vanishing and moving objects.
Judging distance.
Observation of bullet strike.
Use and care of optical sights.
Use and care of telescopes, field glasses, and periscopes.
Use of natural and construction of artificial cover.
Assimilation of colour to surroundings.
Construction of all types of loopholes and bullet-proof cover.
Value of immobility and silence and necessity of patience.
Map reading.
Writing of simple reports.
Eyesight training.
Location by means of flash and sound of hostile riflemen.

Snipers should be kept well informed; they should be shown aeroplane photographs of the enemy's position, and any information of interest to them from intelligence reports, examination of captured prisoners, &c., should be passed to them.

(b) *Choice and Concealment of Positions.*—No definite rules can be laid down as to the best positions for snipers. It must be left to the ingenuity and enterprise of the sniping officer or snipers to discover suitable places and to utilise them skilfully. Many excellent places will be found for observation and sniping in rear of the firing line. The best time to reconnoitre for such points is during the evening light, when the enemy cannot see any distance, but while it is still possible to see whether they command the view required.

The building of loopholes so as to make them secure, invisible, and convenient for observing and firing at definite points is an art in itself and gives endless openings for originality. Loopholes usually have to be let into the parapet by night and this must be practised, as the work has to be done quickly so as to be completed by daylight. The concealment of loopholes is made much easier if the outer face of the parapet is irregular. The Germans in many places take great pains to give an irregular outline to their parapet, using beams, timber, bolsters, mattresses and all sorts of rubbish piled up against it. A tunnel through the parapet, if the opening is carefully concealed, may form a good sniper's post.

The use of veils and coats of a colour to match the background is useful. If near sandbags, an empty sandbag worn over the head is a good disguise. Against an earth background a brown gauze veil, against grass a green one are both difficult to detect. Grass, weeds, wood or branches may give concealment.

Dummy loopholes are of great value to attract enemy's fire.

(c) *System.*—Posts should be so arranged that the whole front of the enemy's line opposite the battalion sector is under observation from dawn till dusk, each post having a definite front to watch. Snipers should work in pairs, one observing while the other is in readiness to shoot. Four men in two reliefs should be told off to each post.

Each post should be made to render a report daily under the following headings :—

Any new work done by the enemy.

Machine guns, trench mortars, snipers, observation posts, new loopholes, &c., located during the day.

Germans seen, place, uniform, apparent age, physique, equipment.

Any of the enemy fired at, any evidence to show they were hit.

Any other information of interest.

All rifles and optical equipment must be carefully cleaned on coming off duty, and should be inspected daily by an officer.

Snipers should not usually be required to do any night work, the duty of constant observation by day is a trying one, and, with the cleaning and care of the equipment, a sniper's time will be fully occupied.

(d) *Discipline.*—Good discipline is necessary to prevent carelessness in giving away posts by exposure or by wild and unnecessary firing. The battalion snipers are apt to develop into "scallywags" in habit and appearance, unless good discipline is strictly enforced.

(e) *Care of Equipment.*—This has already been mentioned above. It must be remembered that telescopic sights are most delicate instruments and require testing and adjustment by an expert if good results are to be obtained.

4. When a battalion is taking over a new line, the battalion snipers should, whenever possible, spend 24 hours in the new trenches with the snipers of the battalion to be relieved, in order to obtain all the information available from them and to become acquainted with the new line.

5. If a line is taken over in which the enemy's snipers have been allowed to get the upper hand, the first task is the location of the hostile snipers' posts. The enemy's loopholes should be searched for systematically all along the parapets, together with any likely sniping-places in rear. The trees, sandbags, &c., in our own trenches should be searched for rifle bullet marks which may show the direction of the hostile snipers. Sentries should be warned to try and discover from what point sniping is coming, and to watch for any flashes at night. When all possible has been done to locate the enemy's sniping, a system of loopholes should be decided on by which every part of the enemy's line can be observed and fired on from some secure position.

6. Co-operation between neighbouring units is essential. Often the best position to observe and fire on a certain portion of the line is in the sector of the battalion on the flank.

7. Fixed rifle batteries for keeping certain points or localities under fire by night are often extremely useful as a means of hampering the enemy's work and causing loss.

33. *Co-operation with Artillery.*

1. *Arrangements for Intercommunication.*—A certain force of artillery is detailed for the support of each infantry brigade holding a portion of the line. Batteries are allotted to sectors, and the points on which guns are normally layed* are selected by the infantry brigade commander in consultation with the artillery. The zones of fire allotted to adjacent batteries should overlap, if possible, at specially dangerous or important points.

The following system of communication between infantry and artillery has been found to answer well :—

> A code number or letter is given to each place on which guns are layed and a sketch showing the code is kept by the company commander in the trenches, by the battalion commander, at the battery O.P., and the battery. A direct line is laid from the trenches (at some selected company headquarters) to the battery. When fire is required at night on any particular point, it is sufficient to telephone down the code letter or number, and the gun concerned opens fire at once. If fire is required on any other place, it should be described with reference to one of the selected points. If this system is used, careful instructions as to the occasions on which artillery fire may be called for and a good understanding on the point between the infantry and artillery are necessary. Infantry must understand that firing by night is apt to give away the gun positions, so unnecessary requests for fire must be avoided ; on the other hand, frequent opportunities arise of doing the enemy damage by artillery fire at night and can only be taken advantage of if there is close co-operation between the infantry and artillery.
>
> In order not to give away permanent gun positions, it has been found to be a good plan to lay out night lines for single guns from positions to be taken up by night to deal with any special target.

The arrangements for the action of the artillery in case of an attack by the enemy are dealt with in Section 41, Chapter IV.

2. *Aggressive Action.*—In order to obtain full benefit from aggressive artillery action, close co-operation between infantry and artillery is essential. Every means must be used to induce the enemy to man his parapets or come out and expose himself and then to catch him with infantry and artillery fire. Various schemes will suggest themselves, and can be worked out between infantry and artillery commanders.

It is a good thing to have a number of schemes both of retaliation and of aggressive action worked out and communicated to all

---

* Usually known as the " night lines."

concerned, so that they can be put into force at once by a message —"Scheme No.   ."

3. *Information.*—The artillery require all the assistance they can get as to location of targets and the effect of their fire. Every endeavour should be made by the infantry to assist, and artillery observing posts should be connected to the front trenches for this purpose.

Infantry officers should be instructed in artillery methods of describing the position of targets, and it is a great advantage both to infantry and artillery if arrangements can be made for every infantry officer in turn to spend a few hours in the artillery observation station overlooking his part of the line. It helps him to know the country from an artillery point of view.

In describing targets, reference should always be made to points in the enemy's line, not to portions of our own line. The same names should therefore be given by infantry and artillery to prominent objects in the enemy's line.

The following rules should always be observed in reports sent by the infantry to the artillery :—

(i) The time and the observer's position must be accurately stated.

(ii) If reporting on enemy's artillery fire it must be stated whether shrapnel or H.E. The direction from which the shells are coming should be given as accurately as possible.

The fuzes of German shells frequently furnish valuable information to the artillery. They should be sent at once to the nearest artillery unit, with a statement as to where they were found.

4. *Artillery Observation Posts.*—Careful instructions are necessary to prevent artillery observation posts being given away by infantry approaching them without precaution. On the other hand artillery have been known to draw fire on infantry positions by approaching headquarters, reserve positions, etc., without concealment.

34. *Sanitation and Care of Feet.*

In view of the length of time during which the same line of trenches frequently has to be occupied, special precaution must be taken to keep trenches in a clean and sanitary state. A latrine system of buckets or tins must be arranged whenever possible. A supply of chlorate of lime will be kept in each trench and used daily. Places for burying all tins and rubbish should be carefully chosen as far from the trench as is practicable and should be marked.

Bodies of dead men will be taken right away from the trenches to be buried.

The disease known as "trench feet" is caused by prolonged standing in cold water or mud and by the continued wearing of wet socks, boots, and puttees. It is brought on much more rapidly when the blood circulation is interfered with by the use of tight boots, tight puttees, or the wearing of anything calculated to cause constriction of the lower limbs.   It can be prevented by :—

(a) Improvements to trenches leading to dry standing and warmth.

(b) Regimental arrangements ensuring that the men's feet and legs are well rubbed with whale oil or anti-frostbite grease before entering the trenches, and that, so far as is possible, men reach the trenches with dry boots, socks, trousers, and puttees.*

(c) By taking every opportunity while in the trenches to have boots and socks taken off from time time to time, the feet dried, well rubbed, and dry socks (of which each man should carry a pair) put on.

(d) By arrangements to give the men some exercise daily so as to maintain the blood circulation.

(e) By the provision of warm food in the trenches when possible, and by the provision of warmth, shelter, hot food, and facilities for washing the feet and drying wet clothes for men leaving the trenches.

It is important to keep 50 extra pairs of boots in a battalion, so that men whose boots need repair can be given another pair while theirs are being mended.   This can be done by battalion or brigade arrangements, a small shoemaker's establishment being kept up, which can go on working while the battalion is in the trenches.

35. *Communications.*

Communications in the trench line are established by telephone, but it must be realised that in the event of heavy shelling all telephonic communication is likely to be interrupted, and an efficient alternative system of visual signalling and a service of orderlies must be arranged and tested.

The Adjutant is responsible for the communications of his battalion.   Battalion signals are reponsible for all communications from battalion headquarters forward. The Brigade Signal Section is responsible for communications from brigade headquarters to battalion headquarters.

It is the duty of all ranks to assist the Signal Service in the following ways :—

(a) Reporting breaks in lines to the nearest Signal Station.

(b) Taking care to prevent damage to lines by troops or wagons, even if lines are badly laid.

(c) Taking into the nearest Signal section any telephone equipment found lying about.

(d) Preventing any unauthorized persons interfering with lines ; anyone seen interfering with cables who has not a blue and

---

* Long gum boots are issued for use in the trenches and should be put on *while the men's feet are still dry.* Gum boots should not be kept on longer than absolutely necessary, as owing to lack of ventilation, men's feet sweat freely, and the inside of the boot becomes wet.

white armlet should be asked his business and sent to the nearest Headquarters if his answers are not satisfactory ; any civilian seen touching lines should immediately be arrested.

Where telephone lines cross roads or tracks used by troops or communication trenches, &c., they must be buried or put up at such a height as not to impede movement. All telephone lines should be labelled at frequent intervals.

An efficient system of communication by orderlies must be arranged, and long messages, unless urgent, should, whenever possible, be sent by orderly to avoid congestion of telephone lines. Within a brigade, each battalion details two permanent bicycle orderlies, who remain with brigade headquarters for the purpose of taking messages to their battalions. Battalions are responsible that they always have at least two orderlies (in addition to the permanent brigade orderlies) who know the way to brigade headquarters. There must also be at battalion head-quarters guides to every trench held by the battalion.

Men should constantly be sent with messages at night so that they may know their way about. They should be able to describe accurately the position of their trench to the persons to whom they take the messages.

Headquarters should never be changed unless absolutely neces-sary, as it causes dislocation of the signal arrangements. Any unit which changes its headquarters must at once inform the unit above, and send an orderly to it to act as a guide to the new headquarters.

The Signal Service is responsible for giving the correct time, and watches should be set by signal time.

36. *Reports.*

Periodical situation reports are required from units in the trenches at stated hours, usually at morning, noon, and evening. The direction of the wind should be given in situation reports, as this affects the possibility or otherwise of a gas attack by the enemy.

Any unusual occurrence is, of course, reported at once, and any important change of wind should also be reported.

A casualty report and fighting strength return are required daily from units as soon after noon as possible.

A list of material required for the trenches should be rendered as early as possible in the morning (see p. 40).

Staffs must avoid burdening units in the trench line with unnecessary returns and correspondence ; units, on the other hand, must remember that delay or carelessness in rendering reports and returns causes unnecessary work to the staff.

CHAPTER IV.

ORGANIZATION OF A TRENCH LINE AND ACTION IN CASE OF ATTACK.

37. *General Considerations.*

The importance of organizing a line of trenches, and the distribution of the garrison within it, on a definite scheme and with a definite object, is sufficiently obvious. There is, however, a tendency, due usually to a lack of guidance from above, and also to the frequent changes of units in a line, to lose sight of this and to remain content to make the best of what is found existing. In such circumstances the defensive line becomes a haphazard collection of trenches, and the organization of their defence or of an offensive movement from them is a matter of great difficulty.

The objects to be sought in the organization of a system of trenches are :—

(*a*) To render the front line invulnerable to any small assaults by the enemy, and to create behind it a defensive zone of such depth as will not only make it .impossible. for an attack, in whatever strength it is made, to penetrate the whole of our defensive system, but will cause the enemy such loss, and so disorganize his attacking forces, as to enable our reserves to inflict on them a decisive defeat.

(*b*) To enable an attack on the enemy's defences to be made under the most favourable conditions and with the minimum of warning to the enemy. To this end our front line of trenches should be pushed within assaulting distance of the enemy's front line, and the arrangement of the trenches be such that the attacking troops can be distributed under the best conditions.

(*c*) In the normal periods of trench warfare, to reduce, by the improvement of the trenches and an economical distribution of the garrison, the wastage in our own forces, both from battle casualties and from disease ; and by skilful sniping and constant small enterprises to harass and inflict loss on the enemy.

Local conditions will largely determine the relative importance of the foregoing considerations. In a line of such length as now exists, there will be certain portions in which there are no objectives of sufficient importance to make an attack on a large scale either by ourselves or the enemy probable ; on such portions of the front the aim is by good organization of the defence and minor offensive enterprises to compel the enemy to

59

keep as large or a larger garrison than ourselves, and to increase his rate of wastage compared to our own. On other portions of the front there may be some objective which is likely to be the aim of a hostile attack, whereas an advance on our part would result in no commensurate gain ; in such a case the organization of the defence is of paramount importance. Or again, these conditions may be exactly reversed.

On a small scale, the same considerations apply to a brigade or battalion front. Certain features are of tactical importance, while certain lengths of trench offer no particular advantage to either side. Thus the distribution of the garrison and the construction of the defences must be founded on clear tactical ideas and not on a uniform distribution of so many men to so many yards of front.

38. *Distribution of Men in Trenches.*

By day, provided there is a good obstacle in front, covered by the cross-fire of machine guns, and supports can be moved up rapidly, the front line should be held lightly, in order to minimise loss from shell fire and the enemy's snipers, and to enable the majority of the men to obtain better rest and shelter in the support and reserve lines. By night, the front line must be held in sufficient strength to repulse raids by the enemy, and to prevent his reconnoitring patrols from penetrating the front line ; and also because in a line held thinly by night the men are apt to become " jumpy."

The question of the number of men placed in the front line of trenches is, however, to a certain extent, affected by the question of upkeep of the trenches. Experience has shown that trenches cannot be kept from falling in unless continuous work on their repair is carried on. In order, therefore, to keep a line of trenches habitable, it is often necessary to keep constantly in them a sufficient number of men to do the necessary work.

The distribution of a battalion in the trenches will usually consist of two or three companies in the front line finding their own supports and two or one companies in battalion reserve. Battalion headquarters should be close to the position of the battalion reserve, and will be connected by telephone to headquarters of companies.

It has been found by experience that in trench warfare it is advisable to make each company self-contained, *i.e.*, each company should have its own trained grenadiers with a sufficient supply of grenades, its own snipers, and men trained in laying out barbed wire, making loopholes, &c. There may be in addition a party of battalion grenadiers or battalion snipers, specially trained and organized for any special work.

39. *Machine Guns.*

1. *Distribution.*—The extra fire power now placed in the hands of brigade and battalion commanders by the increase in the
(B 11870)   D

number of machine guns enables men to be economized in the front trenches and a larger force thus left available for counter-attack.

A natural tendency is to place every available machine gun in the first line trenches, in order to establish an impassable curtain of fire in front of them. In the case of a bombardment, these trenches are liable to be very badly damaged and most of the machine guns may be destroyed. Any which have been located will certainly be put out of action. This tendency must therefore be suppressed.

The object to be aimed at is to place machine guns in such a way that if, after a bombardment or by the use of asphyxiating gas, the enemy succeeds in penetrating our lines, his infantry, at every step of their advance, will be met with fire from machine guns which have been previously echeloned in depth, and will thus be compelled to stop.

It is not so necessary to cover a large area with fire as to arrange for flanking fire from well selected positions; this fire will sweep away the waves of hostile infantry as they try to push forward.

Commanders must therefore divide their machine guns between the front line and the ground in rear of it, and in each particular case must see that the emplacements blend with the surrounding ground and fit in with the general scheme of defence.

The commander of the brigade machine gun company must always make a careful study of the whole sector held by the brigade, with a view to ensuring that the guns are placed to the best advantage. Co-operation must be arranged on the flanks of the sector with the machine gun companies of the neighbouring brigades.

2. *Protection and Concealment.*—A really bomb-proof emplacement for machine guns requires considerable thickness of cover, and in the open this fact will render it liable to be easily located by the enemy, who will be able to destroy it if he thinks it worth while.

Bomb-proof emplacements must therefore only be placed in positions where the enemy cannot observe them, such as on reverse slopes, or where their relief conforms to the folds of the ground, or in woods, &c.

The importance of keeping machine guns invisible in places where a bomb-proof emplacement cannot be concealed necessitates the firing emplacements being made outside the shelters, but they must be near enough for the guns to be brought into action at a moment's notice. The shelters are only to be used to protect the teams, and can therefore be dug as deep as required and so have an almost invisible relief.

Firing emplacements must be *as near the shelters as possible.* They can either be protected against splinters by light overhead cover, or be in the parapet without any head cover at all.

Firing emplacements can also be prepared in holes in the open in front of or behind the fire trench. These holes should be connected with the shelters by underground passages. The gun should be mounted at the last moment on the extreme edge of the hole, either without any protection at all, or, preferably, masked by a shield or gently sloping parapet. If the hole and its surroundings are carefully disguised, it will certainly escape observation by the enemy. Such emplacements should be frequently used behind the first lines (see fig. 22).

When a fire trench is dug on a reverse slope, a very useful method when the amount of work involved is not prohibitive is to dig such holes in front of the ridge and connect them with the trench by underground passages running under the ridge itself.

Machine guns can also be placed in trees in the same way as observation posts.

In order to ensure invisibility, all communication trenches leading to the emplacements must be constructed as blinded saps. It is also essential to prepare a large number of emplacements in order to avoid firing daily from those which are specially constructed for the purpose of repelling an attack.

Machine gunners must never abandon their position in any circumstances. If necessary they must allow themselves to be surrounded, and must defend themselves to the last. A lost position has on many occasions been recaptured quickly thanks to the tenacity and heroism of a few machine gunners. In order to render such a desperate resistance possible, machine gun emplacements must fulfil the following conditions :—

(a) They must be surrounded by irregular barbed wire entanglements, made as invisible as possible.

(b) There must be several emplacements in case one should be rendered useless.

(c) The teams must be provided with protection against gas, and have plenty of food, water and ammunition.

3. *Lewis guns.*—The Lewis gun differs from the Vickers or Maxim by its greater mobility and its inability to sustain a rapid rate of fire for any length of time. Lewis guns should be used in a defensive line to economise infantry and to supplement the Vickers or Maxim guns of the brigade company, not to take their place. They can be used in co-operation with the machine guns of the brigade company to sweep depressions, covered approaches, &c., on which these guns cannot fire. Lewis guns fire over the parapet and can therefore often sweep ground invisible from a machine gun emplacement, which is usually sited near ground level and therefore has a low command. There must be the closest co-operation between the battalions and the commander of the brigade machine gun company over the choice of the positions and tasks for Lewis guns.

As Lewis guns are company weapons, their number in the front line will usually be determined by the number of companies holding it ; it may, however, occasionally be advisable to take the Lewis guns of supporting or reserve companies, if thereby the number of men in the front line can be reduced, and if those companies do not require their guns for other purposes.

Owing to the mobility of the Lewis gun and the absence of a fixed platform, emplacements, in the ordinary acceptation of the term, are not required. The Lewis gun can be fired off its light mounting over any portion of the parapet with very little preliminary preparation, and its fire can be brought to bear on an object very rapidly ; a much greater liberty of action can therefore be allowed to this weapon than to the Vickers or Maxim gun. Although emplacements are unnecessary, definite " firing places " must be prepared, either by means of loopholes or in depressions in the parapet, defiladed from the front if possible.

In allocating Lewis guns to a portion of the defence, certain fronts should be given to them, and the teams should be thoroughly familiar with their " firing places," and the ground to be swept from each.

It is just as essential to keep Lewis guns under cover during a bombardment as it is to keep machine guns and their teams. In the case of the former weapon, however, as there are no definite emplacements, greater choice is possible in the selection of the spot for the shelters, provided the guns can come into action without delay.

40. *Action in Case of Attack.*

1. The measures taken by the defence to meet an attack have already been outlined at the end of Section 2 (p. 7). The main principles are :—

(a) To stop any attack from the outset by a concentration of artillery, machine gun, and rifle fire, the moment the enemy is seen issuing from his front trenches or collecting in them for an attack.* To this end careful arrangements must be made for observation and for communicating to the artillery by telephone or signal the moment the enemy's attack commences.

(b) It must be understood by all ranks that, should the enemy succeed in gaining a footing in our trenches, a counter-attack made at once, and without hesitation, will almost always be successful, even if made by inferior numbers. Counter-attacks by grenadier parties, especially from the flanks, are often particularly effective. On the other hand, if a counter-attack cannot be launched before the enemy has had time to organize and establish himself, then it becomes necessary to wait till an attack with adequate artillery preparation can be organized.

(c) Strong points and keeps organized for all-round defence must be held to the last, even though surrounded, and whatever happens to the rest of the line. They will

---

* A frequent method of attack by the Germans is to send on at first a few men only, and if they are successful to follow up with large numbers.

break up the enemy's attack and give time for a counter-attack in force to be organized.

(d) An attack on any large scale will be preceded by a very heavy bombardment, which may last several days and result in the partial obliteration of portions of the front system of trenches. During such a bombardment, special instructions may be issued by the higher commanders for the temporary withdrawal of the bulk of the garrison from portions of the front line. But strong points and localities organized for all-round defence must always be maintained.

2. All formations and units will have schemes made out for the defence of the portion of the line for which they are responsible. These schemes must always lay down the points of special tactical importance, which it is essential to hold. Arrangements should be made so as to be in a position to launch immediate counter-attacks, organized beforehand, to recapture any of these points which may be lost. If the important tactical points are correctly chosen, their re-capture should make untenable any intermediate portions of the line which may have fallen into the enemy's hands. As far as battalions and brigades are concerned, schemes of defence are based on the following principles :—

(a) The front system of trenches is the main line of defence. Should the enemy, following a heavy bombardment, succeed in penetrating into our line, he must be driven out immediately, before he has time to establish himself there, and our front system of trenches regained by counter-attacks directed against the points of tactical importance.

(b) It is the duty of the immediate supports, without waiting for orders, to reinforce the front line of trenches if required, and if any trench is captured to counter-attack at once without hesitation, and if any trench is blown up to occupy the crater at once, or prevent the enemy doing so by occupying our side of the crater and placing obstacles in the hole.

(c) The battalion reserve is to be used offensively to maintain the front system of trenches by counter-attack. Should the attack be on such a large scale that the battalion reserve is obviously insufficient to attempt the re-establishment of the line, it will be used to occupy a position to check any further advance by the enemy till a counter-attack by the brigade reserve can be organized.

(d) The brigade reserve will be used on similar principles to the battalion reserve.

The brigade scheme of defence will therefore include :—

(a) A definition of the sector for which each battalion in the front line is responsible.

(B 11870)   D 2

64

(b) General instructions as to how the line is to be maintained in case of attack, with special reference to protection of the flanks should the enemy succeed in breaking the line to the right or left.

(c) The distribution of the machine guns of the brigade company, and the manner in which they are to be used.

(d) Arrangements for communication with the supporting artillery, to ensure fire being opened on the enemy's front line immediately.

(e) The state of readiness to be maintained by the brigade reserve, arrangements for instant communication of an alarm to it, and for its action.

The brigade reserve is usually in billets or shelters, one to two miles behind the front line. The defence scheme should arrange for it to move at once up to some position near the line of the battalion reserves by the routes most sheltered from enemy's observation and artillery fire. These routes must be reconnoitred by day and night by the brigade reserve, and guides must know them. While the brigade reserve is falling in, a mounted officer from it should go to brigade headquarters. The position to which the brigade reserve will be directed in case of attack, and the time it should take to reach it, should be known to battalions in front line. Arrangements to communicate with the reserve when it has reached this position must be made.

(f) Arrangements for action of any guns of the brigade machine gun company which are in reserve.

(g) Orders for first line transport.

Battalion defence schemes should include :—

(a) Arrangements for alternative methods of communication if telephone lines are broken.

(b) Action of battalion reserve, and arrangements for co-operation with neighbouring battalions in case of counter-attack by battalion reserves.

(c) Orders to officers in charge of strong points or keeps.

(d) Special arrangements for the action of grenadier parties, if necessary, and for keeping up the supply of grenades.

3. The precautions in case of an attack by gas are given in special instructions issued.

41. *Action of Artillery in Case of Attack.*

To meet a hostile attack by night, in a fog or under cover of smoke and gas, the important thing is to waste no time, but start the guns firing at once. Every gun should be normally laid on its "night line" (see p. 44) when not otherwise engaged, and, on receipt of a pre-arranged signal, will open fire at once on this line, "sweeping" a certain amount where necessary. The officer at the battery then endeavours to ascertain the situation, but, if the wires have been cut, he must use his own discretion as to continuing fire.

An alarm signal is necessary, and the occasions on which it should be used must be clearly understood. Every precaution should be taken to prevent it spreading needlessly to neighbouring units. A visual signal, in case telephone lines are cut, must be pre-arranged.

It is advisable to test the alarm signal arrangements occasionally, but this should only be done by the brigade or division commander in consultation with the C.R.A. The telephone communications between the artillery and infantry should be frequently tested by day and by night, and at least once every 24 hours a round should be fired by the artillery, on a pre-arranged signal, to test the time taken between the sending of the message and the bursting of the shell.

CHAPTER V.

NOTES ON THE ATTACK IN TRENCH WARFARE.*

42. *Need for Careful Preparation.*

Success in an attack on a line of trenches depends on the training of the troops and on the thoroughness of the preparations made.

Confusion is apt to occur in any assault ; it is specially to be expected when attacking a maze of carefully prepared positions, and is the most frequent cause of failure. Unless it can be prevented or minimized by careful preparation and training, the enemy, whose counter-attacks will have been planned and be taking place over familiar ground, will probably succeed in driving the attackers back again.

Time for preparation is available, and full use must be made of this. The attack can, therefore, be said to begin weeks before the day fixed for the assault.

43. *Infantry Preparation for Attack.*

1. *Reconnaissance.*—Units in occupation of a system of trenches must always consider their line and the enemy's defences from the point of view of attack. Constant observation and patrolling will be required to add to the information available. The ground between the opposing front lines must be accurately reconnoitred so that no unsuspected obstacles, such as sunken wire or ditches, may hold up an assault. Every effort must be made to locate machine gun emplacements or strong points in the enemy's line, so as to be able to assist the artillery in the bombardment of the hostile defences. The whole of the enemy's system of defences over which the assault is to go must be made familiar to all ranks. A great deal of information is available from the excellent trench maps compiled from aeroplane photographs, and a study of the photographs themselves.†

2. *Plan of Attack.*—In the plan of attack the following are the chief points to consider from the point of view of infantry units (brigades and battalions) :—

---

* This chapter is not intended to be exhaustive and does not touch on very many most important preparations and arrangements which have to be made in the case of an attack on a large scale. It is intended to serve as a general guide as to the arrangements necessary on the part of brigades and battalions.

† The use of a magic lantern to throw aeroplane photographs on a screen has been found of great value.

(a) The distribution of the attacking infantry, *i.e.*, the number of lines or "waves" required for the attack, the points opposite which the assaulting lines must be strongest to deal with important objectives, the detailing of parties for special tasks ("clearing" parties, carrying parties, parties to dig communication trenches back to our front line, &c.). Definite objectives must be allotted to each body of men down to sections.

(b) The use of machine guns and trench mortars to support the attack, and arrangements to send forward a proportion of these behind the attacking infantry.

(c) The employment of grenadier parties.

(d) The protection of the flanks, and arrangements for co-operation with, and assistance of, neighbouring units.

(e) Arrangements for communication.

(f) Arrangements for supply of S.A.A., grenades, tools, &c.

3. *Training.*—Before taking part in an attack, troops that have been a long time sedentary in the trenches will require special training to fit them for the assault. They will require marching and exercise to harden them. The enemy's defensive lines should be reproduced to actual scale somewhere well behind our lines, and the troops be practised in the assault, with and without officers, till every man knows his role in the attack. The co-operation of grenadiers with the rest of the infantry must be practised.

Signallers will require practice in visual signalling.

4. *Preparation of Trenches for Attack.*—All possible preparation of the trenches should be done long before the attack takes place, otherwise our intention to attack will be made plain to the enemy. Therefore in every system of trenches dispositions for an attack must be considered, and only minor additions should be necessary previous to the actual attack. It should be the aim of every commander to push his front line trenches before an assault as close to the enemy as possible, or at least to within 200 yards. This may be done by sapping and then joining up the heads of saps.

Advantage can sometimes be taken of a dark night and a new trench be dug in front of our old front trench during the night. In this case the party must be large enough to ensure getting cover the first night. This method will also only be possible if the troops holding the line, by stopping the enemy's patrols moving about, have established a superiority in the "debatable ground."

Assembly trenches must be prepared so that the successive waves of assaulting troops can be launched at the required time. These trenches should be prepared gradually. As far as possible use should be made of the existing trenches. A stereotyped form cannot be laid down for assembly trenches. The requisites are :—

(i) There must be easy egress both above ground and by communication trenches.

(ii) The assaulting troops must be close enough up.

(iii) The general line must be perpendicular to the line of advance.

In arranging assembly trenches care must be taken to provide forming up places for the various special parties, such as grenadiers, working parties, &c.

Sidings will probably be required for reserves. These can be suitably made off the "up" communication trenches.

Communication trenches must be provided in sufficient number to avoid congestion. One for up and one for down traffic per battalion frontage at least will be required, and between the last lines the number will require further increase, so that finally there will be one trench leading into the front line about every 50 yards.

Sign boards will be required on all communication trenches showing which are for up and which are for down traffic. Care must be taken to make those intended for evacuation of wounded wide enough and with sufficiently easy curves to allow a stretcher to pass.

Saps should be dug forward to be converted into communication trenches to the enemy's front line when captured. These should be tunnelled under the parapet, and when time allows be continued underground instead of above ground.

Exits from trenches must be prepared. These can either be made out of sandbags or by means of ladders. If ladders are used, all the ladders in one bay should be nailed together top and bottom by planks to prevent a ladder falling. Care must be taken that the tops of ladders do not protrude over the parapet.

In short, the preparation of trenches for assault entails the careful selection of the position of every man prior to the assault, and then the preparation of forming up places to suit.

Our own wire must be cut by parties detailed from the assaulting battalions. It should be cut during darkness the night before the assault.*

Bridges will have to be made over our trenches at certain points to provide for the advance of the artillery.

5. *S.A.A., Grenades, Food, Water.*—Stores of S.A.A., grenades, food, water, tools, and R.E. material must be established in the trenches. They must be conveniently placed for carrying forward to the captured position. One man should be in charge of each store. Special carrying parties will require to be detailed to carry the stores forward. Dumps of stores should be arranged in échelon, so that those in the trenches can be easily replenished.

---

* The fact that our own wire has been cut can be disguised by cutting transverse gaps or by écheloning the original wire thus ___ ___.

69

44. *Equipment.*

Assaulting troops should be as lightly equipped as possible, but it is difficult to reduce the weight carried below the following scale :—*

> 200 rounds S.A.A.
> One day's rations (in addition to iron ration).
> Two sandbags.
> One pick or shovel to every third man.

Extra wire cutters, flares, smoke candles, etc., will be carried by a proportion of the men.

The equipment of grenadier parties is dealt with in the pamphlet on " Training and Employment of Grenadiers."

Grenadiers carry rifle and bayonet and 50 rounds S.A.A.

45. *Preliminary Bombardment.*

The artillery will prepare the way for the assault by battering the enemy's defences and destroying his obstacles. It will be the duty of the infantry to assist the artillery by continually reporting information gained about the enemy's line, and by observing the effect of the artillery fire mainly as to whether strong points or machine gun emplacements are being suitably dealt with, and the success or otherwise of the wire cutting. It is also necessary for infantry officers to make certain that they and the artillery commanders are in agreement as to the places where the wire is going to be cut.

This bombardment will probably take a long time, and during that time the garrisons of trenches should be reduced to avoid the casualties from the enemy's retaliation.

The enemy must be prevented from repairing his obstacles and trenches, after they have been damaged by artillery fire, by keeping the damaged portions under fire of trench mortars, rifle grenades, machine guns and rifle.

Definite tasks must always be allotted to trench mortars, in co-operation with the artillery.

46. *The Assault.*

The bombardment is kept up till the moment fixed for assault, when the artillery lifts, and the assault is launched.

The assaulting troops will consist of successive waves, each wave consisting of men extended at about one man every two yards, and with about 50 yards between waves. The number of waves will depend on the distance from our front trench of the final objective. The pace will be moderate, and on no account must a wild rush be allowed. The assault must be pressed on above

---

*˙Arrangements for storing packs of troops taking part in an attack must be made. Each man's name should be marked on his pack.

ground till its objective is reached, special parties being detailed to clear up the trenches over which the assault passes. These "clearing" parties accompany the assaulting waves, but remain behind in the trenches which they have been detailed to clear, while the assaulting troops press on to the final objective without entering them. "Clearing" parties will be composed largely of grenadiers.

The assaulting troops, on gaining the final objective, proceed to consolidate. R.E. parties and carrying parties to take up the tools and material required must be detailed beforehand. It may be impossible to take up material till after dark.

Parties must also be detailed to consolidate tactical points in rear of the assaulting troops, as they are gained. They will be assisted by the "clearing" parties, when these have finished their task of disposing of the enemy.

Generally speaking, then, attacking troops will consist of :—

(a) The troops detailed to carry through the assault to the final objective.

(b) The clearing parties who dispose of any enemy left behind in the trenches over which the assault has passed.

(c) The parties detailed for the consolidation of tactical points behind the assaulting troops and parties to carry up to the assaulting troops the material required to consolidate the positions won.

Special arrangements will have to be made, and special bodies of troops detailed to form a defensive flank on each side of the front assaulted, and also to attack isolated or semi-isolated strong points encountered on the flanks of assaulting troops.

The relative strength of the various parties cannot be laid down. They vary according to circumstances. The important principle is that every body of troops has a definite task assigned to it and knows what that task is.

47. *Action of Artillery during the Assault.*

At the moment fixed for assault, artillery fire must "lift" from the actual places to be assaulted, but must be kept up on the immediate flanks of the attack. Once the assault has been launched, the duty of the artillery is :—

(a) To keep down the fire of the hostile artillery. This is done by the counter-batteries.

(b) To prevent the enemy bringing up supports and reserves, by keeping up a steady fire on his communication trenches and other lines of approach and places in rear where troops might collect for a counter-attack.

(c) To give continuous support to the infantry during their advance and to deal with obstacles, strong points, &c., which may be holding them up.

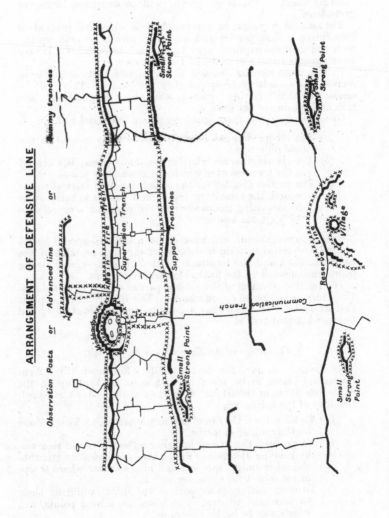

ARRANGEMENT OF DEFENSIVE LINE

DIAGRAM OF FIRE SUPERVISION AND COMMUNICATION TRENCHES.

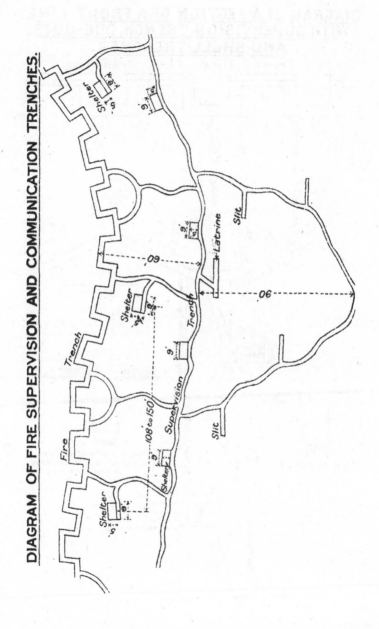

DIAGRAM OF A SECTION OF A FRONT LINE, WITH SUPERVISION TRENCH, DUG-OUTS, AND SHELL TRENCHES.

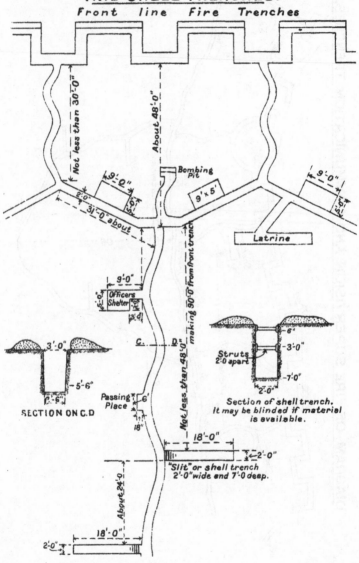

Front line Fire Trenches

Not less than 30'-0"

About 48'-0"

Bombing Pit

9' x 5'

9'-0"

2'-0"

31'-0" about

Latrine

9'-0"

9'-0"

Officers Shelter

5'-0"

3'-d"

making 90'-0" from front trench

C. D

3'-0"

6"

Struts 2'-0 apart

3'-0"

7'-0"

2'-0"

5'-6"

2'-6"

SECTION ON C.D

Passing Place

6'

18"

Not less than 48'-0"

Section of shell trench. It may be blinded if material is available.

18'-0"

2'-0"

"Slit" or shell trench 2'-0" wide and 7'-0 deep.

About 24'-0

18'-0"

2'-0"

74

ALTERNATIVE ORGANIZATION OF A FRONT LINE.

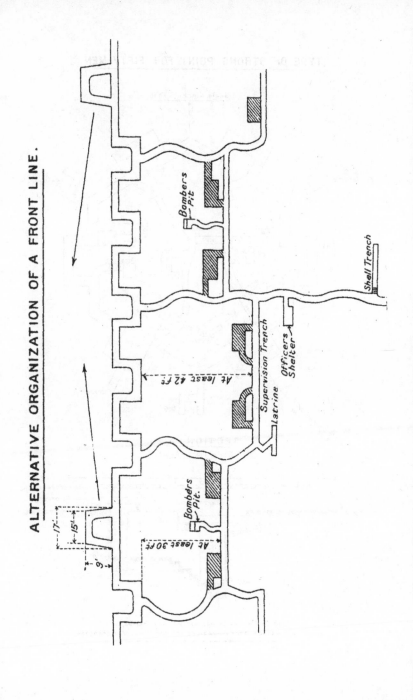

TYPE OF STRONG POINT FOR FIFTY MEN.

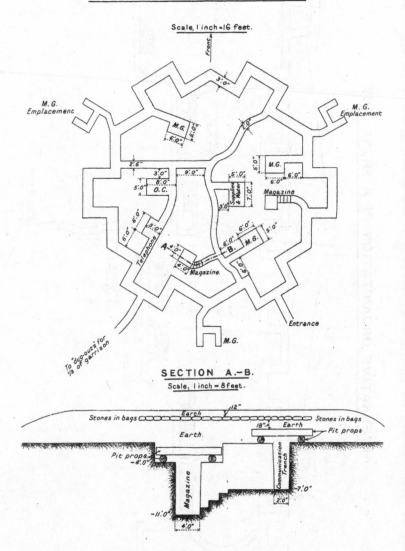

Scale, 1 inch = 16 feet.

SECTION A.–B.
Scale, 1 inch = 8 feet.

In bad soil it may be necessary to use Frames, or struts and walings in the magazines and communication trenches.

SUPPORTING OR STRONG POINT.

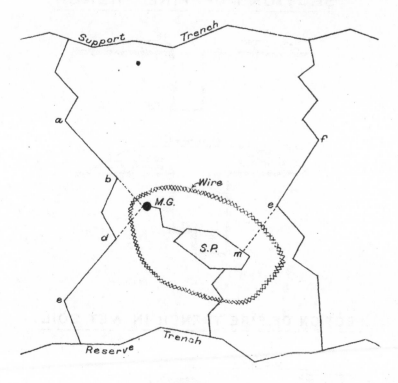

SECTION ON m,e,f.

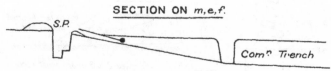

Portions ab-cd-ef- of Communication
Trench enfiladed from S.P. as shown in
dotted lines.
    To increase fire effect trenches
sloping gradually upwards may be constructed
along dotted lines, as in section on m,e,f.

SECTIONS OF FIRE TRENCH.

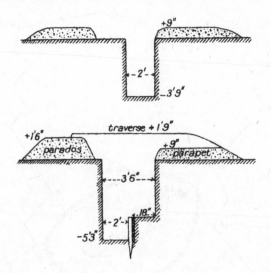

SECTION OF FIRE TRENCH IN WET SOIL.

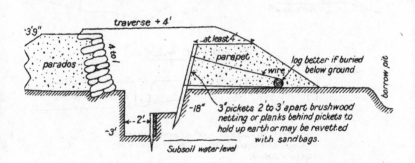

BOMBING PIT.

Scale ½ in = 1 ft.

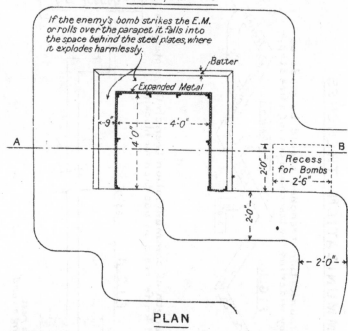

If the enemy's bomb strikes the E.M. or rolls over the parapet it falls into the space behind the steel plates, where it explodes harmlessly.

Batter

Expanded Metal

9"

4'-0"

4'-0"

A ————————————————————— B

2'-0"

Recess for Bombs
2'-6"

2'-0"

2'-0"

PLAN

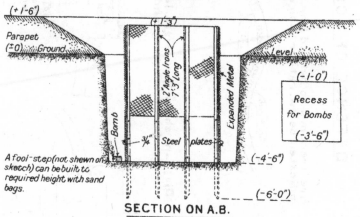

(+ 1'-6")

(+ 1'-3")

Parapet (±0) Ground

Level

2 Angle Irons 7'-3" Long

Bomb

¾" Steel plates

Expanded Metal

(-1'-0")

Recess for Bombs

(-3'-6")

A fool-step (not shewn on sketch) can be built to required height with sand bags.

(-4'-6")

(-6'-0")

SECTION ON A.B.

79

DEFENCE OF COMMUNICATION TRENCHES

Fire trenches to defend communication trenches should be made as indicated below, rather than by widening the trench and cutting a fire step.

FIG. 10.

Diagram showing straight length of communication trench for protection against bombing and knife rests in position for blocking.

FIG. 11.

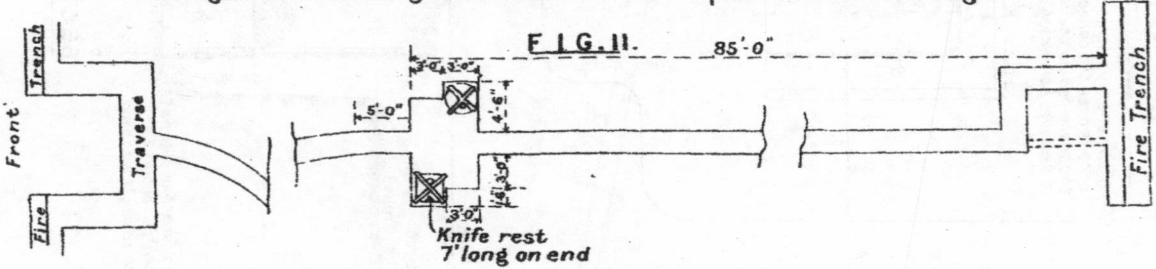

80

ALTERNATIVE FOR 30 YDS. STRAIGHT AT END OF COMMUNICATION TRENCH.

Scale 1 inch = 40 feet.

When the nature of the ground allows it, the following arrangement of the rear end of a communication trench may be substituted for the 30 yds. straight; it will generally be necessary to cut an inclined channel, running from ±0 at the end of the loopholes L^1. L^2. to −4′0 at B^1. B^2 in order to bring fire on the zig-zag portion of the communication trench.

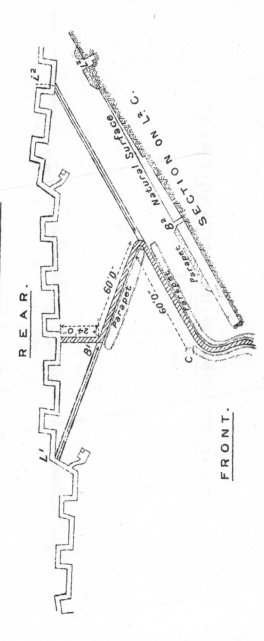

REAR.

FRONT.

SECTION ON L.C.

TYPE OF SUNK WIRE ENTANGLEMENT

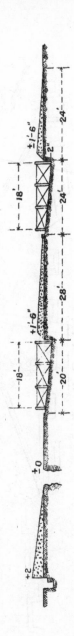

WIRE ENTANGLEMENT.

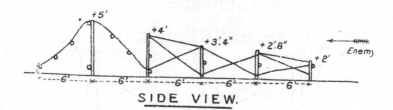

+5' +4' +3'4" +2'8" +2'

Enemy

6' 6' 6' 6' 6'

SIDE VIEW.

PLAN, (WITHOUT LOOSE WIRE)

"KNIFE REST" OBSTACLE.

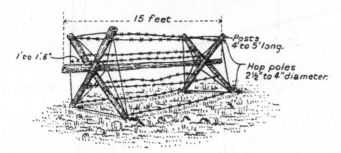

15 feet

1' to 1'.6"

Posts 4' to 5' long.

Hop poles 2½" to 4" diameter.

The efficiency of the obstacle is increased by adding barbed wire wrapped in loose spiral coils round it.

DUG OUTS.
FRAMES.

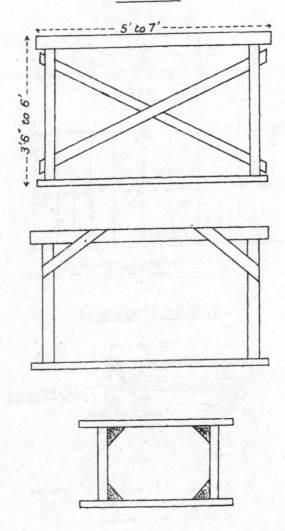

TYPE OF DUG-OUT IN WET GROUND FOR EIGHT MEN.

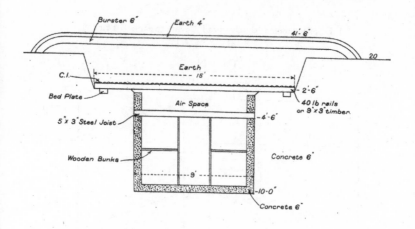

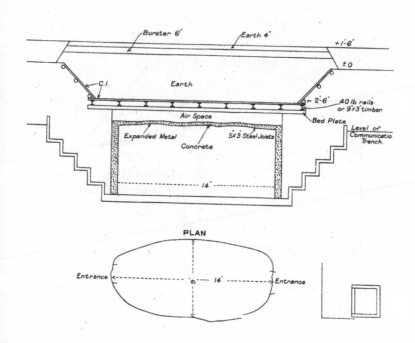

PLAN

MACHINE GUN EMPLACEMENTS.

of minimum dimensions as fixed by Commandant
of M.G. School.

1 Emplacement with Overhead Cover, to fire Sitting.
Scale – ⅜" = 1'.

PLAN.

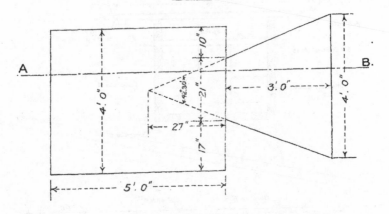

SECTION ON A.B.

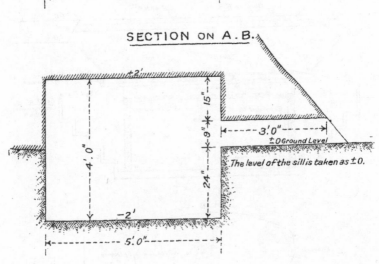

The level of the sill is taken as ±0.

MACHINE GUN EMPLACEMENTS.

of minimum dimensions as fixed by Commandant
of M.G. School.

2 Emplacement with Overhead Cover, to fire Standing.

Scale _ ¼" = 1'.

PLAN.

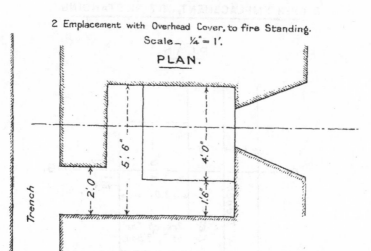

SECTION ON A.B.

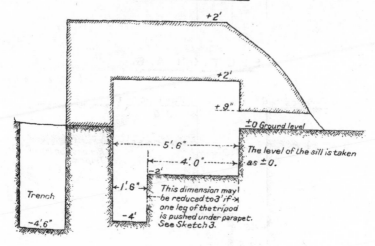

The level of the sill is taken as ±0.

This dimension may be reduced to 3' if one leg of the tripod is pushed under parapet. See Sketch 3.

MACHINE GUN EMPLACEMENTS,

of minimum dimensions as fixed by Commandant of M.G. School.

3 OPEN EMPLACEMENT, TO FIRE STANDING.

P.LAN.

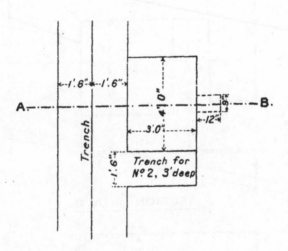

SECTION A.B.

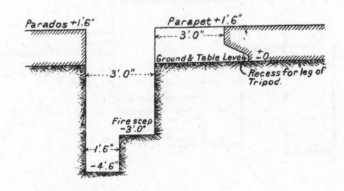

MACHINE GUN EMPLACEMENT.

Scale. ¼ Inch = 1 Foot.

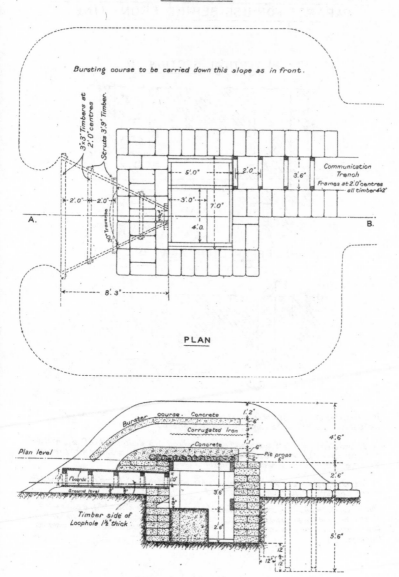

PLAN

SECTIONAL ELEVATION on A.B.

TYPE OF MACHINE-GUN EMPLACEMENT WITHOUT PARAPET FOR USE BEHIND FRONT LINE.

P' VERTICAL SECTION P

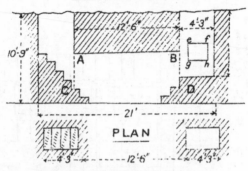

PLAN

P' PERSPECTIVE VIEW P

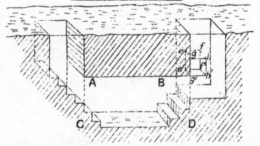

This emplacement consists of two shafts, P and P', rectangular in section. The firing shaft P is 4'3" x 2'-7" x 7'-8", and the entrance shaft P' is 4'-3" x 2'-7" x 10'-9".

These two shafts are 12'-6" apart and are connected by a shelter A, B, C, D, dug or mined, with a casing of 2' planks. One of the walls of the firing shaft P is provided with a recess e, f, g, h, e', f', g', h', which serves for storing ammunition.

To fire, the machine gunner climbs up a ladder placed in shaft P and rests the machine gun on the natural surface of the ground.

There is no parapet, etc., showing above the ground, as the whole of the excavated earth is removed to a considerable distance. The emplacement is constructed away from any communication or other trench and it is impossible for the most skilled observer to discover it.

WINTER AVENUE.
GENERAL TRACE.
Not to Scale.

A.B.C.D.   Points at which general direction changes.

o.p.p.p.   Traverses, and passing places.

d.d.d.   Fire breastwork to cover, borrow ditches;
             12 to 18 ft. long.

     Of same profile as Fig 24 but no back parapet to give
   room for bombing

e.   Returns left open to allow fire from reserve
         trench down the avenue.

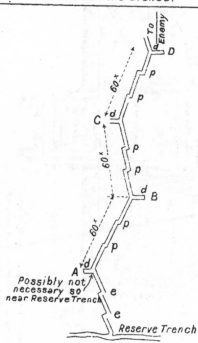

91

WINTER AVENUE.

CROSS SECTION.

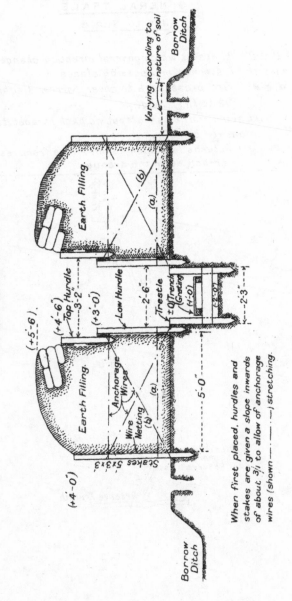

When first placed, hurdles and
stakes are given a slope inwards
of about 3/1 to allow of anchorage
wires (shown ————) stretching.

WINTER AVENUE.
DETAILS OF PASSING PLACE.

SCALE 1˙- 2˙

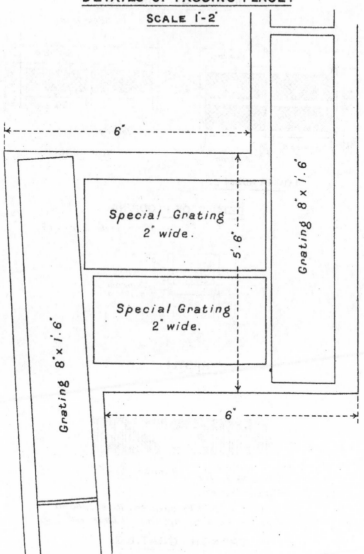

6˙

Special Grating
2˙ wide.

Special Grating
2˙ wide.

5˙.6˙

6˙

Grating 8˙ x 1˙.6˙

Grating 8˙ x 1˙.6˙

WINTER AVENUE.

DETAILS OF HURDLES.

Scale ½ in = 1 Ft

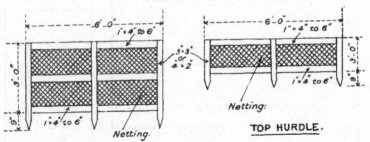

LOWER HURDLE.

TOP HURDLE.

DETAILS OF FLOORING.

Scale ½ in = 1 Ft

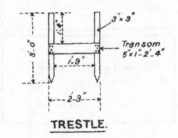

TRESTLE.

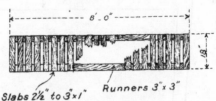

Slabs 2½" to 3" x 1"
about 1½" apart.

Should be covered with expanded
metal to save wear & tear (and fire.)

TRENCH GRATING.

94

WINTER AVENUE.

EXTENSION OF A SQUAD.

(a)

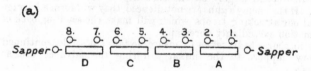

(b)

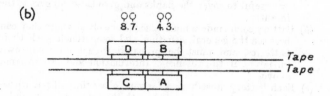

(c)

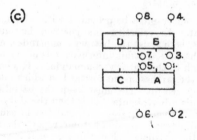

(d)

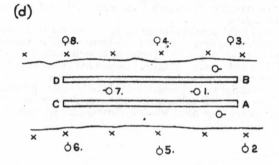

The difficulties of this latter task are almost entirely those of observation and intercommunication. It is often impossible owing to smoke, dust, &c., to see exactly where the infantry have got to, and what is stopping their progress. The obtaining of timely information from the advanced troops presents great difficulties, and will depend largely on the efficiency of our counter-battery work. If the enemy's guns are not silenced, they will form a barrage behind our attacking troops which will make the sending back of information exceedingly uncertain.

The measures to be taken to ensure, so far as possible, continued artillery support to the infantry during the advance are as follows :—

(a) A proportion of field guns dug in close to our front trenches are useful to cover the flanks and give close support to the infantry.

(b) Battery commanders must place themselves where they can best see the general situation and keep touch with their batteries, and must be prepared to act on their own initiative, in the absence of information and orders from above.

(c) Each battery must have a forward observing officer, whose duties are to keep in touch with the infantry commander whom the battery is supporting, to keep the battery commander informed as to the exact position of the infantry, and to assist him in ranging on to anything that is checking the progress of our infantry.

The forward observing officer must be provided with telephone and signalling equipment. In selecting his position he must remember that his business is to assist the battery commander, not to join in the infantry fight, and that his information is of no use unless he can get it through to the battery commander. His best position will normally be the farthest point forward to which good communication has been opened up. He must keep the battalion commander informed of his whereabouts. It is then the duty of the infantry to let him know their requirements, and the measure of support they receive will depend largely on their reports being clear and intelligible to the artillery. For this reason it is very necessary that infantry officers should understand what information the artillery require.

Some form of light signal, visible to aircraft and artillery through smoke and mist, is required to let everyone know when the infantry have gained a certain objective. It should be sufficiently portable to be carried by every man. Flags and screens have been used, but they often get left behind and are then very misleading.

A proportion of light trench mortars should be brought up behind the infantry as soon as possible, and it may sometimes be possible to use them against some point which is checking the advance.

48. *Employment of Machine Guns.*

The role of machine guns in the attack is —

(*a*) To assist the artillery in the preparation of the attack, if required ;
(*b*) To cover the assaulting infantry with their fire and to keep down flanking fire ;
(*c*) To fill up gaps that may occur either laterally or in depth ;
(*d*) To assist in the consolidation of the position and repulse hostile counter-attacks.

It is most important that all machine guns are allotted a definite task and given definite orders. The guns of the brigade company may be allotted as follows :—

(*a*) Some to cover advance by firing on the enemy's parapet, keeping down fire against flanks of attack, and sweeping ground in rear of enemy's first line, till masked by the advance of the infantry ;
(*b*) Some to follow up the assaulting infantry. A proportion of these guns should accompany the parties detailed to consolidate tactical points in rear of the assaulting troops. Usually, Lewis guns only will go forward with the assaulting infantry at first. But some of the guns of the brigade company must be brought up as soon as possible after the assault has reached its final objective. These guns should not fire before the advance ; the line of advance of each gun should be carefully selected beforehand ;
(*c*) Some may be detailed to fire from positions in rear on points where enemy are likely to collect for counter-attack.

Lewis guns, owing to their mobility, are very suitable at the opening of an attack to provide covering fire from the front. Under cover of darkness, smoke, or artillery bombardment, Lewis gunners can creep out in front of the trenches and establish themselves in shell holes, ditches, long grass, &c., where it will be difficult to detect them. They may thus be able to cut wire which the artillery have been unable to cut and to fire on hostile machine gun emplacements, loopholes, and parapet.

Lewis guns will accompany the assaulting troops, but not in the first line, and will assist to keep down the enemy's machine gun fire, cover the re-organization of the infantry, consolidate the ground won, protect the flanks, and repel counter-attacks.

49. *Use of Grenadiers.*

Grenadiers will principally be employed in clearing trenches, after these have been successfully attacked, and also to check and destroy hostile bombing parties attempting to counter-attack.

They will be required to clear a portion of a trench from the flanks when its capture from the front has failed.

Full instructions on hand and rifle grenades and their employment are to be found in "The Training and Employment of Grenadiers." Emphasis may here be laid on the necessity of new units arriving at the front with thoroughly trained grenadiers, and also on the necessity for organizing with great care the supply of grenades during an attack.

50. *Communications.*

Buried telephone wires will previously have been installed in our front line system. These should be carried on up to the front line, and wire be ready to run across to the hostile line when captured. These wires will, however, be very exposed, and cannot be relied on.

Visual signalling and runners will therefore often be the only means available. The issue of discs, rockets, flares, or other improvised signals and their use must therefore be arranged. Receiving stations for visual signalling must be arranged for in our trenches, and these must be suitably protected.

APPENDIX A.

WINTER AVENUES.

(*Breastwork Communication Trenches.*)

1. The "avenue" shown in the figures 23–27 is primarily designed for construction in winter in ground where deep communication trenches are impossible and the difficulties of digging are increased by the soil clinging to the shovel and preventing a long "throw."

2. *Trace.*—The trace (fig. 23) is designed to reduce labour by combining protection from enfilade fire with passing places. A change of direction is made about every 60 yards to safeguard the avenue from being swept from end to end. Each arm is broken twice in its length at the passing places. These are made sufficiently wide to permit of stretchers passing the angles. The breaks are right-handed to enable a man to fire down the trench whilst keeping most of his body covered. In the arm nearest to the trench whence the communication starts, part of the inner breastwork of the passing places is omitted so that each section of the arm can be enfiladed from the parapet.

The avenues and borrow pits are flanked by means of short breastworks projecting from the elbows of the parapet.

3. *Profile.*—The profile is given in fig. 24. The height of the parapet will depend on depth below the surface of the ground at which the trench gratings will be clear of the subsoil water. Six feet of cover at least must be provided, and the more of this there is below ground the less the labour required for the parapet. But even if submerged, the gratings, being wired to the transoms, give a good foothold ; and they can always be raised by putting another transom on the trestle, the parapet being heightened correspondingly.

A trench is, however, always advisable, even if the gratings are to be at ground level, as it acts as a drain and supplies some earth for the parapet. The sides of the trench should be revetted by slipping planks, brushwood or netting between them and the trestles, stakes being added if necessary.

The borrow pits should be as far as possible from the breastwork consistent with the power of "throw" in the particular ground. A 2-feet berm is the absolute minimum.

4. *Time of Construction.*—The avenue can be made in from 10 to 12 hours by two to three reliefs, and so can be completed in one night.

5. *Preparation.*—The most careful preparations must be made, materials calculated out beforehand, and transported to the nearest

convenient place under cover. There they must be laid out in such a manner as will ensure rapid and easy issue in the dark.

Working parties must be carefully calculated and divided up into small gangs.

The officers and men for each relief should be carefully practised by rehearsal by day, in their roles in the operations on which they will be employed.

It will hasten the work and prevent confusion if the avenue is started from both ends, and a stores dump is made at each of them.

It is generally inadvisable to extend a working party of 100 men from one point at night. The line of the proposed avenue should be divided into sections by marking stakes or other means, and each party led direct to its starting stake by its officer.

6. *Tracing and Reconnaissance.*—The R.E. should reconnoitre the ground at dusk on the preceding night, and mark out with tapes the lines along which the hurdles are to be placed.

If there is any danger of the tapes being observed by the enemy during the day, tracing must be done at dusk on the actual night.

The infantry officers in charge of parties should accompany the tracing officer and should familiarise themselves with the approaches to the dumps and starting points.

7. *Men and Tools and Materials.*—The men and tools and materials are as follows :—

First Relief (5 *hours*)—

	Per 4 yd. run.	Per 100 yd. run.
R.E.	2	50 (2 officers, 5 N.C.Os.).
Infantry	8	220 (5 officers, 20 N.C.Os.).
Shovels	8	220
Picks	8	200
Pliers	2	50
Measuring rods ...	1	25
3 ft. hurdles ...	4	100
5 ft. pickets ...	8	200 (3-in. diameter).
	(2 extra for first hurdles.)	
Wire (14 S.W.G.)...	1,056 ft. (18 lbs.)	26,400 ft. (450 lbs.)
3 ft. rabbit netting	8 yds.	200 yds.

Second Relief (5 *hours*)—

R.E.	⎫	
Infantry	⎬ As in first relief.	
Tools	⎭	
18-in. hurdles ...	4	100
15-in. rabbit netting	8 yds.	200 yds.
Sandbags	70	1,750
Wire (14 S.W.G.)...	264 ft. (4½ lbs.)	6,600 ft. (112½ lbs.)

Third Relief—

		Per 4 yd. run.	Per 100 yd. run.
R.E.	... ...	2	50 (1 officer).
Infantry	... ...	4	110 (2 officers, 10 N.C.Os.).
Shovels	... ...	4	110
Picks	... ...	4	100
Trestles	... ...	3	76
8 ft. gratings*	...	$1\frac{1}{2}$	38
Planks for revetting		48 sq. ft.	1,200 sq. ft.
Mauls	... ...	$\frac{1}{2}$	12

Note 1.—The length of third relief depends on whether the full amount of digging has been carried out in the first and second reliefs. If the full amount has been done there is no necessity for a third relief, as the trench gratings can be laid by the R.E. next morning.

Note 2.—No mauls in first two reliefs on account of noise.

Note 3.—Reliefs are reckoned from time of leaving dumps.

8. *Organization of Working Party.*—The most convenient unit of organization is a squad consisting of two R.E. and eight infantry. This unit is completely equipped with tools and materials as in column 1, para. 7, and does 4 yards of avenue.

    (*a*) Every five squads as above should be formed into an officer's party, with four N.C.O.'s and four spare men, and does 20 yards of avenue, or just the length between the breaks (fig. 23), for which special squads could be provided if necessary.

    (*b*) If the tactical situation permits, the infantry should leave their equipment at the dump, and carry rifle and cartridge slings only.

    (*c*) In the first relief each infantryman carries pick and shovel slung. Slings of spun yarn or cord should be attached to these beforehand by the party preparing the stores. In addition, a hurdle is given to every two infantrymen.

        The two sappers carry the measuring rod, pliers, pickets, wire, and rabbit netting.

        (*Note.*—Netting being in rolls would usually be carried down by the four spare men in every officer's party.)

    (*d*) In the second relief four infantrymen in each squad carry the light hurdles and the other four carry the sandbags. R.E. carry the wire and netting (but see note to (*c*)). Tools are taken over from first relief on the ground.

9. *Extension.*—(*a*) A squad should march to its work as in fig. 27 (*a*).

---

    * Special gratings for passing places to be calculated and 8 ft. gratings to be decreased accordingly.

The men are numbered and the hurdles lettered for purposes of reference.

(b) When the leading squad reaches the farthest forward end of the section allotted to the party, the hurdles are placed on the ground netting downwards and feet to the tape as in fig. 27 (b).

The men lay their arms 5 yards from the tape.

(c) The R.E. then measure the distances of the picket holes from the tape. The infantry then dig holes with the picks for the pickets and hurdle feet as in fig. 27 (c).

While the infantry are making the holes the R.E. prepare the wire.

(d) When the holes are complete, hurdle feet and pickets are put in them and the earth pressed down. (If the earth is so hard as to necessitate hammering, mauls must be brought and muffled, but only in circumstances of a very special nature must hurdles be mauled in, as the process strains them.)

(e) Nos. 1 and 7 then hold the hurdles, the R.E. put on the wires marked a and b in fig. 24 and the rabbit netting, assisted by the remaining infantry. The work will be greatly accelerated if the infantry have had previous practice.

(f) As soon as the netting and the ties marked a and b are fixed, the infantry are placed as in fig. 27 (d) and dig. While they are doing so the R.E. fix the other ties, and see that the borrow ditch is kept 2 feet or more as ordered from the netting stakes.

(g) When filling in the parapet, care should be taken to keep the weight of earth against the rabbit netting greater than that against the hurdles, in order to avoid forcing the latter over towards the trench.

10. *Tasks.*—In the first relief the number of cubic feet of earth in the parapets of the squads' task is 360 cubic feet (*i.e.*, 4×6 ft. $\times 5$ ft. $\times 3$ ft.). This will be too much for the men to do in the time at their disposal after completion of wiring, etc., but they should be able to fill up to a height of $2\frac{1}{2}$ feet.

In that case :—

Parapets = 300 cubic feet.
Two men in the trench dig 30 cubic feet each = 60 cubic feet.
Five men in borrow ditches dig 40 cubic feet each = 240 cubic feet.

In the second relief there are 60 cubic feet of the lower part of the parapet to be done (as above), and the top parts of the parapets amount to 210 cubic feet, a total of 270 cubic feet. This should easily be completed by the eight infantry in four hours, including filling the sandbags.

11. *Action of Reliefs.*—At the end of the first relief the infantry stand at their tasks. The second relief extend beside them and take over their tools. The first relief then put on their equipment and file off. Not until after they have gone will the second relief lay down their rifles and equipment.

R.E. hand over tools and duties in similar manner.

12. The work should be easily completed in one night *if careful preparations have been made*, and if not greatly interrupted by fire.

Until the end of February a third relief is always possible before dawn. *It should be provided.* At the end of the first relief it can easily be seen if the third relief will not be required, and message to that effect sent.

APPENDIX B.

Rapid Wire Entanglements.

The following are two methods of putting up wire entanglements, when rapidity is essential.

First Method (used by French).

Bays of wire fencing about 90 feet long are prepared beforehand, using light posts 7 feet 6 inches apart with horizontal top and bottom wires and diagonal wires (see fig. 28). For the top wire and one of the diagonals barbed wire is employed, plain wire about 0·15 inch thick for the others. Each bay is then rolled up and weighs about 90 lb. ; it can be carried easily by two men if a stick is passed through it.

To put up the entanglement—unroll the bays along the front at 90 feet intervals and drive in the posts. This gives the front row of the obstacle (see fig. 28). In rear of it unroll and place more bays, zigzag fashion, so as to form a series of equilateral triangles with the original line. In this portion two rolls of fencing are required for each roll in the front row (see fig. 29). Repeat the same process to form additional sections.

Light posts are necessary from considerations of weight, but as there are three posts alongside each other where the straight and zigzag portions meet (except in the front and back row of fencing, when there are only two) a strong support is formed if the posts are bound together (see fig. 29).

Second Method.

See figs. 30, 31, 32, which sufficiently explain the method used.

As a variation of this method, work may be commenced by making the fence on the front line of posts first (work of Nos. 5, 6, 7, 8), then joining the first line of posts by criss-cross wires to the second (work of Nos. 1, 2, 3, 4, in fig. 29), and lastly making the fence on the rear posts. The advantage of this alternative method is that the working party then has the obstacle between them and the enemy the whole time they are working, instead of having to carry stores and work in the second stage in front of the obstacle erected by Nos. 1, 2, 3 and 4 in the first stage.

APPENDIX C.

ILLUMINATION OF OBSTACLES AND FOREGROUND.

The lighting up of the foreground and obstacles at night is of great importance.

The usual means adopted for this purpose is the Verys light, of which a liberal supply is now available, but occasions may arrive when the undermentioned methods will prove of value. These lights should be so arranged that they can be put in action instantaneously when the enemy approaches the obstacle : they must illuminate the whole of the obstacles and the foreground while leaving the defenders in shadow.

Bonfires.

Bonfires are effective when fuel is to be had. They may be built close to the line of the obstacle, with screens behind them.

A bonfire should be so built that it cannot easily be pulled down by the enemy. A stout post may be fixed upright in the ground, and the fuel built up round it in the form of a cone. Or three posts may be erected, three or four feet apart, with sticks nailed to them horizontally so as to form a cage, and the fuel piled inside. A heap of shavings or dry leaves should be placed at the bottom, and means of lighting arranged in connection with it. For this purpose a length of instantaneous fuze may be used, with one end in a small bag of gunpowder, under the heap of shavings, and the other inside the work. But the fuze must be kept in thoroughly good condition. Friction tubes form an excellent means of ignition. They can be fired by the release of a weight which is attached by wire to the eye of the pin. The tubes must be rigidly fixed, and strong wire used for suspending the weight. The blast from a friction tube being considerable, the end of the instantaneous fuze nearest the tube should be one inch away from it. Both ends of the fuze may be packed with quickmatch to ensure ignition. Another method is to arrange a match under the shavings so that by a pull on a cord the match will be rubbed against an igniting surface. The shavings must be enough to make a bright flame at once, and petroleum or pitch should be added to them if available. Materials for renewing the bonfire should be kept at hand. Small pieces of canvas should be fixed over the firing arrangements to protect them from weather.

Lights, Illuminating Wreck.

Lights, Illuminating wreck are articles of store. They can be lit with either instantaneous or safety fuze. Instantaneous fuze should be stripped at the end to ensure good contact with the light. They illuminate a circle of about 100 yards diameter and burn for about 20 minutes.

Alarms and Flares.

Where night attacks may be expected, automatic alarms and flare light are useful adjuncts. They are usually combined with the obstacle. One of the simplest alarms is a row of tin pots, each containing a pebble, hung on a wire fence so as to rattle when the latter is disturbed. A piece of tin, 2 inches to 3 inches in diameter, such as the top of a jam pot, may be bent round the wire, and will answer the same purpose. Trip wires can be arranged to fire a rifle, or to fire a cartridge which, in its turn, will ignite a flare.

It must be borne in mind that flares lighted within a few yards of the perimeter of a camp, or close to a parapet, are difficult to screen effectively and are likely to be a source of greater danger to the defence than to the attack; they should therefore be used with great caution. At night troops have a tendency to concentrate their fire on any brilliantly illuminated area. A number of flares capable of burning from two to five minutes are preferable to one or two bonfires; a better effect is obtained from flares by placing them at some height above the ground. Convenient trees may be used for this purpose.

Arrangements for automatic alarm signals, in connection with entanglements or intermediate fences, generally have to be improvised on the spot with whatever materials are available.

A trip flare that has been found to work satisfactorily consists of a balanced board fixed in a trench having at one end the flare and at the other a heavy weight which is temporarily supported. The trip wire having been pulled, the support beneath the weight is withdrawn, and the end of the beam falls. By this means the flare appears above ground, and the jerk given to the beam fires a friction tube attached to the flare by instantaneous fuze, and so lights the flare. (*See* Fig. 33.)

The flare is composed of a mixture of nitrate of potash, sulphur and orpiment (Lights, G.S., long, Mark III).

Fig. 34 shows a similar device for the firing of a mine or bonfire outside the pit. A bonfire composed of straw, dry wood, &c., is readily set on fire by a small one-ounce cartridge composed of five parts white sugar and four parts chlorate of potash enclosed in grease-proof paper, fired by either instantaneous fuze or electrically by No. 14 fuze, with metal cap with the meal powder removed.

APPENDIX D.

INFANTRY AND ARTILLERY INTER-COMMUNICATION.

Apart from the unreliability of telephones, a difficulty, in the event of attack, is to ensure that a trained officer who can gauge the situation is at the infantry end. Infantry officers are liable at times to call prematurely for artillery support. Artillery are therefore on occasion perhaps slow in rendering the necessary assistance. Here the question of where the infantry end of the wire should be run to comes in. Some are against its being run into a fire trench, especially at night, for the following reasons :—

(a) The trench commander, who may be a junior subaltern, *thinks* he is going to be attacked, calls for artillery fire, and starts every gun in the Division firing. The whole Division is turned out unnecessarily and moral suffers. All commanders are short circuited.

(b) Wire run into a fire trench is constantly being broken. In case of attack it is almost invariably broken by the enemy's preparatory shell fire.

(c) The trench may be rushed and the instrument left in it. This has actually happened and the enemy may have listened to our messages until it occurred to somebody, some time later, to disconnect the wire at battalion headquarters.

Therefore it is best to run the wire to headquarters of battalions in trenches, or at furthest to a support trench well in rear.

The above is quite apart from the question of running a wire into an advanced trench for *observation* purposes, but here again there is a temptation to use it unnecessarily.

A better system at night is for an artillery officer, an orderly and telephonists to sleep at the headquarters of the battalion in the firing line. The former communicates with the battery by telephone *and* by orderly when the battalion commander requires artillery support. Artillery fire is immediately opened on the night lines while the officer makes his way to the observing station, connects up the communications with the battalion headquarters and the battery, and is ready to make alterations in the direction of fire when required.

Selection of battery position.—A battery which shows itself or allows its flashes to be seen at once comes under such a heavy and concentrated shell fire that any effective reply is out of the question, if, indeed, it is not put out of action entirely in a few minutes.

German artillery methods.—The Germans have a good system of observation, and trained observers with telescopes are constantly on the watch for any signs of movements in our positions and keep a special look out for artillery observing parties. Defilading from view of ground, observers must, therefore, take account of the highest ground in the enemy's position, although it may be distant.

Our infantry in support and reserve are apt to be very careless and often give themselves away, as the following extracts from a report show :—

(a) One morning I was coming away from a battery observing station. After crawling along a dirty ditch for some hnndreds of yards, I came to some houses. where a few of our infantry were loafing outside their billets in view of the German high point, miles away. I warned them, but did not loiter in the vicinity. The billets were shelled the same morning.

(b) A few infantry showed on the skyline near one of our observing stations which was promptly shelled.

(c) A battery commander incautiously showed himself at a window of the house from which he was observing. He was promptly shelled out of it.

It is most important that the enemy's notice should not be drawn to the localities in which the artillery observation stations are situated. Good observation stations are very scarce, and they are useful for the battalion commanders to view the hostile lines. No one should be allowed to go to the look-out place unless on duty, and then the greatest care must be exercised to get there unobserved.

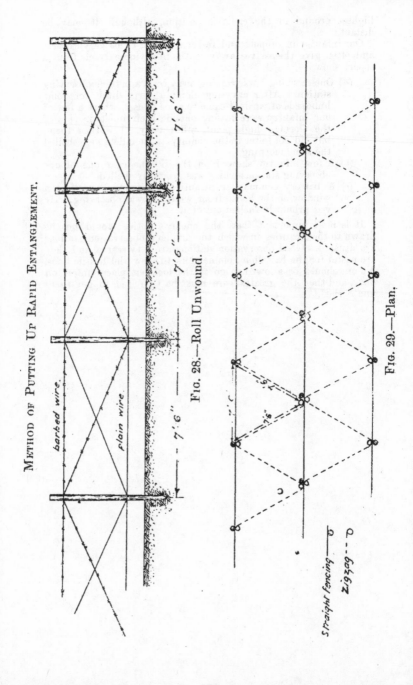

METHOD OF PUTTING UP RAPID ENTANGLEMENT.

FIG. 28.—Roll Unwound.

FIG. 29.—Plan.

Straight fencing ———
Zigzag - - - -

108

METHOD OF PUTTING UP RAPID ENTANGLEMENT.

FIRST STAGE.

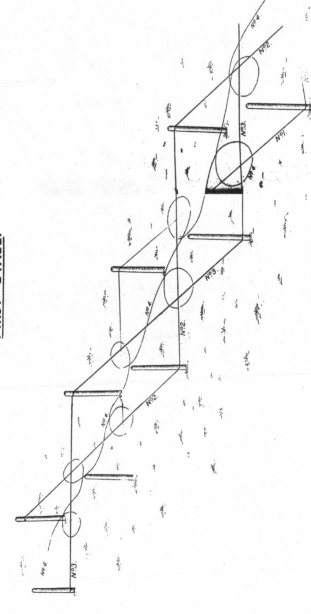

SECOND STAGE.

Completed Entanglement

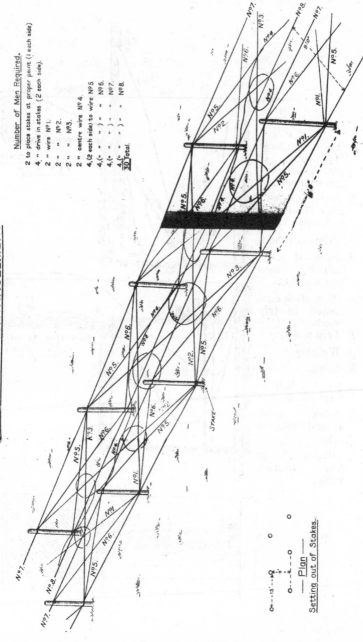

Number of Men Required.

2 to place stakes at proper point (1 each side)

4 " drive in stakes (2 each side).

2 " wire No 1.

2 " " No 2.

2 " " No 3.

2 " centre wire No 4.

4 (2 each side) to wire No 5

4 (" " ") – " No 6.

4 (" " ") – " No 7.

4 (" " ") – " No 8.

30 Total.

o   o

o - - -15"- - - o - - - 15"- - - o

———— Plan ————

Setting out of Stakes.

111

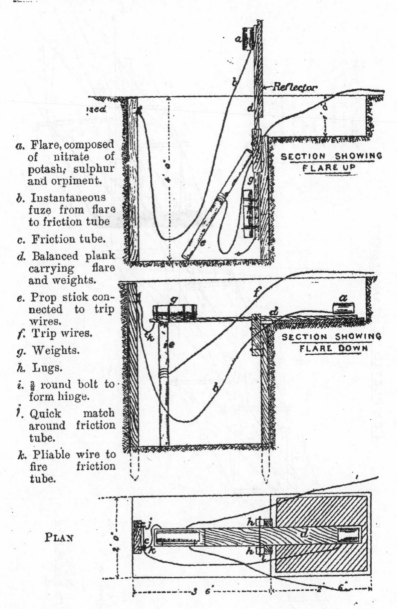

a. Flare, composed of nitrate of potash, sulphur and orpiment.

b. Instantaneous fuze from flare to friction tube

c. Friction tube.

d. Balanced plank carrying flare and weights.

e. Prop stick connected to trip wires.

f. Trip wires.

g. Weights.

h. Lugs.

i. ⅜ round bolt to form hinge.

j. Quick match around friction tube.

k. Pliable wire to fire friction tube.

SECTION SHOWING FLARE UP

SECTION SHOWING FLARE DOWN

PLAN

FLARE PIT.

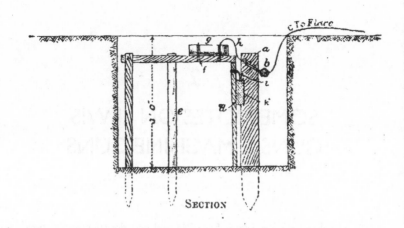

SECTION

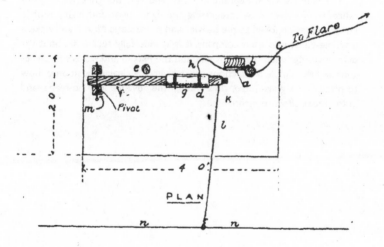

PLAN

REFERENCE.

a. Friction tube placed so that pull comes at a right angle.
b. Quick match.
c. Instantaneous fuze to flare.
d. Prop stick.
e. Guide stake.
f. Pivotted arm 2' 6" × 2" × 2".
g. Weight attached to arm and connected by flexible wire or spun yarn to friction tube.
h. Flexible wire or spun yarn.

i. Flexible wire or spun yarn from prop stick to weight.
k. Weight connected by flexible wire or spun yarn to prop stick and thence to wire "*l.*"
l. Wire connected to "cut" or "trip" wire.
m. Wire pin through two uprights and acting as pivot for arm on which weight "*g*" rests.
n. "Cut" or "trip" wire.

2

SOME NOTES ON LEWIS GUNS & MACHINE GUNS

SS 122 was issued in September 1916 and was designed for infantry officers who were now integrating the lightweight and highly mobile Lewis gun (as opposed to the heavier and more static Maxim and Vickers machine-guns) into each company. It is wonderfully technical about the differences between the Lewis gun, and the Maxim and Vickers machine-guns and the simple illustrations give a brilliantly clear exposition of how to place Lewis guns in trenches and on the advance into no-man's-land in the most effective manner.

SOME NOTES ON LEWIS GUNS AND MACHINE GUNS.

I. PRINCIPLES OF EMPLOYMENT.

1. Now that two Lewis guns are added to the equipment of each company, any officer may find himself in command of this new weapon, and he should therefore have some notion of the best use to which it can be put.

These notes are designed to help officers in this. A good many of the remarks may be platitudes to the more experienced officers, but I know that many have had little opportunity of studying any form of machine gun.

2. The principles of machine guns in their simplest form necessarily come into such a subject, and I have dealt with them at some length for three reasons:

   (1) A Lewis gun is a form of machine gun and takes over some of the work previously done by Maxim and Vickers guns. Some of this work they do as well as a Vickers, some better, some worse. An officer commanding a Lewis gun ought to know what work is best left to a machine gun and what he can take on better himself.

   (2) Machine guns work so closely with infantry that much misunderstanding can be removed if the infantry officers know something of the principles on which they are used.

   (3) One of the main jobs of Lewis guns is knocking out enemy machine guns. And to hunt anything successfully you must know its habits.

II. CHARACTERISTICS OF LEWIS GUNS AND MACHINE GUNS.

1. *Lewis guns share with machine guns* the following characteristics:

   (1) They can at any moment open a heavy concentrated fire, and the volume of fire is not decreased till more than 66 per cent of the team become casualties.

   (In a company every casualty sustained lessens the volume of fire.)

      (ii) They can give a maximum volume of fire from a mini-mum of front.

          (For a short burst the fire of a Lewis gun equals that of about 20–30 rifles, and it can be fired from a single loop-hole or, in the open, from a frontage of two men.)

    (iii) Fire control is easy, since all the firing is done by one man.

2. *Lewis guns differ from machine guns* as follows:

      (i) They are cooled by air and not by water. They therefore get hot much sooner and will be red hot if 700 or 800 rounds are fired rapidly. If more are fired, they may burst. Company officers, therefore, if requiring only one gun, should use both alternately. Again, if one company has a hot time while another has nothing to do, the latter should be prepared temporarily to exchange guns with the former.

      (ii) They are more open, and therefore more exposed to dust, wet, and mud than machine guns. They also contain a greater number of easily broken parts.

    (iii) The magazines are more easily damaged than the belts of machine guns. If a full one is dropped on hard ground, it will probably be so dented that it will not fit the gun. The bulk of the magazines therefore must be carried in boxes sufficiently strong to protect them, and these are very heavy.

          (845 rounds in the boxes issued to us weigh 102 pounds, while a box of 1,000 rounds of S. A. ammunition in bandoliers only weighs 75 pounds more. Boxes carrying 1,000 rounds of machine-gun ammunition in belts weigh 78 pounds.)

    (iv) The main advantage claimed for Lewis guns over machine guns is that, needing no water, they are lighter and so more mobile.

But company officers must remember that the mobility of a gun depends largely upon the mobility of its ammunition. They must therefore be prepared to provide men to lend a hand with the heavy magazine boxes in case of a long, rapid advance or of casualties among the section carriers.

3. To sum up, a Lewis gun is rather like that inevitable starter in the Grand National about which all the prophets say that " it

will win if it stands up." That generally means that it hasn't a chance unless it has a first-rate training with a real good jockey. In the same way stoppages and breakages in a Lewis gun can only be prevented and minimized by having real good men, who will keep their guns in order and use them properly. Company officers, in selecting men, should imagine that they have a new motor car and wish to choose one of their men to be trained as chauffeur. A Lewis gun is a more delicate piece of mechanism than a motor car and needs more constant attention. A rough, stupid man can put it out of action for a long time in cleaning it, and a careless, irresponsible man will waste endless ammunition if he fires it, and will have his gun red hot at the critical moment.

III. TACTICAL HANDLING.

The simplest way to arrive at the purposes to which Lewis guns may be put is to consider first the work machine guns have done in the past, and then see what part of this work Lewis guns should take over, and also if there is any further work for which they are specially adapted.

(I) TRENCH DEFENSE.

1. In normal times in the trenches the first duty of machine guns is defense. For this purpose brigade machine-gun officers make arrangements for their machine guns in the front trenches to join in forming what is called a "belt of fire" across the entire front. Every machine-gun officer, on taking over a sector of the line, is shown or provided with a map something like figure 1.

If this belt is properly constructed, it is clear that no considerable body of the enemy can cross "No-man's land" without terrific losses, so long as the machine guns remain in action. The emplacements from which machine guns fire to form this belt of fire are called "battle emplacements"; they must be well concealed and strong enough to resist anything but a direct hit from a large shell. Each gun should have an alternative battle emplacement covering the same allotted field of fire, in case one should be knocked in. "Defense" emplacement would probably be a better name than "battle" emplacement, for these emplacements are designed for defense, and for an attack different positions would often be selected.

2. Two points should first be noted about the siting of these emplacements:

    (i) The guns all fire diagonally.

    This is for three reasons. (*a*) They cover more ground. A greater space of " N .-man's land " can be swept without altering the aim, and together they form a belt of fire through which the enemy attack must pass. Fewer men will thus be needed to hold the trench. (*b*) They are less likely to be seen, because they are defiladed from the nearest part of the enemy's trenches. (*c*) They enfilade an enemy attack, and shots which miss or pass through a near party may hit the next.

Hence it follows that a gun sited in one company is probably looking after the front of another company or even another battalion. The men on duty with machine guns must not, therefore, be looked on by company officers as sentries in the ordinary way. Their only concern is to keep their guns tuned up to prevent anyone from tampering with them, and to look out *along their line of fire.* We had one emplacement for instance, in the middle sector at Ypres, where the sentry could only watch his line of fire at night through the loophole in his emplacement.

    (ii) Each gun has its own particular ground to cover, which may be large or small, and so long as it covers that satisfactorily it fulfils its main purpose.

    Company officers sometimes look through an emplacement and criticize it adversely on the ground that it has a small field of fire. Such criticisms can not be intelligently made unless the critic knows the purpose for which the gun has been so placed.

3. The formation of such a belt of fire looks very easy on a map, but in practice many points have to be considered. In the first place all the guns, so far as possible, must be sited for grazing fire and not for plunging fire. In other words, the trajectory of the bullet should coincide with the slope of the ground for as long a distance as possible. One of the great advantages of the Maxim or Vickers gun is its fixed platform. The gun can be laid along its line at dusk and fired with effect at any hour of the night, but this advantage is lost if the aim of the gun has to be continually changed. (The German front-line machine guns rarely traverse at all. The traversing fire that sometimes comes over our lines is generally from a reserve

trench.) It follows, therefore, that a high commanding position is a disadvantage for a front-line gun, especially at night. (See fig. 2.)

4. When your trench line runs up a slope, it is generally better to cover the front by siting your gun at the bottom and firing up the slope for the following reasons: (i) You are more likely to get an attacking party at night on the sky line. (ii) The emplacement at the top of the slope would be more easily spotted, and when spotted will be more easily shelled. (iii) When firing down a slope the bullets that miss their immediate object generally bury themselves in the ground. When firing up over a ridge the outside bullets of the cone may do damage on the other side. In fact one can generally site a gun with this secondary object in mind, and work out the aim with a map, clinometer, and compass so that such bullets are likely to fall somewhere useful either to enfilade an enemy trench farther up the line or hit a village, headquarters, dump, or crossroads behind.

" Mad Alick," of ——, the generic name of a family of machine guns in that neighborhood, is a good instance of this practice. He fires at the top of our parapet where he can partially enfilade it, but is so placed that shots which pass over it will fall in the neighborhood of ——. Luckily he has mistaken the contours and can not get observation of his fire, with the result that the center of his effective beaten zone is generally halfway up the tower of —— Church. If he retired two or three hundred yards and fired at the same mark and elevation, he would make —— Street a much more unpopular promenade.

5. This is an important point for Lewis guns as well as machine guns. The main criticism that can be brought against both is that they fire so rapidly that every shot can not hit and therefore they are wasteful of ammunition. This charge can largely be answered by so firing that the outside shots of the cone have a reasonable chance of hitting a secondary target. To accomplish this successfully the directing gunner must have a good bump of locality and a thorough knowledge of the map.

(II) STRAFING IN TRENCHES.

1. While the formation of a belt of fire, to economize infantry in defense, is the first duty of machine guns posted in front-line trenches, a certain amount of useful strafing can also be done on occasions. But only in exceptional circumstances should this

be indulged in from the battle emplacements or they will soon be discovered. This work can generally be best done by reserve guns from rising ground behind the trenches. Dumps, approaches, crossroads, etc., can often be fired on. But if an attack is contemplated, any approaches or communication trenches that can be reached should be left alone till the day of attack, or the enemy will defilade them with traverses or choose a safer line.

2. Patrols, working parties, or gaps in the enemy's parapet can be strafed from the front line, and for this purpose less elaborate emplacements may be made, often in commanding positions.

(III) LEWIS GUNS IN TRENCHES.

1. Now arises the question, what part of the machine-gun work in the trenches can Lewis guns usefully take over?

The "belt of fire" business is, in the main, best left to machine guns when these are available, because owing to their fixed platforms they can better cover their lines by night; but there are occasions when Lewis guns can usefully supplement them. For instance, your trench line may run over a flat-topped ridge. Both slopes may be swept by machine guns shooting upward, but neither may sweep the flat top. The top would be an unsuitable place for a permanent emplacement, and in any case it would be wasteful to retain a machine gun for so small a space. A Lewis gun placed near would make this secure. (See fig. 3a.) Again, in the middle sector at Ypres there was a hollow with a hedge in it running at right angles to our trenches, and we had to keep one machine gun solely to watch it. (See fig. 3b.) Here a Lewis gun would do the work perfectly well.

2. But it is in the strafing that Lewis guns will be most useful. There is practically no front-line strafing that can not be better done by Lewis guns. The work does not need long-continued fire, and two or three Lewis guns could quickly be concentrated to join in such work without leaving any gaps in the belt of fire, as would occur if front-line machine guns were moved for this purpose.[1]

3. Again, any work in front of our own lines is more suited to Lewis guns. At Fleurbaix last June the Germans used often to work in the daytime on a new trench 40 yards in front of

---

[1] *Note by General Staff.*—Lewis guns are not, however, suitable for "strafing" by indirect fire and should not be used for this purpose (see S.S. 106, Appendix A, 3 (a)).

their line—dead ground from our parapet. I asked permission to take out a Maxim through the long grass to stalk them, but the colonel refused because if we were surprised by an enemy patrol we would have difficulty in getting so heavy a gun away. Here was an ideal opening for a Lewis gun. Similarly in an enterprise on the German trenches two Lewis guns pushed out into " No-man's land " on either side of the point of attack would keep clear the raiding party's line of retreat.

(IV) THE ATTACK FROM TRENCHES.

1. In any attack the duties of all forms of machine guns are (i) to cover the advance of the infantry by keeping down or unsteadying the enemy's fire; (ii) to prevent or delay the enemy from bringing reinforcements to the threatened points; (iii) to help in the fight for superiority of fire before the assault.

In a trench attack (iii) will not occur. The necessary superiority must be obtained beforehand by greater weight of artillery and by holding the supremacy of " No-man's land."

Let us picture a typical trench attack and see how machine guns and Lewis guns can attain the first two objects.

FIRST PHASE.

2. In the preliminary bombardment, Lewis guns can do nothing and machine guns very little. I have seen it suggested that machine guns should enfilade any communication trenches that they can in order to catch Germans retiring to the shelter of the second line. I do not agree with this. Impatience is a very general fault on our side. When we see a chance of inflicting some small damage on the enemy we are far too apt to do it at once instead of saving up the blow for some time when it will have a real importance. As an example of this when officers in the front line spot an enemy machine gun, even if it is doing no damage, they often call on the artillery to shell it. Even if our guns knock it out, another will quickly be brought up to sweep the same ground from a safer position and nothing material has been gained. On the other hand, if the gun were left in fancied security till the morning of an attack, and then knocked out, the Germans probably could not replace it in time

to be of any service. In just the same way, by enfilading communication trenches early in a bombardment you may catch a few men. But the trench can be easily cleared and will be marked as dangerous. If you leave it alone and strafe it when the enemy are returning to the front line to meet our attack, the effect wil be far greater. You may block the trench and upset the German organization.

3. When the bombardment ceases, our infantry goes "over the top." As soon as the enemy sees them, every loophole will be opened and parapets manned. An intense fire will be poured upon our men, both from the enemy's front line and from any positions behind commanding "No-man's land." However severe our bombardment, some machine-gun emplacements are sure to be left, and it is from these that the greatest losses will be dealt.

4. The Vickers in rear can deal with the enemy's second-line positions; they can also delay reinforcements; they can do this by enfilading communication trenches; by shooting over others which can not be directly enfiladed they will make the enemy stick to the trench instead of coming up more quickly over the top. They can also often search ground which the artillery can not effectively shell, as it is here that reinforcements will probably be collecting.

5. But before the arrival of Lewis guns it was always very difficult to silence the enemy's front line. It is clear that this can not be properly done from our own trenches, because our fire would at once be masked by our own attacking troops. As a suggestion, gaps might be left in our attacking line, especially in a salient opposite well-shelled trenches, for machine guns to fire through. (See fig. 4.) But this covering fire must chiefly be done by guns placed well in front of our own trenches, which can continue firing till the infantry is past them. For this purpose the light and easily concealed Lewis gun is particularly well adapted, and Vickers guns can also be used in the most favorable positions for cover. How these guns get there is immaterial provided that they reach their places unseen before the attack. They may go out the night before, dig themselves in, and stop there; or they may prepare their shelter at night and crawl out to it in the later stages of the bombardment or under cover of a smoke cloud. They should get as far forward as possible so long as they are out of bombing distance of enemy saps and not in the line of fire of our own wire-cutting

guns. Since they will fire diagonally, a position behind a hillock where they are covered from the trenches opposite might be a good one. But each position must be chosen on its merits.

6. If Vickers guns and Lewis guns were used together, the Vickers guns should sweep the enemy's parapets and their breastworks at loophole height, since they are more suited to sustained traversing fire.

7. The special job of Lewis guns is knocking out machine guns. But to do this one must study their habits. If a Lewis gunner hears a machine gun firing straight opposite him it is a great temptation to fire at the sound; but this would almost always be useless because German guns, like our own, fire diagonally and are defiladed from the front.

German front-line machine guns have narrow loopholes because they traverse very little. They all have strong head cover, coming low down in front so that they can only be hit by short range fire. They fire diagonally so that they can only be hit from the direction in which they are firing. Lewis gunners, therefore, have the best chance of putting out the gun whose bullets are coming nearest themselves; and the strike of machine gun bullets on the ground is the best guide to the place from which you can put that machine gun out. German machine gun loopholes are generally near the ground level.

8. Every gun, Vickers or Lewis, must have assigned to it its own particular length of enemy trench before it is sent out. The Vickers guns will cover, between them, the whole parapet; while Lewis guns would be given a particular length of parapet to watch for machine guns. All these lines should be diagonal. (See Fig. 5.)

9. Only two men should go out with the gun, the rest waiting in the trench behind ready to bring on ammunition when the gun advances. With the gun must be sufficient ammunition for its immediate purpose as well as a load for No. 2 to take forward.

SECOND PHASE.

10. The Lewis guns, having ceased fire as the infantry passed, would remain in position until they were assured that the trenches had been carried. In case of failure they would cover the retreat. As soon as the infantry were well into the front trench the guns would move forward and join their companies.

101862°—17——13

11. If the attack was proceeding further they would endeavor to cover the next advance precisely as they covered the first. If, however, they have to meet a counter-attack at once, they must be arranged to form a belt of fire across the front precisely as machine guns do in the trenches, and they will continue to do this until a further advance is to be made, or the machine guns come up to consolidate the positions won. Occasionally a Lewis gun may be used to defend a straight communication trench; but these are rarely found near the front line; generally these trenches twist too much and are better defended by bombers, while the Lewis guns prevent a direct rush over the top. If the counter-attack comes before you have time to organize a belt of fire across the whole battalion, companies should separate their Lewis guns to fire inward across each other's front.

12. It may happen that X Battalion captures its trench, but Z Battalion on its left fails to do so. One or two guns of X Battalion may then be usefully employed with the bombers working their way along the trench to the left. A good position for such a gun is shown in figure 6. In any case where one battalion finds itself in front of the general alignment, the Lewis guns of the middle companies must be prepared to form the belt of fire by themselves across the entire front, because the guns of the flank companies may have to be drawn back to protect the flanks of the battalion.

13. The best positions for the Lewis guns should always be chosen before the guns themselves follow up the attack. It is very dangerous to move guns laterally across the firing line. The guns, following up from the rear, should always be directed straight to their positions. Company commanders should arrange with their Lewis gun officers as to who is to carry out this important duty. In the authorized personnel of a Lewis gun team, no provision is made for scouts, range takers, or observers. I suggest that Lewis gun officers should have a liberal allowance of runners trained in this work.

14. Provided the gun is not overheated, ammunition may be used freely from the first position the guns occupy. But the moment guns go forward they must fire more sparingly. Once you are in the enemy's trenches every round of ammunition increases 10 times in value, and must be economized accordingly. All further supplies will have to pass through the enemy's curtain fire.

(V) LEWIS GUNS IN OPEN FIGHTING.

1. The main principles that govern the use of Lewis guns are the same in open fighting as under the circumstances already described.

2. The guns will sometimes have to be used for covering fire. If, for instance, the company is surprised by rifle or machine-gun fire while in artillery formation, all Lewis guns will at once get into action to cover the deployment.

3. Similarly in an attack, where the infantry has to advance over an exposed piece of ground, Lewis guns will be pushed ahead secretly to cover the movement. In former times companies would pass such ground by advancing by alternate platoons or sections, one platoon firing while the next advanced. Now Lewis guns can provide the necessary fire and the whole company can pass quickly over without halting. But where there is a long stretch of open ground, the covering can better be done by the overhead fire of machine guns. Machine guns can fire far more continuously and can put in accurate shooting at ranges up to a mile and a half. At this distance their bullets have a steep angle of descent and are therefore better calculated to demoralize troops in trenches. Still, for short distances of exposed ground Lewis guns are better, because, by the use of prearranged signals, they can open fire at the exact moment that the infantry advances.

4. Lewis guns are also useful for shifting hostile advanced pickets or unexpected machine guns.

5. Such covering fire often has to be used when no clear target presents itself, but even so it may be of real value. In South Africa the men of the squadrons used to jibe at our machine guns and say they never hit anything, but they added " We like to hear them popping because they make the Boers shoot so badly."

6. Though in a war like this covering fire often has to be used, gunners must never lose sight of the real object of all kinds of machine guns, which is the annihilation of a body of the enemy. They are weapons of opportunity, and in general must lie low till they can get the greatest effect. They must get as near as they safely can to the enemy when our side is advancing, and conversely they must allow an attacking enemy to come as near as they can without undue risk. This margin of safety varies according to circumstances. An enemy patrol

of 50 men might be allowed to approach within 50 yards. If there are several patrols converging on the gun, this distance must be increased. The distance would be lessened if there were concealed barbed wire in front of the gun, and so on.

7. If one gun is firing at a party of the enemy, it should open fire at that part of the enemy nearest to likely cover and traverse inward. The enemy will probably run into the line of fire in trying to reach cover.

8. If two or more guns are used for the same purpose, each must have a separate point of aim. With two guns, each would start at an extreme flank of the party and traverse inward. If there were four guns, the other two would lay on the center and traverse outward to left and right. All these points of aim must be settled beforehand.

9. It is impossible to go over all the situations that may occur in open fighting, but the following remarks may cover some of them.

The best mark a Lewis gun can have is cavalry. Cavalry has no terrors for any machine guns if the latter are ready for action.

Except in the case of covering fire, it is a general rule for Lewis guns that they should not open fire unless they have a reasonable chance of inflicting very severe losses. There are times, however, when this rule will not hold good, viz: (1) In a rearguard delaying action, guns would open at extreme range to delay the enemy by making him deploy early. (2) If an enemy is retreating, a lucky burst of fire at long range may turn the retreat into a panic. In such a case there is no object in waiting, because your target will get no nearer. (3) It is worth having a long shot at particularly tempting marks. A battery limbering up, a machine-gun section on the move, a general and his staff, should, like a woodcock, be strafed by everybody.

If there is a gap in our line, a Lewis gun on either side of it, shooting diagonally across each other's front, will prevent an enemy getting through till it is filled up.

In any organized scheme of attack or defense (as opposed to patrol work or small enterprise) each Lewis gun must be given its own particular line to deal with, and from this line of fire it must only move in exceptional circumstances. Such a case might be a local raid by the enemy. If the raiding party seemed likely to gain a footing in A sector, and B sector was not attacked, the gun defending B sector might be swung round to help the defense of A. But in all such cases one man of the gun team must be ordered to keep watch along the original line, so that he can switch the gun back the moment a target presents itself on that line.

In defense Lewis guns should not be ordered to cover too wide a stretch of front. This would only lead to an inefficient watch, while if several targets presented themselves the gun would be constantly changing from one to the other and do little real damage to any. It is much better to give a gun a smaller line—say, one field and a hedge—even if the whole line is not covered. For if you prevent the enemy from crossing two fields here and two fields there, you will break up and disorganize his line, and he will attack your infantry with little chance of success.

Finally, Lewis guns should be handled as a sailor handles a submarine. In a square, straight fight with a Vickers a Lewis gun stands no more chance than a submarine in a similar encounter with a battleship. Both only succeed by popping up unexpectedly, delivering a rapid crushing blow, and then, when they are discovered, trusting to escape by their mobility and invisibility to some other unexpected place from which they can repeat the dose.

IV. GENERAL REMARKS.

1. The question may be asked, Is it worth while to try to work this somewhat elaborate organization? Why not use the Lewis guns as a kind of superior rifle, just like any other rifle is used now?

To this there are two answers.

(i) At the present moment rifles are not, in practice, used to the best advantage. The most important principles summed up in the expression "Fire control" are, owing to the extreme difficulty of applying them in action, in grave danger of being disregarded. Even in trenches one sees sentries at night firing off rounds haphazard in the direction of the opposite trench, instead of each bay being given some definite aiming mark along which its occupants can fire with greater chance of success. But with Lewis guns fire control is greatly simplified, since only one man is firing the equivalent of 20 rifles, and therefore the fullest attention devoted to this subject is never wasted.

(ii) All automatic rifles and machine guns are extremely wasteful of ammunition unless used on the principles already described. It is only by such methods that they get their full effect. Hitherto we have been far behind the Germans in material of this kind; now we may be about equal to them. But even if we get a preponderance the advantage will largely be lost unless we get out of every weapon the full work of which it is capable.

2. And from this another point arises. It has been said that Lewis guns and machine guns get their best effects by diagonal fire. Why not carry this to its logical conclusion?

Many of us saw something of the fiasco of the 9th of May, 1915. I got full accounts from men who went through and came back. All of them told the same story—that, once they were through the German front line, they were swept by machine guns from both flanks, but not a man could tell me even roughly where those machine guns were situated.

3. And if you think of our own practice attacks, it is easy to see how such a thing happened. We are given a compass bearing on which to march. The officers find some object at which the flanks of their command are to aim, and their best N. C. O.'s are wholly occupied in keeping this direction. The officers divide their attention between seeing that the direction is kept, studying the dangers and difficulties of the ground to be traversed, and looking for signs of the enemy in their objective. The remainder are watching for the officer's signals. But nobody is looking to the place from which casualties will come—the flanks, half right and half left, where machine guns may be lying safely defiladed from their own front.

Now, this sidelong glance might well be the special duty of Lewis gun teams. In their position in the fourth line they have few anxieties about direction. If a few guns with a small supply of ammunition were sent forward to assist the advance, the remainder of the teams carrying heavy ammunition would suffice to mark the line which the guns could rejoin as the battalion passed. Similarly no injury would be done to the direction of the line if spare men of Lewis gun teams were sent forward to points of vantage from which they could watch our flanks and signal the guns forward if they saw signs of any danger from those directions. I feel confident that if some such arrangement were made, our losses in an attack would be very greatly lessened, and no German machine guns would inflict heavy casualties upon us, as they did on May 9, without being in any danger themselves.

FIGURE 1.

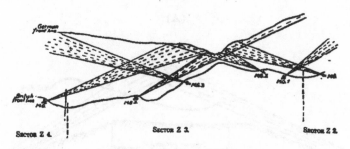

Example of chart given to machine gun officer on taking over a sector of trenches (Z 3), showing lines of fire which his four guns must cover from their battle (i. e., defense) emplacements.

FIGURE 2.

MACHINE GUN DEFENDING A LINE.

(A) Machine gun in a commanding position.

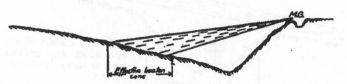

(B) Machine gun in low position.

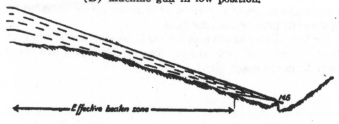

(Remember that both guns are shooting diagonally, so that (A) position would leave many gaps through which an enemy might pass. In (B) position there are no gaps.)

FIGURE 3.

(A)

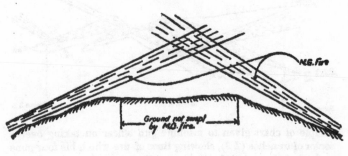

(B)

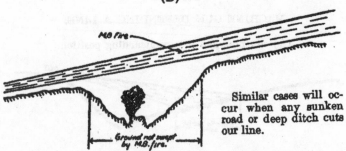

Similar cases will occur when any sunken road or deep ditch cuts our line.

Examples of ground in front of trenches better defended by Lewis guns than by machine guns.

(In both cases you are supposed to be looking straight to your front out of your own trench. The machine guns are firing away from you diagonally.)

FIGURE 4.

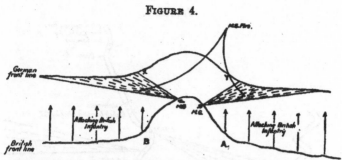

Example of machine guns covering a trench attack, when a gap is left in the line of attack A—B—a British salient. The infantry can get more than half-way across before masking the M.G. fire. The enemy's line must be well bombarded between X—Y, to prevent them from making this a rallying point for reserves, and must be watched by Lewis guns from M.G. emplacements. (Conventional drawing to show arrangement.)

FIGURE 5.

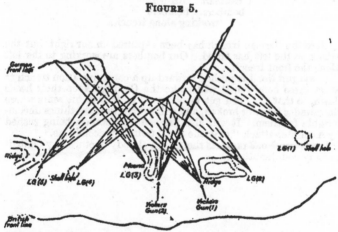

Example of arrangement of Lewis (5) and Vickers (2) guns to cover attack on German salient. The Vickers sweep the whole length of the parapet in their zones. The Lewis guns are allotted sections which they must watch for M.G. emplacements. These are always likely to be found in the sides of a salient.

FIGURE 6.

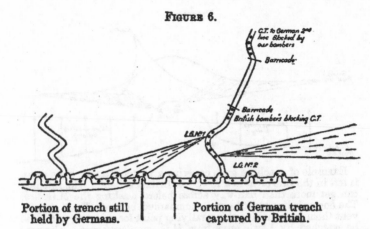

Portion of trench still | Portion of German trench
held by Germans. | captured by British.

NO MAN'S LAND.

German   British
bombers.   bombers
working along trench.

Here the German trench has been captured on our right, but the attack on the left has failed. Our bombers are working to the left along the front trench.

Lewis gun No. 1 is pushed forward up a communication trench to assist these bombers; it will make the Germans keep their heads down, so that they can get no observation, it may hit some where the parados is low or broken, and will generally make things uncomfortable for them. It will also prevent our bombers being rushed by a counter-attack " over the top " from the second line.

Lewis gun No. 2 protects the trench already captured by enfilading any counter-attack.

3

INFANTRY MACHINE-GUN COMPANY TRAINING

By the time this manual was published in 1917 the machine-gun was of critical importance on the Western Front, its deadly effectiveness as a killing machine proven on the first day of the Somme, 1 July 1916. I have left out from this rather exhaustive manual (over one hundred pages) the sections on how to organise machine-gun companies and to train and drill them in favour of the business end chapter on 'machine-guns in battle'.

Chapter VI.

MACHINE GUNS IN BATTLE.

32. *Introductory*.

1. The general principles laid down in Infantry Training, Chapter XV, for the employment of machine guns in battle remain unaltered by the introduction of the machine-gun company organization and the substitution of Lewis gun detachments for machine-gun sections in battalions. But the new organization and the increase in the number of machine guns with infantry units have rendered necessary certain modifications in detail which are discussed in the present chapter. A certain amount of repetition and rearrangement of matter that is already dealt with in Infantry Training has been found necessary in order to avoid too frequent reference to paragraphs or sentences in that manual.

2. The special characteristics of Lewis guns and the manner in which these characteristics affect their employment must be studied by machine-gun officers, as they have to cooperate closely with Lewis guns. These characteristics, therefore, are discussed in

sections 33 and 34.[1]   Detailed instructions for Lewis guns are given in Lewis Gun Training.[2]

3. The special principles which govern the employment of machine guns in the phase of operations known as trench warfare are dealt with in Notes for Infantry Officers on Trench Warfare.

4. It must be remembered that in Infantry Training a machine-gun section means two guns, whereas under the present organization it means two subsections each of two guns, or four in all.

33. *Characteristics of machine guns and Lewis guns compared.*

1. The principal characteristic of the machine gun is its ability to produce *rapid and sustained fire*.   Provided water and ammunition are available, a machine gun is capable of keeping up a rapid fire for a very considerable period.

On the other hand, the Lewis gun, though capable of extremely rapid fire, is incapable of sustaining this fire for long.   This necessitates, therefore, the use of short bursts of fire as the normal practice.

Its inability to sustain fire is primarily due to the fact that a water jacket is not provided (in order to economize weight) and the gun consequently becomes hot very quickly.   Further, owing to their lightness, the working parts will not stand constant vibration to the same extent as those of the machine gun.

2. A further difference between the two weapons is in the type of mounting used.   The machine gun is provided with a heavy tripod which enables the gun to be used for overhead and indirect fire. This mounting also allows of the gun being laid on a fixed point, and fired at any time, by day or night, without further preparation.   By this means it is possible to form "bands of fire" through which any enemy attempting to pass must suffer heavy loss.

The Lewis gun is fired from the shoulder, a light bipod providing a support for the barrel; there is no traversing or elevating gear; and aim is taken and altered as when using a rifle, the conditions are, therefore, not suitable for overhead or indirect fire, nor for creating "bands of fire."

3. The machine gun, owing to its weight, and that of its mounting, is less mobile than the Lewis gun.   The latter being specially provided with a light bipod to increase its mobility, can be carried like a rifle, and fired with very little preliminary preparation, so that

---

[1] Infantry battalions are provided with Lewis guns organized in Lewis gun detachments of 1 noncommissioned officer and 12 men each, with 2 Lewis guns.

[2] To be issued shortly.

after movement its fire can be brought to bear on any object much more rapidly than that of a machine gun.

34. *The employment of Lewis guns.*

1. Owing to its greater mobility a much greater liberty of action can be allowed to this weapon than to the machine gun. It must, however, be clearly understood that the Lewis gun can not take the place of the machine gun. It is a supplement to and not a substitute for the latter type of weapon.

2. It is adapted for even closer cooperation with infantry than the machine gun, as the Lewis gunner can move and appear to the enemy as an ordinary rifleman. Its distribution as a battalion and company weapon provides a mobile reserve of fire available for the smallest unit commander wherever an infantry soldier can go.

3. It is specially adapted for a concentrated enfilade fire on a definite line such as a hedge or wall, or to cover a road or defile where it is not possible to deploy a number of rifles, and for places where it is difficult or impossible to bring up a machine gun unobserved. When wider fronts have to be swept with fire or heavier fire is required at longer ranges machine guns can be more usefully employed.

4. Although the expenditure of ammunition is not so great as with machine guns, the difficulty of getting ammunition up to the more exposed positions to which Lewis guns can go will be much greater. It is important, therefore, to withhold fire as long as possible and to use the power of the gun to develop unexpected bursts of fire against favorable targets.

35. *The tactical handling of infantry machine guns.*

1. The tactical principles laid down in Infantry Training, sections 160, 161, and 162, apply generally, but the organization and distribution of the machine guns with a brigade there discussed need modification to suit the new organization and distribution of machine guns.

2. The introduction of the machine-gun company organization, while facilitating the collective employment of machine guns, does not mean that they should always be so employed. It may sometimes be advisable to detach machine guns under the orders of battalion commanders and this should be done if the tactical situation requires it. (See sec. 36 (2) (3).). In this case the battalion commander concerned should clearly understand the reasons why the guns are attached to him. Definite instructions should be given

by the battalion commander to the machine-gun officer as to what is required of him, but the latter should be allowed as much freedom as possible in the execution of his task.

3. *Command and control.*—The various tasks which the machine-gun company has to carry out demand the most careful preparation and organization on the part of the company commander.

He must insure that all section commanders fully understand the part they have to play, and he must be always on the watch to regain control, at the earliest possible moment, of any guns temporarily detached, in order to provide a reserve for his brigade commander.

During action the machine-gun company commander will keep in the closest possible touch with the brigade commander, and it is important that section officers should keep in close touch with the commanders of units to which they may be attached and under whose command they come. Machine-gun officers must carefully observe this principle in order to avoid dual control and consequent misunderstanding.

It is unsafe to rely on telephones, especially in open fighting. Steps must, therefore, be taken to maintain communication by visual signaling and by orderlies.

4. *Cooperation.*—Cooperation is an essential feature in machine-gun tactics, both between the machine guns and other arms and between the guns themselves.

Grouping machine guns into companies by centralizing control facilitates the execution of a comprehensive scheme of machine-gun cooperation in accordance with the needs of the tactical situation. When this is to be effected the machine-gun company commander must be thoroughly conversant with the situation. He should take every step to insure cooperation, not only between the guns of his company, but between his company and machine guns on the flanks.

5. *Concealment.*—

(a) *During movement.*—To insure concealment when on the move machine gunners should try to disguise their identity as such by adopting the formation of the neighboring troops. This, and any other means of escaping detection, should be constantly practised.

When machine guns are moving, they should watch and avoid areas that are being swept by shell fire.

(b) *When in position:*

(i) As few men as possible should be near the gun. It will usually be found that two men are quite sufficient.

(ii) When time, implements, etc., are available, guns should be dug in, but, unless it is possible to construct a really satisfactory emplacement, it is better to seek cover from view. A hastily made emplacement will merely serve to draw the attention of the enemy.

(iii) Masks and gloves will often facilitate concealment, especially when facing strong sunlight.

Every effort must be made to prevent machine guns being located by artillery. If, however, machine guns are shelled, their action will largely depend on the tactical situation. They may make a change in position of about 50 yards or they may temporarily cease fire, the guns and detachment getting under cover; the latter will often deceive the enemy into thinking that they have been destroyed and enable the guns to obtain a good target later. A careful distribution of the gun numbers will minimize casualties.

36. *Machine guns in the attack.*

1. In order to obtain the best results, the machine-gun company commander must be thoroughly acquainted with the plan of operations and must make a careful reconnaissance of the ground.

By use of maps and study of the ground through a telescope from positions in rear or on the flanks, he should endeavor to make himself familiar with the nature of the ground, the correct use of which may prove of decisive value. (See Infantry Training, sec. 161.)

Having made his reconnaissance, and having received instructions from the brigade commander (Infantry Training, sec. 160 (13)), the machine-gun company commander will give definite orders to his section officers.

2. *Distribution of machine guns in the attack.*—The machine-gun company commander may divide the guns under his command into groups, some to go forward with the Infantry, some to cover their advance, others as a reserve.

3. The machine guns that go forward with the attacking Infantry will be placed under the control of the Infantry commander to whom they are attached. (See Infantry Training, sec. 160 (13).)

The rôle of these guns will be to—

    (a) Assist the Infantry in obtaining superiority of fire.

    (b) Make good the positions won.

    (c) Pursue the enemy with fire.

    (d) Cover reorganization of the Infantry.

    (e) Repel counterattack.

    (f) Cover retirement in the event of the attack proving unsuccessful.

The number of guns to be sent with the Infantry will be governed by two factors, viz, the length of front and the nature of the ground.

The *time* of their advance will be determined by the nature of the ground and progress of the Infantry. The progress of the Infantry must be carefully watched so that the guns may be brought forward at the earliest possible moment. They should very rarely advance with the leading line of Infantry. This is the duty of the Lewis guns, the fire of which should suffice to hold the position won until it can finally be consolidated by the machine guns.

4. The guns detailed to cover the advance of the Infantry will normally be under the control of the machine-gun company commander, who acts under the instructions of the brigade commander. The rôle of these guns will be to provide covering fire for the Infantry up to the last possible moment in the following ways:

(a) By fire from the flanks or through gaps in the line.

(b) By overhead fire.

(c) By indirect fire.

Great care must be exercised in (b) and (c) in order to avoid endangering our own troops.

Orders to the machine guns detailed for this task may, if necessary, include general instructions to govern their action, after the task has been completed, pending receipt of further orders from the machine-gun company commander. It must, however, be remembered that it is usually dangerous to prescribe to a subordinate at a distance anything that he should be better able to decide on the spot, with a fuller knowledge of local conditions, for any attempt to do so may cramp his initiative in dealing with unforeseen developments. (See F.R.S., Part I, sec. 12, par. 2.)

5. Guns kept as a reserve will be under the control of the machine-gun company commander, acting under the instructions of the brigade commander. Owing to their characteristics, machine guns are valuable as a reserve of fire power, and when kept in reserve in the hands of the brigade commander may prove of the utmost value at the critical moment. It must be remembered, however, that a great development of fire power is most useful in the opening stages of an attack, to cover the advance of the infantry, and it is a mistake to keep guns in reserve if they can be usefully employed in supporting the advance. These guns may be used for long range searching fire on ground behind the enemy's line, which is likely to hold supports or reserves, but must be available to move forward at once, when required.

6. The great fire power of machine guns relative to the space they occupy, the rapidity with which they may be brought into or out of action and the ease with which they can change the direction

of their fire render them especially suitable for the protection of threatened flanks and for filling gaps which may appear laterally or in depth. Any of the guns mentioned in the previous paragraphs may at times be employed in this manner.

7. During an attack it may be advisable to continue to hold certain tactical points, which have been captured, until the attacking troops have made good their next objective. The characteristics of machine guns fit them for this duty; their use will avoid diminishing the strength and dash of the attacking infantry.

8. *Limbers and ammunition reserve.*—Gun limbers will generally remain under the orders of section or subsection officers, but ammunition limbers would, as a rule, be placed under the officer in charge of the brigade ammunition reserve (Infantry Training, sec. 166 (2)), or under a machine-gun officer, who should keep thoroughly in touch with the progress of the machine guns so that he may be able to keep the wagons as close up as possible.

When machine guns are attached to battalions, a proportion of ammunition limbers will accompany them if required.

It must be remembered that ammunition limbers are far less mobile than gun limbers.

37. *Machine guns in the defense.*

1. When it has been decided to consolidate a position for defense a reconnaissance should be carried out, the machine guns being generally allotted on the following principles.

2. Some guns should be posted as soon as possible in accordance with the nature of the ground to form a complete belt of flanking machine-gun fire along the front of the position. Important concealed approaches and folds in the ground should also be covered by machine guns.

Cooperation must be arranged with the Lewis guns of battalions, which can cover the less important approaches or small depressions or hollows which the machine guns can not sweep.

3. A proportion of machine guns should be kept in reserve. When the ground is suitable, these may be used for indirect overhead fire if the results are likely to justify the expenditure of ammunition, and the readiness of the guns to take up other tasks is not impaired. It will often be found advisable to prepare machine-gun emplacements at important tactical points in rear of the front line and to detail guns for their occupation, if necessary. Preparation in this respect will facilitate a rapid readjustment of the line at any point.

4. Secondary positions and lines of retirement must be reconnoitered, and steps must be taken to insure that the detachments are familiar with them. In case of a withdrawal becoming necessary, machine guns in supporting positions will cover the retirement of the Infantry and guns in the front line. When the latter have occupied their secondary positions, they, in their turn, will cover the movement of the guns originally in support.

5. Arrangements for firing at night should be made. The day and night gun positions will probably be different; the change from the one to the other should be made just after dark and just before dawn.

6. Communication must carefully be arranged throughout machine-gun sections. Machine-gun officers must keep in touch with battalion commanders and the machine-gun company commander. (See sec. 35, par. 3.)

7. The following points should also be noted:

(a) The position of the ammunition limber should be determined and the arrangements for ammunition supply made known to all concerned.

(b) Range cards should be made for each gun.

8. The variations that arise during the protracted defense of a position are dealt with in Notes for Infantry Officers on Trench Warfare.

38. *Machine guns with an advanced guard.*

1. The functions of an advanced guard make it necessary that great fire power should be available when required. A large proportion of machine guns should therefore be allotted to advanced guards.

These machine guns should move well forward in the column, so that they may be able to get quickly into action.

2. The principal duties of machine guns with the advanced guard are to—

(a) Assist in driving back enemy forces by rapid production of great fire power at any required point;

(b) Assist in holding any position gained until the arrival of the Infantry;

(c) Cover the deployment of the main body by holding the enemy on a wide front.

3. The characteristics of machine guns render them as a rule more suitable for employment with the main guard than with the van-

guard, but the size of the vanguard may necessitate machine guns being attached to it.

39. *Machine guns with a rear guard.*

1. As rear guards will usually be required to hold positions with the minimum of men, a large proportion of machine guns should be allotted to them.

2. Experience has shown that well-placed machine guns, supported by a few Infantry only, will frequently hold up an advance for long periods.

3. In occupying a rear guard position with machine guns the ordinary principles of defense apply, but the following points should be specially noted:

(*a*) As wide a field of fire as possible should be selected.

(*b*) Guns must be concealed in the least obvious places.

(*c*) Covered lines of retirement must be reconnoitered.

(*d*) Gun limbers should be close up to facilitate a hasty retirement.

(*e*) Positions in rear must be chosen before the machine guns retire from their forward positions.

(*f*) A proportion of the machine guns should occupy the positions in rear before all the machine guns retire from the forward position. Thus the retirement of the last gun can be covered.

(*g*) Pack transport is very useful.

40. *Village fighting.*

1. As soon as the infantry have made good one edge of a village, machine guns should be brought up in close support. They should then search windows, doorways, roofs, etc., likely to be held by the enemy.

2. Machine guns should be used to command cross streets, etc., so as to guard against attack on the flanks or rear of the infantry. They should also be posted on the edges of the villages to prevent flank attacks, and when possible should be pushed forward well on the flanks, so as to command the exits from the village.

3. During village fighting use may be made of windows, doors, etc., as machine-gun positions. If a good field of fire can not be obtained from existing doors and windows, and time is available, small holes can be made in the outside walls of the upper stories of buildings, enabling a good field of fire to be obtained.

101862°—17——6

41. *Occupation of various positions.*

1. Machine guns may be hidden in almost any position, but it is advisable to avoid places which are either obvious or easy to recognize, such as cross roads or single objects, or places which can easily be located on the map. It is important that guns should merge into the surroundings, and straight edges or distinct shadows should not be made.

2. Banks of rivers, canals, and railways, ditches, folds in the ground, hedges, palings or walls, also mounds of earth, may be used either to afford a covered line of approach and supply to a gun position or else a gun position itself. When firing over the top of the cover, greater protection is given if hollows are scooped out for the front tripod legs. (Pls. XII to XIV.)

3. Houses may be employed in the following ways:

The gun may be placed in rear, firing through windows or doors in line or past the sides of the house. When firing from a window, door, or hole in the roof, the gun should be placed well back for concealment. (Pl. XVI.) A damp piece of cloth hung in front of the gun helps to conceal the flash. When firing from a cellar, care should be taken not to cause a cloud of dust to rise and give away the position. A means of retirement and alternative emplacements should be arranged. Overhead fire and observation may often be obtained from high buildings.

4. Woods and crops provide cover from view, facilities for communication, and good lines of approach or supply. In neither case should guns be placed too near to the front edge. In woods it will often be possible to construct hasty overhead cover.

5. If a barricade has been constructed across a road, machine guns should not be put on the barricade itself but, if possible, in a concealed position to a flank from which they can sweep the road.

6. Haystacks do not as a rule afford a very satisfactory position, but guns may be placed in a hollow in front, or behind, firing past the side, or else in a hollow on top, firing through the front face of the stack. A machine gun concealed in a field which is covered with cornstalks, manure heaps, or mounds of roots is very hard to locate. (Pl. XV.)

7. Wood stacks, planks, logs of trees, and farm implements may be used to conceal guns; cover from fire can often be obtained by the addition of bricks or sandbags. (Pl. XV.)

8. Trees generally provide better observation posts than machine-gun positions.

42. *Signals.*

In many cases observation will be impossible from the gun position, and it will be necessary for observers to signal results from a flank. The following semaphore code is used in signaling the results of observation of fire:

O = Fire observed *over*.

S = Fire observed *short*.

R = Fire observed to *right* of target.

L = Fire observed to *left* of target.

K = Fire observed *correct* (target or range).

W = Fire unobserved or "Washout."

PLATE XII.

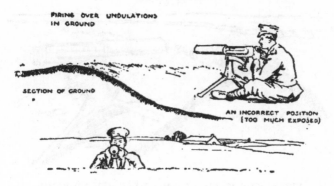

FIRING OVER UNDULATIONS IN GROUND

SECTION OF GROUND

AN INCORRECT POSITION
(TOO MUCH EXPOSED)

PLATE XIII.

SECTION OF GROUND

A CORRECT POSITION
(GOOD COVER)

PLATE XIV.

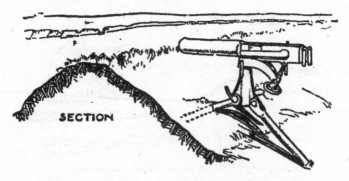

SECTION

VICKERS OR MAXIM GUN MOUNTED BEHIND BANK.

PLATE XV.

GUN EMPLACE-
MENT DUG OUT
OF HEAP OF ROOTS
WITH INSIDE WALLS
OF SAND BAGS

STACK OF WOOD USED AS
GUN EMPLACEMENT

PLATE XVI.

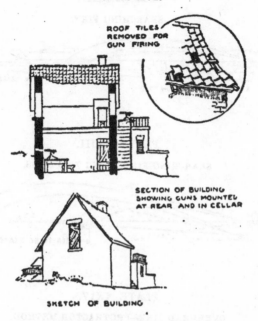

ROOF TILES
REMOVED FOR
GUN FIRING

SECTION OF BUILDING
SHOWING GUNS MOUNTED
AT REAR AND IN CELLAR

SKETCH OF BUILDING

PLATE XXI.

USE OF COMBINED SIGHTS.

PLATE XXII.

SEARCHING FIRE.

L OF S FOR Y.

L OF S GIVING ELEVATION TO X

AREA TO BE SEARCHED

PLATE XXIII.

SEARCHING FIRE, USING TWO GUNS.

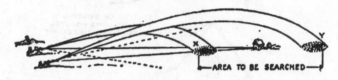

AREA TO BE SEARCHED

PLATE XXIV.

OVERHEAD FIRE—PROTRACTOR METHOD.

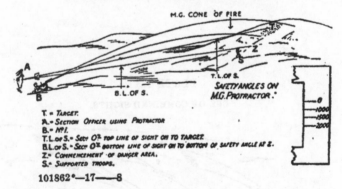

M.G. CONE OF FIRE

T.L.OF S.

SAFETY ANGLES ON M.G. PROTRACTOR.

B.L.OF S.

T. = TARGET.
A. = SECTION OFFICER USING PROTRACTOR.
B. = Nº I.
T.L. OF S. = SECº Oº TOP LINE OF SIGHT ON TO TARGET.
B.L. OF S. = SECº Oº BOTTOM LINE OF SIGHT ON TO BOTTOM OF SAFETY ANGLE AT Z.
Z. = COMMENCEMENT OF DANGER AREA.
S. = SUPPORTED TROOPS.

101862°—17———8

148

PLATE XXV.

OVERHEAD FIRE—TANGENT SIGHT METHOD.

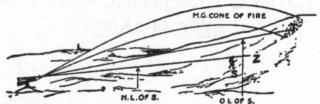

T = TARGET
O. L OF S. = ORIGINAL LINE OF SIGHT ON TARGET WITH CORRECT ELEVATION ON GUN
N. L OF S. = NEW LINE OF SIGHT ON TO BOTTOM OF SAFETY ANGLE AT Z
S. = SUPPORTED TROOPS.

PLATE XXVI.

INDIRECT FIRE—GRATICULE METHOD.

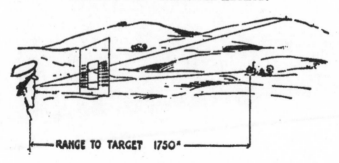

← RANGE TO TARGET 1750ʸ →

4

NOTES ON IDENTIFICATION OF AEROPLANES

Not the first aircraft recognition materials issued by the British in the First World War (this one was published in 1917) but the most comprehensive. The first of the war was in fact an aircraft recognition 'card' which after some issues between Captain Partridge's Army Printing and Stationary Services and the War Office was issued to every man in the British Expeditionary Force (BEF) in January 1915 – 250,000 copies in all!

NOTES ON IDENTIFICATION OF AEROPLANES.

DEFINITIONS.

Monoplane.—An aeroplane with one wing on each side of the body.

Biplane.—An aeroplane with two wings on each side of the body.

Triplane.—An aeroplane with three wings on each side of the body.

Tractor machines.—Machines having the air screw in front of the wings.

Pusher machines.—Machines having the air screw behind the wings.

Nacelle.—The term used in pusher machines for the body which carries the engine, controls, observer, and pilot. The *Caudron*, although it is a tractor, is constructed after the pusher type. In "pusher" machines, the nacelle projects well in front of the wings.

Under carriage.—The part of the structure connecting the wheels to the nacelle.

Fuselage.—The body of a tractor machine, which carries the pilot, observer, and engine, and extends back as far as the tail. All fuselages now are covered with canvas or three-ply wood.

Tail.—The small horizontal plane at the end of the fuselage.

Rudder.—The small vertical plane or planes attached to the tail.

Fin.—A small vertical fixed plane on the top of the fuselage and tail. · The rudder is usually attached to the near end of the fin.

Dihedral.—An aeroplane is said to have dihedral when the wings, as seen from the front, are set at angle to each other on either side of the body.

Stagger.—An aeroplane is said to have stagger when the lower wings are not set vertically below the upper wings.

Leading edge.—The front edge of the wings of an aeroplane.

Trailing edge.—The rear edge of the wings of an aeroplane.

Ailerons.—Flaps fitted to the trailing edge of the main plane in order to give lateral control. Ailerons are sometimes very conspicuous.

Overhang or extensions.—An aeroplane is said to have overhang when the upper wings are longer than the lower wings.

Sweep back.—An aeroplane is said to be swept back when the wings, as seen from above or below, are not set in a straight line. Sometimes the leading edge is swept back while the trailing edge is straight.

Cut back.—When the trailing edge is longer than the leading edge.

Wedge shape.—When the leading edge is longer than the trailing edge.

Struts.—The wooden supports joining the upper wings to the lower wings.

These notes should be studied in conjunction with the latest edition of "Silhouettes of Aeroplanes."

GENERAL INSTRUCTIONS.

1. Success in the identification of aeroplanes can only be attained by an exact knowledge of the characteristics of the different types of plane and by constant practice in observing all types of machines at all angles of flight.

Machines which can easily be identified at some angles often present at other angles no distinguishing characteristics to any but a trained observer. In order to pick up the characteristics of the different types the observer should employ a definite system of identification, and he should be acquainted with the specific purpose for which each type is employed.

Even a moderately trained observer should be able to distinguish between a hostile and a friendly machine at a distance of not less than 5,000 yards. If an observer is not able to do this, machine-gun detachments will continually be having to "stand tó" only to dismiss a minute later when it is realized that the plane is friendly; while for antiaircraft artillery work it is essential that on a clear day planes should be identified at ranges of not less than 10,000 yards.

CLASSIFICATION.

2. Aeroplanes can be divided into two main classes—those designed for reconnaissance, artillery observation and bombing work, and those designed as chasers and scouts.

The former are usually comparatively large, stable, two-seater machines. Modern two-seater machines have a speed as high as 120 m. p. h. The *R. E. 8* has a speed of about 90 m. p. h.

Although artillery machines may fly at heights from 8,000 to 10,000 feet, the machines doing long recon-

24997°—18——2

naissance will frequently get much higher, i. e., to 18,000 feet.

Scouts are smaller and faster machines, carrying a pilot only. Their flying speed is anything from 80 to 140 miles an hour; the normal height for scouts is over 12,000 feet, and for the later types usually over 15,000 feet. These machines are essentially fighters, and by adopting offensive tactics on the enemy side of the lines seek to prevent his machines from doing their work and to enable our own to do theirs. Very often they fly at great heights in order to be able to dive effectively on to slower machines flying at lower heights.

CHARACTERISTICS.

3. Many allied machines employ tail booms, while up to date there are no German machines of this type of construction. No doubt therefore should be entertained of any machine having an open structure connecting the wings to the tail. This open structure is frequently referred to as open fuselage.

The wings, being the most conspicuous part of an aeroplane, are usually examined first.

The special characteristics of British reconnaissance machines are dihedral and stagger; of French reconnaissance machines, great span, i. e., length from wing tip to wing tip compared to width of planes, and open-tail booms; of German reconnaissance machines, overhang with closed fuselage. In the majority of modern German machines the top and bottom planes are of equal length.

Only four allied machines when flying show both these German characteristics. They are, *B. E. 2E, R. E. 8, Caudron R. 4*, and *Caudron G. 6*.

With regard to the scouting class it is impossible to lay down any hard and fast rule by the wings alone.

The tail and rudder, for most types, are the surest guide for distinguishing allied from hostile machines.

The vast majority of allied machines have rectangular or modified rectangular tails, while the German machines have in most cases either the fish tail or the heart-shaped tail.

These distinctions apply equally to reconnaissance and scout machines.

4. MACHINES EMPLOYED FOR RECONNAISSANCE WORK.

ALLIED.	GERMAN.
F. E. 2B.	Albatros.
F. E. 2D.	Aviatik.
B. E. 2E.	D. F. W. Aviatik.
R. E. 8.	Rumpler.
Morane Parasol.	L. V. G.
Martinsyde.	Gotha.
Armstrong Whitworth Beardmore.	New Type.
De Havilland 4.	
Bristol Fighter.	
Handley Page.	
Voisin.	
Maurice Farman.	
Farman Freres.	
Single Caudron.	
Twin Caudron.	
Caudron R. 4.	
Caudron G. 6.	
Paul Schmitt.	
Avion A. R.	
Letord.	
French Morane.	
Moineau.	

MACHINES EMPLOYED FOR FIGHTING PURPOSES.

ALLIED.	GERMAN.
De Havilland 5.	Fokker.
Sopwith Biplane.	Roland.
Sopwith Scout.	Halberstadter.
Sopwith Triplane.	Albatros Scout No. 1.
Sopwith Camel.	Albatros Scout No. 2.
S. E. 5 with clipped wings.	S. S. W.
*Nieuport.	
*S. P. A. D.	
†Morane Monocoque.	

WINGS.

5. In examining the wings of an aeroplane there are six characteristics for which the observer should be on the lookout:

(a) Dihedral.   (d) Overhang.
(b) Sweep back.   (e) Wing tips.
(c) Stagger.   (f) Ailerons.

6. Dihedral is most noticeable in a machine coming straight in or going away. It is also distinctly noticeable when traveling obliquely, but at certain angles machines with swept-back wings may appear to have dihedral. Care is required to differentiate between these two characteristics.

7. Sweep back is seldom noticeable until a machine has reached an angle of sight of about 45°, except when banking. A very critical examination should always be made of a machine when banking, as many

---

*Flown by both British and French.
† Flown by French only.

special characteristics, such as the shape of the wing tips and tail can then be best observed.

The *Nieuport* is, at present, the only allied plane having swept-back wings.

8. Stagger is most conspicuous when an aeroplane is traveling obliquely or at right angles to the observer. In those positions the inclination of the struts is very obvious.

The effect of stagger is to cause the planes to appear rather wide apart.

The *Roland* and *Halberstadter* machines have slight stagger; otherwise stagger can be regarded as a characteristic of allied aeroplanes. In the *De Havilland 5*, *Avion A. R.*, and *Letord* the stagger is reversed—i. e., the top plane is behind the lower plane.

9. Overhang is best seen when a machine is coming straight in or going away. On oblique courses it is difficult to decide whether a machine has overhang or not.

10. Wing tips may be divided into four main classes—round, square, cut back, and wedge shape.

The wings of British machines are chiefly of the round, cut-back, and wedge-shape types, the only exception being the *S. P. A. D.*

French machines have either square or cut-back tips.

Many German machines have square tips, but the *Fokker, Roland, Halberstadter,* and *Albatros Scout No. 2* have the cut-back type.

11. Few machines have ailerons which can be detected from the ground, with the noticeable exception of the *Voisin*.

Old types of *Albatros* had noticeable ailerons. These took the form of a thickening of the wing tips. A lookout should be kept for ailerons in new pattern German machines.

TAILS.

12. There are five main types of tail, although there are many variations of these types.

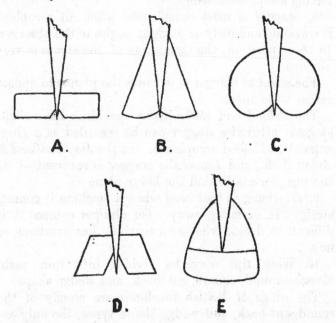

A.   **B.**   **C.**

D.   **E.**

Type A is the rectangular. It is by far the commonest British type. It becomes modified into the following three types:

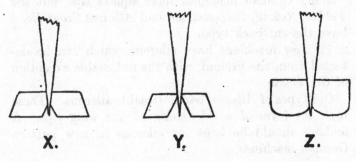

X.   **Y.**   **Z.**

Two German machines, the *Halberstadter* and the *Fokker*, have tails of type Y.

Types B and C are essentially German, but one British machine, the *De Havilland*, has a tail of type C.

Type C has developed into type E, which is now one of the commonest types of hostile tails.

Type D is employed by two allied machines, the *Nieuport* and *Moineau*, and by one German machine, the *Roland Scout*.

Tails can best be observed when a machine is banking or is directly overhead.

BRITISH.

F. E. 2b and 2d.—There are a considerable number of machines of this type. They are easily distinguished by their large size, open-tail booms, and marked dihedral. The engine also has a loud purr, which is readily distinguishable after a time.

BRITISH.

B. E. 2e. and B. E. 8.

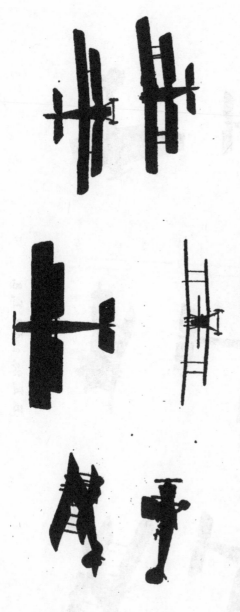

BRITISH.

B. E. 2e and R. E. 8.—These machines, except for a difference in the rudders, are difficult to distinguish. Their characteristics are marked stagger, dihedral, and overhang and the particularly blunt cut-back tips to their wings. The engine is fairly silent.

The rudder of the *R. E. 8* joins the fuselage almost at right angles, while that of the *B. E. 2e* has a fin in front of it which slopes away to the fuselage.

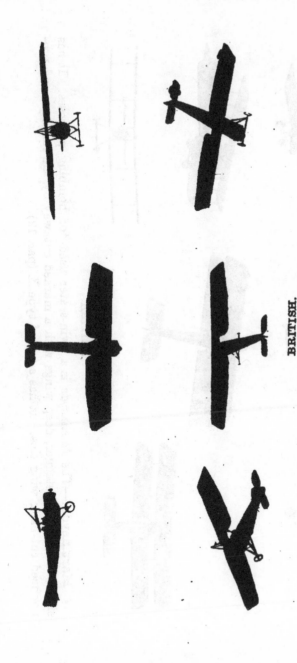

Morane Parasol.—The *Morane Parasol* is a large two-seater monoplane with the fuselage suspended well below the wings, giving it the form of a cross when approaching and receding.

163

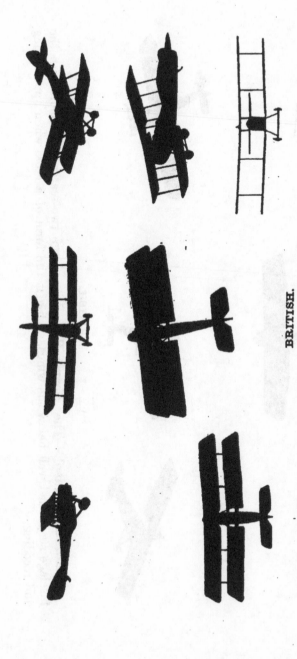

BRITISH.

Martinsyde.—The *Martinsyde* is a twin-seater used for bombing purposes. It has slight dihedral and stagger, deep wings with a marked cutaway by the fuselage, and pronounced cut-back wing tips. It has a tail of type X (par. 12).

BRITISH.

Armstrong Whitworth.—This is very similar to a *B. E. 2c*, but it is larger and the planes have a much greater width from front to rear in proportion to their length (from wing tip to wing tip), the tips being markedly wedge-shaped.

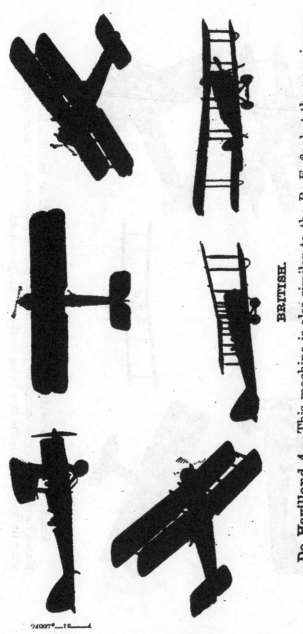

BRITISH.

De Havilland 4.—This machine is also similar to the *B. E. 2c*, but the nose is very square and projects a considerable distance in front of the planes.

The tail plane is also slightly different and the wing tips are cut back.

24007°—18———4

166

BRITISH.

Bristol Fighter.—The *Bristol Fighter* is a two-seater tractor biplane with closed fuselage.

The leading edges of the planes are longer than the trailing edges, the tips of the wings are rounded, it has dihedral and stagger, and the tail is of type D (par. 12) but with the corners rounded off.

BRITISH.

Bristol monoplane.

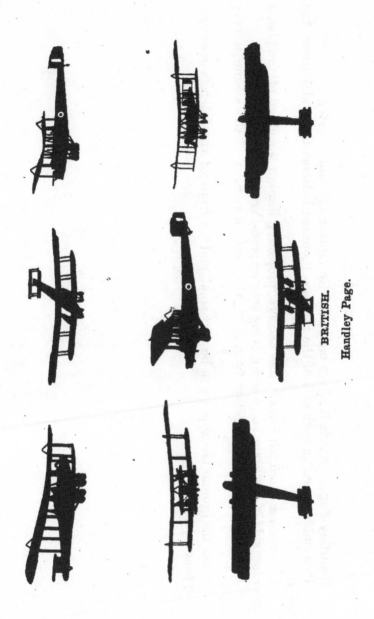

169

Handley Page.—Single fuselage machine with biplane tail and elevator.

Two rudders, one on each side of the fuselage, mounted between top and bottom tail planes.

Two engines mounted stream line nacelles, projecting beyond the chord of the planes on either side of the main body and driving tractor propellers.

At close ranges the projection formed by the balance portion of the aileron is very marked.

From the ground tail appears to be very small and the front of the fuselage snoutlike in appearance.

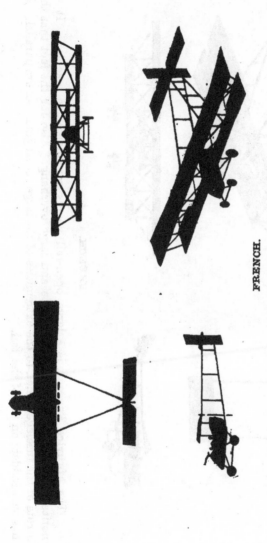

FRENCH.

Voisin.—The *Voisin* is another large open-tail booms machine, chiefly flown on long reconnaissances. It is easily picked up by its marked ailerons and by its long and narrow tail. The tail, with the long, narrow rudder, forms a perfect cross. It has slight overhang. This machine has a very noisy engine. The planes are very long in comparison with the vertical distance between them.

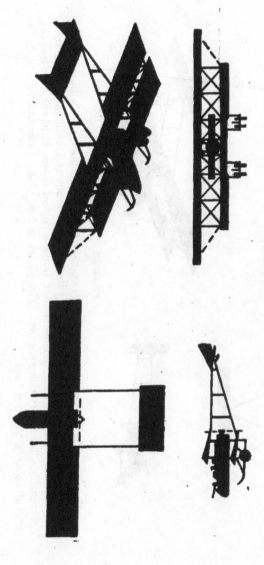

FRENCH.

The **Maurice Farman** is a large open-tail booms reconnaissance machine. It is noticeable for its very square wing tips and large overhang. Also for the fact that the struts of the fuselage joined to the extremities of the large rectangular tail are parallel. It has two rudders on top of the tail.

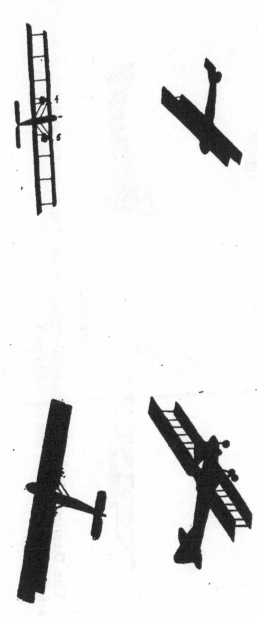

FRENCH.

Caudron R. 4.—The *Caudron R. 4* is another twin-engine reconnaissance machine of very large size. It has very long and narrow wings with a slight overhang, and has a closed fuselage. The tail is rectangular, very long and narrow, type Y (par. 12), with a single rudder and fin.

FRENCH.

The **Caudron G. 6** is a large twin-engine tractor reconnaissance machine, with a big overhang, closed fuselage, and tail of type Y.

FRENCH.

The **Paul Schmitt** (type **VI**) is a big tractor reconnaissance machine, with closed fuselage, rectangular tail, and square rudder. The tips of the upper plane are cut back and those of the lower plane wedge-shaped.

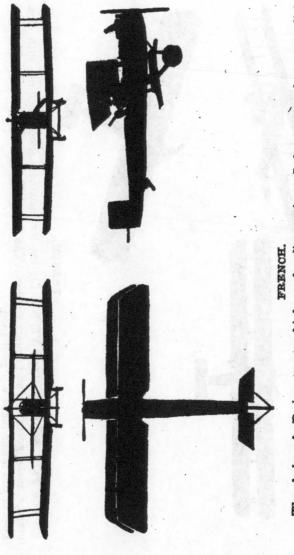

FRENCH.

The Avion A. R. is a tractor biplane of ordinary size. It has reversed stagger, slight dihedral on the lower plane, closed fuselage, large square rudder, and small tail similar to type Y.

FRENCH.

The **Morane Monocoque** is a single-seater monoplane flown by the French. It is not a parasol. The wing tips are cut back, and there is no piece of the planes cut away near the fuselage. The tail is of type Y, the rudder projecting considerably beyond it.

24997°—13——4

177

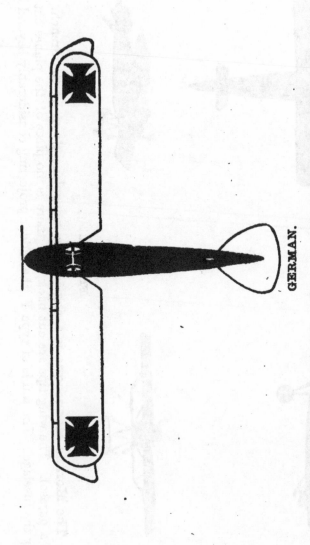

GERMAN.

New Type (probably *Albatros*).—This machine has slight overhang and no dihedral or stagger. The upper plane is cut back, the lower plane rounded. The tail is of the *Albatros Scout* type and the rudder of the ordinary *Albatros* type.

178

BRITISH.

Sopwith Scout.—The *Sopwith Scout* is a fast one-seater machine. The wing tips are wedge shaped. It has stagger, dihedral, and closed fuselage.

24997*—18. (To face page 60.) No. 1

179

Sopwith Triplane.—The *Sopwith Triplane* has three planes, and the wing tips are cut
the *Scout*, except that the corners are very slightly rounded. The tail rudder are similar to
of the *Sopworth Scout*.

BRITISH.

The Sopworth Camel is a small single-seater machine. It has stagger, but no overhan
upper plane is straight, but the lower has a marked dihedral, the tips of both being cut back.
is of type X, and the rudder is similar to that of the *Sopworth Scout*.

24997°—18. (To face page 60.) No. 3

De Havilland 5.—The *De Havilland 5* is a unique British type in that it has a reversed stagger. It also has a closed fuselage.

BRITISH.

Sopwith Biplane.—The *Sopwith Biplane* is a small and fast two-seater machine. It may be distinguished by closed fuselage, slight dihedral, stagger, and kidney-shaped rudder. It is also the only machine with a tail of type Z (par. 12). The engine has a loud and distinctive ringing note.

BRITISH.

S. P. A. D.—The *S. P. A. D.* is a tractor biplane with closed fuselage and is perhaps the most difficult of all allied planes to distinguish.

The wings are square cut; there are two pairs of struts on either side of the nacelle, which appear to be of equal length, but in reality there is a slight overhang.

The tail (see sketch) is the safest guide to the identity of this machine.

The *S. P. A. D.* is liable to be mistaken for a hostile plane by unskilled observers, and the greatest care must therefore be exercised in establishing its identity.

BRITISH.

The **S. E. 5** is a single-seater tractor biplane. It has a marked dihedral and stagger; the tips of the wings almost square cut, no overhang, and one pair of struts on either side.

The tail is the same as the *R. E. 8*, but the rudder is large and triangular with the top point cut off. Care must be taken not to mistake the machine for the *Halberstadter*.

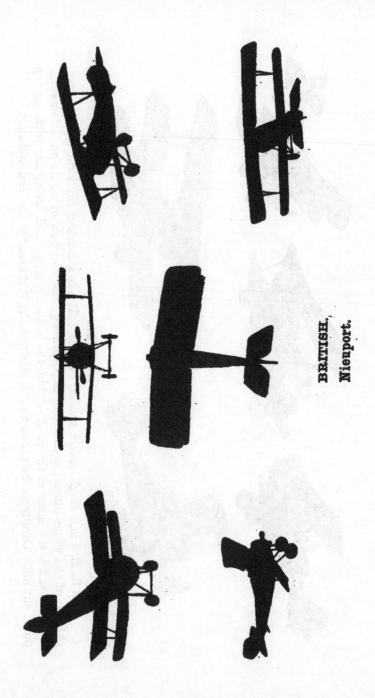

BRITISH.
Nieuport.

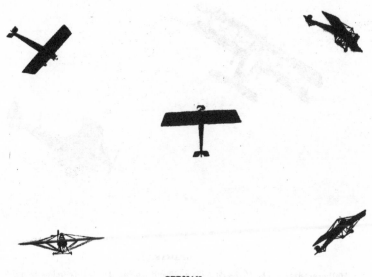

GERMAN.

Fokker.—The *Fokker* is a fast monoplane scout, having cut back wings and rectangular tail, type Y (par. 12). The round rudder cocked up above the tail is its chief characteristic.

GERMAN.

Halberstadter.—The *Halberstadter* is a difficult machine to identify unless seen sideways, and then its high, triangular rudder is extremely prominent. Some uncertainty exists as to the exact structure, but most observers agree as to the slight dihedral and stagger, while the tail is certainly of type Y (par. 12), this having been a common cause of confusion when the machine first appeared. As soon, however, as the rudder can be seen, no further doubt is possible.

Nieuport.—The *Nieuport* is a fast, single-seater scout, very difficult to identify at certain angles.

Its most marked peculiarity is the very narrow under plane, which is shorter than the upper plane, and has dihedral. Once this is picked up doubt is at an end, but when coming straight in, the overhang and dihedral of the under plane give it an extremely Hun-like appearance.

The tail is of type D (par. 12) and must be carefully watched, but the rudder, which is on top of the tail and projects well in rear of it, is easily distinguishable. The wings are slightly swept back and the narrow under plane necessitates a distinctive placing of the struts, thus—

Despite these numerous peculiarities, the *Nieuport* has many times been mistaken for a German machine, and should always be carefully watched.

189

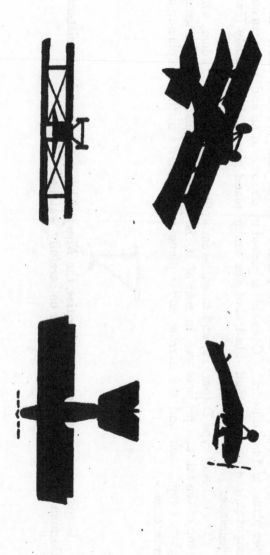

GERMAN.

Roland.—The *Roland Scout* is a fast machine. Its peculiarity is that it has one large strut on each side of the fuselage in place of the usual pair. The rudder is triangular, and the rather large tail is similar to type D (par. 12) with the rear edges rounded. This plane does not fly much nowadays.

GERMAN.

Albatros Scout.—The *Albatros Scout* is a small and very fast machine. It has a slight overhang, but is most easily distinguished by its pear tail, similar to type C (par. 12), although with a blunt end, there being no notch cut out in the middle for the rudder. It is very easy to mistake the *S. P. A. D.* for this machine if the tail is not visible, the chief point of difference being that the *S. P. A. D.* has two pairs of struts on each side of the fuselage, and the *Albatros Scout* only one.

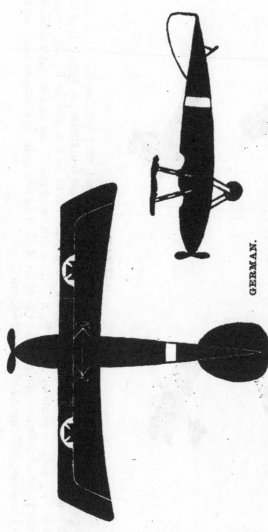

GERMAN.

The **Albatros Scout No. 2** resembles in many points the *Nieuport Scout*. It has overhang and a narrow under plane, necessitating the same arrangement of struts as on the *Nieuport*. The planes are not swept back; the tips are markedly cut back. The rudder is a cross between the usual *Albatros* type and the *Albatros Scout No. 1* type, while the tail is similar to that of the latter machine.

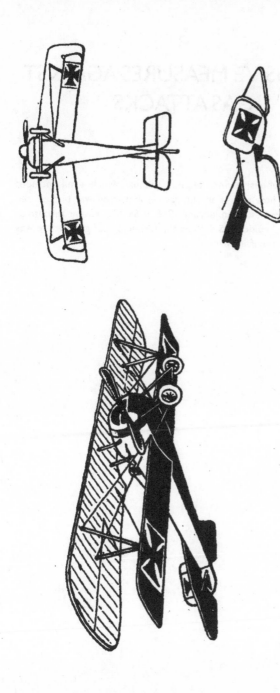

GERMAN.

The S. S. W. (Siemens Schuckert Werke) is almost an exact copy of the French *Nieuport.*

193

5

DEFENSIVE MEASURES AGAINST GAS ATTACKS

A very comprehensive and detailed manual which even includes instructions on how to use an anti-gas respirator on war horses (see appendix III)! First issued in January 1916 as SS 388, it went through at least one revised edition (SS 419) as the technology of gas warfare was progressing at a terrifying pace.

DEFENSIVE MEASURES

GAS ATTACKS.

I. — INTRODUCTION.

A. — GENERAL CONSIDERATIONS.

1. The following notes on defensive measures against hostile gas attacks have been compiled for the guidance of officers in instructing their men and giving orders on the subject.

2. In the absence of suitable protection the gases used in war are extremely deadly. Breathing only very small quantities may cause death or serious injury. Hence, it is essential that no time be lost in putting on the respirators or masks when a gas alarm is heard.

It cannot be too strongly impressed on all that the measures which have been elaborated to meet hostile gas attacks afford **perfect protection**, and if they are carried out properly and promptly no one will suffer from gas poisoning.

3. The whole basis for protecting troops against gas lies *a)* in keeping the appliances in perfect working order; *b)* in learning to adjust them rapidly under all conditions; and *c)* in ensuring that every man is given immediate warning. These results can only be attained :

1) **By frequent and thorough inspection of all protective appliances. The inspections to be daily in the trenches.**

2) **By thorough instruction and training in their use.**

3) **By every man understanding and complying with all Standing Orders on the subject of defense against gas.**

If these are effectively carried out, there is nothing to fear from hostile gas attacks. Officers must impress this on their men, since an important object of all anti-gas instruction should be to inspire complete confidence in the efficacy of the methods adopted.

STANDING ORDERS FOR DEFENSE AGAINST GAS.

I. — Carriage of Respirators.

a) *Within 12 miles of the front line* a box respirator or mask will always be carried.

b) *Within 5 miles of the front line* a box respirator will always be carried, and every man will be clean-shaven, except that a moustache may be worn.

c) *Within 2 miles of the front line and within areas specially exposed to gas shelling,* the box respirator and mask will always be carried. The respirator will be carried in the "Alert" position. It will be worn outside all clothing, and nothing will be slung across the chest in such a way as to interfere with the quick adjustment of the respirator. The chin strap of the steel helmet will be worn on the *point* of the chin.

d) Military Police will report all cases of infringement of the above orders.

e) The above-mentioned zones will be conspicuously marked by each Corps, in such manner as to attract the attention of persons entering them.

f) When not carried in the "Alert" position, the box respirator will be carried over the left hip, the sling passing over the right shoulder. Nothing shall be worn so as to interfere with the immediate *shifting* of the respirator to the "Alert" position. If the mask is also carried, it will be over the right hip, so as not to interfere with shifting the box respirator to the "Alert" position, the sling passing over the left shoulder but under the sling of the respirator.

II. — General Precautionary Measures.

Within the two mile limit the following will be observed :

a) Box respirators will be inspected *daily*.

b) Gas N. C. O.'s will inspect daily all gas alarm appliances and anti-gas stores. They will see that gas-proof dugouts are in good order and the blankets kept moist.

c) All sentries will act as Gas Sentries and will be provided with alarm appliances to give warning in case of gas shelling or a gas cloud attack.

d) Each sentry group will have a definite area to alarm in the event of a gas cloud attack or bombardment.

e) Sentries must be posted to give warning to men in dugouts.

f) All working parties of 10 or more men will have a sentry posted to give warning in the event of gas being used by the enemy.

g) Precautions will be taken to protect ammunition from the corrosive action of gas.

h) Stores of fuel will be kept for clearing dugouts.

i) Units in the line will make wind observations, and sentries will be warned to be on the alert for signs of cloud gas *whenever the wind is in a dangerous quarter.*

In the area between two and twelve miles from the front line the following will be observed :

j) Anti-gas appliances will be inspected at least once a week and immediately before men proceed to any point within the two mile limit.

k) All sentries, traffic control men, military police, etc., when on duty will act as gas sentries and will be provided with suitable alarm devices where necessary.

l) Men may be allowed to take off their respirators when sleeping, but must keep them within reach.

m) Arrangements will be made by Commanders of units and Area Commanders to communicate a gas alarm rapidly to all ranks.

III. — Action to be taken in the event of an enemy Gas Shell or Trench Mortar Bombardment.

a) At the first sign of *gas shell* of any kind or on hearing the alarm, the breath must be held and the respirator adjusted immediately without waiting until the presence of gas is recognized.

b) The alarm will be spread immediately to all troops in the neighborhood :

1) By gongs, rattles, or klaxons;
2) By shouting " Gas shells "—after the respirator has been adjusted ;
3) By runners where necessary.

Strombos Horns will *not* be used.

Men in dugouts, observation posts, and mine shafts must be warned and sleeping men roused.

c) Gas-proof dugouts will be closed immediately, and any fires burning in such dugouts put out. Care must be taken that men do not enter protected dugouts if their clothing has been exposed to gas.

d) Sentries will be posted at suitable points to warn men to put on their respirators before entering the shelled area. These sentries will not be withdrawn until the area is free from gas.

IV. — After a Gas Shell or Trench Mortar Bombardment the following precautions will be observed.

a) *Respirators will be worn until permission to remove them is given by an officer.*

b) Gas may remain in liquid form on the ground for several hours after a bombardment. When it is impossible to withdraw men from an infected area, respirators will be worn until the ground is clear. *Gas shell holes* will be *covered with fresh earth* when possible, or with chloride of lime if available.

c) Closed spaces such as dugouts and cellars may retain gas for many hours and must be cleared by means of fires. Men will not enter such places without wearing respirators until permission has been given by an officer.

d) When a man is close to the burst of a gas shell his clothes may become contaminated with liquid. When possible the clothes will be removed and exposed to the air. Care must be taken that men sleeping in closed spaces are not gassed by long exposure to small quantities of gas brought in on their clothing or equipment.

e) Men affected by gas will be spared exertion as much as possible and casualties will not be allowed to walk to the Dressing Station.

f) Transport will move from the shelled area when possible. Horse respirators will be adjusted on all animals remaining in the shelled area.

V. — Action to be taken in the event of an enemy Cloud Gas attack.

The Alarm.

a) Alarm will at once be given by all means available : — by Strombos horns, gongs, rattles, telephone, and, if necessary, by orderly. Sentries will warn all ranks in the trenches, dugouts, observation posts, or mine shafts.

b) Sentries on Strombos Horns will sound the horn (1) when they detect *cloud* gas, (2) when they *hear other Strombos Horns* sounding. Strombos Horns will *not* take up the alarm from gongs and rattles.

c) In order to restrict the spread of false alarms, when possible, Strombos Horns in back areas will be placed so that they need not be sounded until the alarm is confirmed by telephone.

d) Should the gas cloud be unaccompanied by an infantry attack, no S. O. S. signal will be sent, but the letters G. A. S. will be telephoned or telegraphed, followed by the name of the trench opposite to which the gas is being liberated.

This message will **not** be sent in case of a *gas shell bombardment only*.

e) Arrangements will be made for an immediate report of a hostile gas attack to be sent to all formations within 40 kilometers (25 miles) giving the map reference of the point of attack, as follows :

Divisions will warn :

    Corps H. Q. ;

    All other Divisions of the same Corps;

    (If a flank Division) Neighboring Division of adjoining Corps.

Corps will warn :
Army H. Q. ;
All other Corps of same Army ;
(If a flank Corps) Neighboring Corps of adjoining Army.

f) Arrangements will be made for the warning to be repeated, where necessary, to an officer in each village or camp within a radius of 40 kilometers of the point of attack, who will be responsible for warning units billeted there.

g) Corps will arrange to warn civil authorities who are responsible for the protection and warning of all civilians within the Corps area.

Action on the alarm being given.

h) *There should be as little movement and talking as possible.*
All ranks will at once adjust their small box respirators. Men in dugouts will do so before leaving dugouts.

i) The blanket curtains of protected dugouts and cellars will be properly adjusted, and fires in such dugouts put out.

j) Troops in the front lines, and wherever the tactical situation demands, will stand to arms.

k) In rear lines there is no objection to troops remaining in dugouts, where the tactical situation permits, with the exception of sentries and of officers and N. C. O.'s on duty.

l) All bodies of troops or transport on the move will halt, and working parties will cease work until the gas cloud has passed.

m) If a relief is in progress, units should stand steady as far as possible until the gas cloud has passed.

n) Supports and parties bringing up ammunition and grenades will only be moved up if the tactical situation demands.

Action during an Enemy Cloud Gas Attack.

o) The troops in the front trenches will open a slow rate of rifle fire at once against the enemy's trenches, and occasional short bursts will be fired from machine guns to ensure that all weapons are in working order.

p) Corps will arrange a suitable artillery program to be carried out in the event of a *cloud gas attack.*

Action after an Enemy Cloud Gas Attack.

q) Trenches will be cleared of gas with Anti-gas fans and sandbags.

r) Respirators will be worn until permission to remove them is given by an officer.

s) *A sharp lookout will be maintained for a repetition*

of the attack as long as the wind continues in a dangerous quarter. Men will sleep on the fire-step within reach of a sentry.

t) The instructions given in Section 4 (*c*) above, with regard to entering dugouts, etc., will be observed.

u) No man suffering from the effects of gas will be allowed to walk to the Dressing Station, or exert himself in any other manner.

v) The clearing of trenches and dugouts must not be carried out by men who have been affected by the gas.

w) After a gas attack, troops in the front trenches are to be relieved of all fatigue and carrying work for 24 hours, by sending up working parties from companies in the rear.

x) Horses which have been exposed to the gas will not be worked for 24 hours if it can be avoided.

y) Rifles and machine guns must be cleaned after a gas attack. Oil cleaning will prevent corrosion for 12 hours, but the first opportunity must be taken to clean all parts in boiling water containing a little soda.

z) Small arms ammunition must be carefully examined. All rounds affected by the gas must be replaced by new cartridges immediately. The rounds affected will then be cleaned. Especial attention must be paid to the brass clips.

zz) Expended air cylinders of Strombos Horns will be replaced by full ones.

VI. — Anti-Gas Trench Stores.

a) These comprise :
Extra supply of respirators and masks (5 % of strength);
Strombos horns and other alarm devices;
Wind vanes ;
Gas-proof coverings for dugouts ;
Anti-gas fans ;
Stores of fuel for clearing dugouts;
Vermorel Sprayers ;
Gas sampling apparatus.

b) Commanders of formations or units relieving one another are responsible that trench stores are duly turned over and receipted for, and that they are in good condition, and in proper positions for use or replacement.

c) The actual taking over should be done by company (battery) Gas N. C. O.'s, who will go up with the advance party (if possible in daylight) for this purpose. They will report any defects to their Company (battery) commander.

d) As soon after the actual taking over as possible the Regimental Gas Officer will make an inspection of all anti-gas arrangements and stores. He will call the attention of Company Commanders to any defects or deficiencies for correction. He should collect all possible blind gas shells to be sent to the laboratory for test.

GENERAL PRINCIPLES OF TRAINING IN GAS DEFENSIVE AGAINST GAS SHELL BOMBARDMENTS.

What to expect. — Every man should know what to expect, and should be told to regard as gas shells all those which burst with a small detonation, and to remember that gas shell is difficult to detect when fired with high explosive shell as it usually is.

The enemy has recently been firing large caliber shells with both gas and a large amount of high explosive so that it is practically impossible to tell which are gas shells and which are not. Hence, each man must be prepared to wear his mask during every bombardment.

Gas alarm. — Every man must be practiced in spreading the alarm by shouting "Gas shell" as soon as he has adjusted his respirator. Warning must be conveyed to troops to the leeward of the area bombarded. Sentries should be posted to warn men to put on their respirators before entering affected areas. Arrangements must be made to warn men who are asleep, immediately a gas bombardment begins.

Wearing box respirators. — Box respirators must be adjusted properly during gas shell bombardments and **must not be removed** after the bombardment is over **except on the order of an officer.** If removing respirators is left to the judgment of individual men, casualties are bound to occur.

Respirator Drill. — It is important that men should be practiced in adjusting the small box respirator while wearing steel helmets by going through the necessary motions even when not wearing the steel helmet. **Practice in prolonged wearing** is necessary, as many instances have occurred of men having to wear the small box respirator for five to eight hours. This condition will get worse as the war continues. Men must also be practiced in moving in the dark, and in speaking while wearing the respirator.

Realistic training. — It is important that the **actual training should be made realistic,** and combined with ordinary work; e. g., a party engaged on night operations might suddenly be given the alarm " Gas shell ", whereupon the correct action should be taken, and respirators worn for an hour without interrupting the operations.

Night practices are essential, because gas shelling nearly always occurs at night. Specialists and men of all arms must be able to perform their duties in the dark while wearing their respirators.

Gas-proof Dugouts. — All ranks must be acquainted with the proper method of adjusting the blankets at the entrances to gas-proof dugouts. The adjustment of the blankets should be practiced in the dark when wearing box respirators.

The value of gas-proof dugouts and cellars has been clearly demonstrated. This should be borne in mind in view of the inflammation of the skin produced by mustard gas. Billets and dugouts into which gas has entered must not be occupied until they have been completely cleared of gas by fires or fans.

Fans must be used only when fire is impossible, as they are far less efficient than a brisk fire for a few moments. 1 lb. of dry wood for each 100 cu. ft. of space in the dugout burned briskly for 10 to 15 minutes will clear it of all gas.

How to detect gas and what to do when it is detected.

1. With the present wide use of gas in artillery shells, trench mortars, bombs, cloud gas waves, and even hand grenades, it is a very difficult matter to be sure there is no gas around.

2. Everywhere within the reach of artillery : front line, communication trenches, batteries, billets, or, in fact, wherever a body of men are likely to be found, gas shell bombardment is to be expected and guarded against. Salvos of gas shells are sent over in the hope of catching bodies of men unprepared or unwarned. Such a bombardment is apt to be heavy, especially at first, in order to develop a strong concentration of gas. Not only will gas shells be sent, but also frequently a large proportion of high explosive shells in an attempt to conceal the former or to detract attention. Also, gas shells are sometimes now made with such a large amount of high explosive that their burst cannot be told from ordinary high explosive shell.

a) Gas shells usually make a peculiar "wobbling" noise when they come through the air, due to their being filled with liquid instead of a solid.

b) Generally in the case of both gas artillery shells and gas trench mortar bombs, the sound of the burst is very small and they are therefore sometimes considered as "duds" (high explosive shells that fail to burst).

c) When a gas shell explodes most of the liquid gas turns into vapor, sometimes in the form of a white cloud. However, this is not true of all kinds of gas.

d) If a gas shell bursts 20 yards or less to windward of a body of men they have no time to wait for any alarm, and unless each acts for himself he will be killed. *Each must hold his breath and get his respirator or mask on as quickly as possible.* In doing so, follow the methods described in Drill "B" or Drill "C". *Whenever putting on a mask*, do so according to the methods given in the Drills, because these have been worked out with great pains to save loss of time.

Mustard Gas (Dichlorethylsulphide). — The slight smell of mustard gas and the absence of any immediate effect on the eyes and lungs make it necessary that precaution against gas shell should be taken when any shells are falling nearby, even if no gas be smelled or recognized.

3. Cloud gas is usually, if not invariably, phosgene or phosgene mixed with chlorine. Both have a very distinct irritating odor like that given by chloride of lime, well known as a disinfectant. Both are irritating to the throat and cause coughing. There is no difficulty in recognizing them, but **one full breath of a phosgene cloud will kill a man, therefore, hold your breath while putting on your respirator or mask.** The responsibility for recognizing cloud gas rests with the sentries in the front line trenches. The actual gas cloud is frequently preceded a few seconds by a hissing sound like the escape of steam; this noise, however, can not always be heard on account of artillery or machine gun fire. In the day time these gas clouds are visible at quite a distance and readily recognized, but as they are now used only at night or when there is a fog, it is seldom that they can be seen more than five seconds away.

Summary.

There are three things to do :
First : Hold your breath.
Second : Keep on holding your breath until your respirator or mask is fully and accurately on.
Third : Give the alarm for all your comrades.

B. — NATURE OF GAS ATTACKS.

I. — Gas clouds.

4. This method of making a gas attack is entirely dependent on the direction of the wind. The gas is carried up to the trenches as a liquid in steel cylinders. These are dug or set in the trench and connected with pipes leading out over the parapet. When the valves of the cylinders are opened, the gas escapes, usually with a hissing sound, which, on a still night, can frequently be heard at a considerable distance. It mixes with the air and is carried by the wind towards the opposing trenches, spreading out as it goes forward. A continuous wave of gas and air is thus formed, the color of which may vary :

a) Because of the weather conditions. In very dry air it may be almost transparent and slightly greenish in color, while in damp weather it forms a white cloud.

b) Because it may be mixed with smoke of any color.

5. A cloud attack can only take place when there is a steady but not too strong wind blowing from the enemy's lines towards our own. A wind between 4 and 8 miles an hour is the most likely condition. An 8-mile wind will carry the gas cloud twice as quickly as a man walks rapidly.

Gas attacks may occur at any time of the day, but are most likely to be made during the night or in the early morning.

Rain is without appreciable effect on a gas attack. Fogs have hardly any effect, and may, in fact, be taken advantage of to make an attack unexpectedly. Watercourses and ponds are no obstruction to a gas cloud.

6. The gas used by the enemy is generally a mixture of chlorine and phosgene, or pure phosgene, both of which are strongly asphyxiating. The gases are heavier than air, and therefore tend to flow along the ground and into trenches, shelters, craters, and hollows. The gas cloud may flow around slight rises in the ground, thus leaving patches of country which remain free from gas.

7. Even when very dilute, chlorine can be recognized by its peculiar smell, which is like chloride of lime, but stronger ger and more irritating.

Both chlorine and phosgene also exert a strongly corrosive action on metals, so that the metal parts of arms must be carefully protected by oiling them.

8. The speed with which the gas cloud approaches depends entirely on the wind velocity. Gas attacks have been made with wind velocities varying from 3 to 20 miles per hour, i. e., from 1 1/2 to 10 yards per second. In a 9-mile wind, the gas would reach trenches 100 yards distant in 20 seconds.

Gas attacks have been made on fronts varying from 1 to 5 miles. Their effects at points up to 12 miles behind the front trenches have been sufficiently severe to make it necessary to wear masks.

II. — Gas projectiles.

9. The use of these depends very little on the direction of the wind. In gas projectiles such as shells, hand grenades, and trench mortar bombs, a part or whole of the explosive charge is replaced by a liquid which is converted into gas by the explosion. The explosive force and noise of detonation of these projectiles is generally less than that of the ordinary kind, and a large number of them are usually discharged into a comparatively small space. After the explosion, the liquid gas forms a small cloud, though some of it may sink into the ground and remain active for a considerable time. Mustard gas may so remain for 12 to 48 hours or even longer in cool weather.

For gas shells, the best condition is calm, or with a wind of low velocity.

Gas projectiles can be used in all types of country.

Woods, tall grass, bushes, cornfields, and clumps of buildings may hold the gas active for a considerable time.

Several kinds of shell gas are used by the enemy :

Poisonous Shells : Immediate death. — The gases in some shells may cause instant death if a single breath is taken. These usually contain Hydrocyanic Acid (Prussic Acid) or an allied substance which causes death by action on the nervous system, paralyzing the respiration and resulting in convulsions, coma, and death. These are little used now.

Delayed death and delayed blindness. — Phosgene, chloropicrin, and mustard gas by destroying the lungs cause death from a few hours up to several days, especially if there has been any exertion after breathing the gas.

The new "Mustard Gas" (Di-chlor-ethyl-sulphide), after several hours, causes the eyelids to swell up so that sight is lost for one to four weeks with intense pain in the eyes ; the skin is also burnt by it, though death is only caused by its action on the lungs.

Its danger lies in its insidious nature, because no appreciable irritation is caused at the time. It has a slight odor like mustard or garlic though even this smell may be disguised. The respirator and mask afford perfect protection against it.

Lachrymators. — These shells contain various substances of a nature irritating to the eyes, which makes them water and which causes immediate pain. While their immediate action is strongly irritant to the eyes, they may also cause a delayed general poisoning resulting in death. Respirators or masks must always be put on whenever an area is shelled by these missiles. Gas shells are occasionally sent alternately with High Explosive, the latter masking the presence of the former.

III. — Smoke.

11. The enemy may make use of smoke, either in the form of a cloud or emitted from shells and bombs. Smoke may be used with gas or between gas clouds ; it may also be used alone to distract attention from a real discharge of gas, to cover the advance of infantry, or merely as a false gas attack.

IV. — Mine and explosion gases.

12. The poisonous gases which occur in mines, and which are formed in large quantities when high explosive goes off in an enclosed space (e. g., from a direct hit in a dugout, or from the explosion of a charge in a mine) are not protected against by the ordinary anti-gas appliances. The chief of these gases is carbon monoxide. Protection against such gases will not be considered in these notes.

II. – ORGANIZATION OF GAS DEFENSE.

13. Commanding Officers are held responsible that all the anti-gas appliances for protecting their men are maintained in perfect condition, and that all ranks under their command are thoroughly trained in the use of these appliances and in all other measures which may affect their safety against gas.

Summary of protective measures.

14. *a*) Respirators and masks for each man.

b) Inspection of respirators and masks and training in their use and instruction in all other measures of gas defense.

c) Protected and gas-proof shelters.

d) Weather observations to determine periods when the conditions are most favorable to a hostile gas attack.

e) Arrangement of signals and messages for immediate warning of a gas attack.

f) Appliances for clearing gas from trenches and shelters.

A. – ORGANIZATION OF ANTI-GAS DUTIES.

15. All ranks must be fully conversant with the measures to be adopted for defense against gas attacks as laid down in the Orders of their formation or unit (*).

A Chief Gas Officer is appointed in each Division, so that technical advice is readily available on all matters connected with gas defense. Apart from this, the following scheme of anti-gas duties should be adopted within units.

B. – ANTI-GAS DUTIES WITHIN AN INFANTRY REGIMENT.

(To be modified for other units to suit their organization and duties.)

16. The Commanding Officer will be directly responsible for all measures against gas attacks, and Company Commanders will be responsible to the C. O. for all anti-gas measures within their companies.

Regimental Gas Officer. — To aid the Regimental Commander in seeing that all anti-gas measures are efficiently carried out, Regimental Gas Officers are appointed on the Regimental commander's staff.

The special duties of the Regimental Gas Officer will be fully laid down in special instructions that will be issued from time to time by the Chief of the Gas Service.

In each Company one N. C. O., who has been trained at an Anti-Gas School, and who should be recommended by the Division Gas Officer as suitable for duty as " Company

(*) For typical Divisional Standing Orders, see Appendix IV

Gas N.C.O.", will be specially detailed to assist the Company Commander in anti-gas measures. At least one other similarly trained and recommended N.C.O. will be immediately available to take the place of the Gas N.C.O. in case of need.

A similarly trained Gas N.C.O. will be detailed to Battalion H. Q. for duty with H. Q. details.

17. The special duties of Gas N.C.O.'s will be definitely laid down in Regiments (*). Other duties may, however, be performed, provided that these do not interfere with the gas duties laid down.

18. In order to secure the necessary training in all matters pertaining to defense against gas attacks, the following officers and N.C.O.'s should attend a course at a Corps or other Anti-Gas School.

a) *Officers*.

1) The Commanding Officer or Second in Command, and the Medical Officer.

2) All Company Commanders.

3) Other Officers where possible.

b) *N.C.O.'s*.

1) Two per Company and 2 per Battalion H.Q.

2) Supplementary N.C.O.'s, to be trained whenever possible, so as to have a reserve from which to draw to replace Gas N.C.O.'s, in case of need.

The selected N.C.O.'s, who attend the Anti-Gas Schools will be reported on by the Officer in Charge as follows : At the end of the course the Director of the Gas School will, if the N.C.O. is, in his opinion, suitable for duty as " Company Gas N.C.O." , notify the C.O. concerned to this effect. The latter will then cause the words " passed Anti-Gas School " to be entered on his service record. Only N.C. O.'s, who have been thus reported on favorably should be detailed for duty as Company Gas N.C.O.'s.

19. C.O.'s will facilitate in every way the duties of the various officers of the Gas Service in visiting their lines and inspecting anti-gas arrangements, testing Strombos horn cylinders, etc. They should take every opportunity of consulting with officers of the Gas Service on all technical questions relating to anti-gas measures within their lines.

C. — PERSONAL ANTI-GAS EQUIPMENT.

I. — Equipment carried.

20. Each man is provided with a small box respirator and a mask. He must be made to realize that these appliances are personal equipment, that they are of importance second

---

(*) For typical Standing Orders for Company Gas N.C.O.'s, see Appendix V.

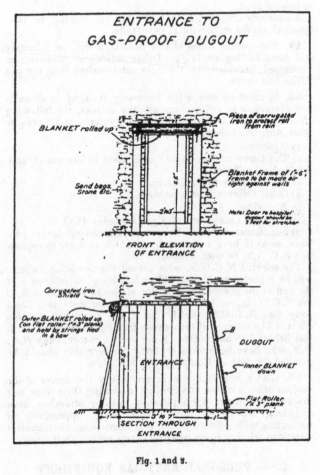

ENTRANCE TO GAS-PROOF DUGOUT

Piece of corrugated iron to protect roll from rain

BLANKET rolled up

Blanket Frame of 1"×6"; frame to be made air tight against walls

Sand bags. Stone etc.

Note: Door to hospital dugout should be 3 feet for stretcher

2'×3'

6'

FRONT ELEVATION OF ENTRANCE

Corrugated iron shield

Outer BLANKET rolled up (on flat roller 1"×3" plank) and held by strings tied in a bow

A

DUGOUT

B

ENTRANCE

6'

Inner BLANKET down

Flat Roller 1"× 3" plank

3' to 7'

SECTION THROUGH ENTRANCE

Fig. 1 and 2.

208

only to his weapons, and that his life may depend on looking after them and keeping them in good order.

21. The small box respirator is the most important protective apparatus. It is always to be used first in case of a gas attack, unless special orders are issued to the contrary. It will protect against all poisonous gases with the exception of mine and explosion gases, and will not become exhausted for hours, even in concentrations of gas generally unobtainable in the field.

22. The mask is an emergency or reserve defense. It is only to be used if the owner should not have a box respirator or if the latter should be found, for any reason, to be defective.

II. — **When and where carried.**

23. a) Both respirator and mask should be carried within 5 miles of the front line.

b) When the wind is safe, working parties during work and at the discretion of the officer in command, may take off their box respirators between 2 and 5 miles from the front line, provided they are placed conveniently at hand for use in case of a sudden gas shell attack or change of wind. The mask will always be carried.

c) At distances greater than 5 miles the mask only need be carried, the box respirator being kept with the equipment under arrangements by the C. O. of the Unit.

D. — PROTECTION OF SHELTERS.

I. — Methods of protection.

24. The fundamental principle to remember is that gas will follow the smallest current of air and make the dugout dangerous.

25. Conversely, if the entrances to the dugout are so arranged as to prevent air currents, the dugout remains safe for many hours even when there is a strong concentration of gas outside.

26. For these reasons, where tactically practicable, it is desirable to have only one entrance with double doors to each dugout, and no chimney.

27. If a chimney is necessary it must be so arranged that the stove pipe can be readily removed and the chimney opening quickly closed airtight. Great care should be taken in fitting this opening so that it will be air-tight, as otherwise well constructed dugouts are rendered unsafe. All entrances must be protected by double doors with an air space between. The best way of arranging such an entrance is shown in the diagram page 20.

a) The frames A and B made of 6″ × 1″ planks, are fitted

to the entrance to the dugout at such a slope that the bottom of the frame is out about 1 foot for a height of 5 feet. Care must be taken in fitting in these frames to leave no cracks between the frame and the earth or the sandbags forming the sides or roof of the entrance.

b) Blanket cloth cut to the proper size is nailed to the top of the frame with a lath to prevent tearing. The blanket cloth must overlap the face of the frame by at least 3, and better still 6 inches.

c) A *flat* roller, made of 1 inch board about 3 inches wide is nailed to the bottom of the blanket on the outside so that when the blanket is unrolled it lies tight against the outside bottom part of the frame, but not touching the ground.

d) The frames of the inner and outer doors should not be less than 3 feet apart in order to allow a man to enter the air space and adjust the first blanket before passing through the second. For medical dugouts the air space should be 8 feet long and 3 feet wide to allow a stretcher to pass through.

e) It has been found useful to sew small metal weights along the sides of the curtain, which fall over strips nailed on the face of door-frame sides, top, and bottom. This causes the curtain to close more tightly.

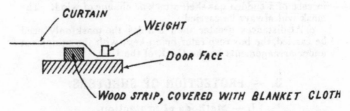

Fig. 3.

Another method for closing those dugouts that are not used during attack is to nail two strips along the face of the door and another to fit in the space between the two.

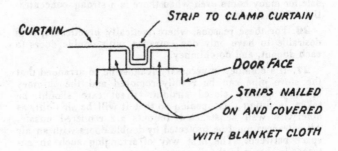

Fig. 4.

f) When not in use the blankets are to be kept rolled up and so held that they can be instantly released. For the outer door a piece of galvanized iron or other sheet metal is placed across the top of the doorway to protect the blanket from rain when it is rolled up.

g) To render blankets completely air tight they must be kept wet; therefore a Vermorel sprayer or a simple can of water should be kept in a special niche in the air space for moistening the blankets. Chemicals for neutralizing the gases are not necessary, but some substance like glycerine is good, as that tends to hold water and to absorb it from the air. Material wet with a solution of water and glycerine does not dry readily.

h) Men must pass through each doorway quickly, and immediately readjust the curtain before touching the second curtain.

i) On gas alarm being given, all fires in dugouts must be put out, the chimney opening closed *tight*, and the entrance curtains let down and sprayed. All persons in the dugout must be awakened and *all must put on their masks*, as some gas may leak in through faulty construction of the dugout, or by some one coming in with gas on his clothes.

II. — Shelters or dugouts which should be protected.

28. The following should always be protected with gas-proof entrances :

Medical aid-posts and advanced dressing stations, Company, Battalion, Regimental, and Brigade Headquarters, Signal Shelters, and any other place where work has to be carried out during a gas attack.

29. In addition to the above, it is desirable to protect all dugouts, cellars, and buildings within shell fire area, particularly those of artillery personnel. It should be noted, however, that the protection of dugouts for troops in the front line of trenches is usually inadvisable on account of the delay involved in getting men out in time of attack. It is desirable to protect stretcher bearers' dugouts with a view to putting casualties in them.

E. — PROTECTION OF WEAPONS AND EQUIPMENT.

30. Arms and ammunition and the metal parts of special equipment (e. g., telephone instruments) must be carefully protected against gas by oiling them or keeping them completely covered. Otherwise, particularly in damp weather, they may rust or corrode so badly as to refuse to act. A mineral oil must be used for this purpose. The following, in particular, should be protected :

I. — Small arms and small arms ammunition.

34. Machine guns and rifles must be kept carefully cleaned and well oiled. The effects of corrosion of ammunition are of even more importance than the direct effects of gas upon machine guns and rifles themselves.

Ammunition boxes must be kept closed. Vickers belts should be kept in their boxes until actually required for use. The wooden belt boxes are fairly gas-tight, but metal belt boxes should be made gas-tight by inserting strips of flannelette in the joint between the lid and the box.

Lewis magazines should be kept in some form of box, the joints of which are made as gas-tight as possible with flannelette.

A recess should be made, high up in the parapet if possible, for storing ammunition and guns. A blanket curtain, moistened with water or Vermorel sprayer solution, will greatly assist in keeping the gas out.

II. — Hand and rifle grenades.

32. Unboxed grenades should be kept covered as far as possible. All safety pins and working parts, especially those made of brass, should be kept oiled to prevent their setting from corrosion by the gas.

III. — Light trench mortars and their ammunition.

33. As far as the supply of oil permits, the bore and all bright parts of light trench mortars and their spare parts should be kept permanently oiled. When not in use, mortars should be covered with sacking or similar material.

Unboxed ammunition should be kept covered as far as possible, and the bright parts oiled immediately after arrival. Ammunition which has been in store for some time should be used up first.

IV. — Guns, medium and heavy trench mortars, and their ammunition.

34. The protection of artillery and artillery ammunition is dealt with in par. 109.

V. — Signal equipment.

35. The protection of signal equipment is dealt with in par. 116.

F. — WIND OBSERVATION.

36. The Meteorological Service reports to Headquarters of Corps and Divisions whenever the wind passes into a dangerous quarter, showing the direction and strength of the wind. As a result of these reports, "Gas Alert" is ordered by Corps or Division H. Q. These general reports, however, refer to large tracts of country, and it is possible that on isolated lengths of front, conditions of terrain or the alignment of the trenches may permit of local air currents which are favorable to the enemy. It is essential, therefore, that the troops themselves should be on the look-out for the possibility of a gas attack.

The wind frequently changes its direction at night, thus creating conditions different from those existing in the day time.

The cooling of the air from midnight till dawn produces downward currents, and hence so far as air currents are concerned makes the period just before dawn the best for gas attacks.

A wind blowing down a steep slope into a valley tends to follow the direction of the valley and may thus be changed as much as 90 degrees in direction.

To make necessary wind observations, there should be a good wind station every 1/4 mile within 100 yards of the front line. Each should be so situated as to give conditions outside of trenches rather than inside but should not be close enough to headquarters to subject it to shell fire in case it is sighted by the enemy.

Observations have shown the wind to be mostly in our favor during the summer and fall and mostly in the enemy's favor during spring.

Company Commanders are responsible that wind observations are made on their Company front every three hours, or oftener if the wind is in, or appproaching, a dangerous quarter, and the reports forwarded through the usual channels to Brigade H. Q. For the method of making these observations and preparing the reports, see Appendix V.

G. — THE GAS ALERT PERIOD.

I. — Order for gas alert.

37. Gas alert will be ordered when the wind is in the dangerous quarter, no matter what the strength of the wind.

The order "Gas Alert" will be sent out to all units by Corps H. Q. (or, if authority has been so delegated, by Division H. Q.), but Brigade or Regimental H. Q., or Battalion Commanders are empowered to order a "Gas

Alert" as a result of wind observations forwarded by Company Commanders. Such action will be reported immediately to the next higher formation.

Gas Alert notices should be posted at the entrance to each main communication trench and at other suitable points within Divisional Areas.

II. — **Precautions during gas alert.**

a) *Inspection.*

38. All box respirators and masks should be carefully inspected, and the inspection should be repeated daily. Steps must be taken to ascertain if al gas alarm appliances are in their positions and in good ord

b) *Alert position of respirators an 4 masks.*

39. All ranks within two miles of the front line must carry their box respirators (or their masks, should they have no box respirators) in the alert position. The press buttons of the flap of the box respirator satchel must be unfastened.

During gas alert the chin strap of the steel helmet must be worn on the point and not under the chin, as it will impede the rapid adjustment of the respirator or mask.

c) *Sentries, etc.*

40. A sentry should be posted at each Strombos horn or other alarm device and instructed in its use, and all working parties should have a sentry posted to give instant warning of a gas attack.

A sentry should also be posted at every large shelter or group of small shelters and at each Headquarters, Signal Office, and independent body of men.

Arrangements must be made by the officer in charge of the trench for warning the Artillery Observation Post if there is one in the trench.

Commanders of units in billets within 8 miles of the front line trenches must organize a system of giving the alarm and rousing all men in cellars or houses.

At night sentries should have at least two men within reach of them, so that the alarm can be spread rapidly.

d) *Sleeping.*

41. When a gas attack is probable, men in front line trenches should sleep on the fire.step instead of in dugouts. Men sleeping in rearward lines, or in works where they are allowed to take off their equipment, must sleep with their box respirators on the person.

e) *Company Gas N. C. O.'s.*

42. Company Gas N. C. O.'s will report to Company

H. Q. in readiness to assist the Company Commander should a gas attack occur.

f) *Officers and N.C.O.'s.*

43. Officers and N. C. O.'s in command of any unit or party must see that the above orders are strictly carried out, both for troops in front line trenches and for detached bodies of troops (working and carrying parties, etc.).

III. — Removal of gas alert.

44. Gas alert will not be taken off without the authority of the Corps Commander or the Division Commander to whom authority has been delegated.

On the receipt of orders for the removal of gas alert, the notices on the subject will be amended accordingly.

H. — CLOUD GAS ALARM.

I. — Method of giving the alarm.

45. For the purpose of giving the alarm the Strombos horn, which is audible for very long distances, is the most important appliance. Its main use is for conveying the alarm to troops in support and reserve lines. In addition, some local appliance, such as a gong or suspended rail, must be fastened up at every sentry's post for the purpose of rousing the men in the immediate vicinity and for conveying the alarm to the sentries in charge of the strombos horns.

Strombos horns should be in the front line, at intervals ordinarily not greater than 400 yards, and at such other points behind the front as required to ensure transmission of warning. As much use as possible should be made of the telephone for transmitting the gas alarm, though it can not be relied upon owing to the possibility of its breaking down.

No reliance can be placed on methods of giving the alarm involving the use of the lungs; e. g., bugles or whistles.

46. Sentries must be prepared to give the alarm on the first appearance of gas, as a few seconds delay may involve very serious consequences. Signals must be passed along by all sentries as soon as heard.

The earliest warning of a gas cloud attack is generally given :

a) By the noise of the gas escaping from the cylinders

b) By the appearance of a cloud of any color over the enemy's trenches. If the attack takes place at night, the cloud will not be visible from a distance.

c) By the smell of the gas in listening posts.

II. — Action to be taken in the trenches on gas alarm.

47. a) *Respirators* to be put on immediately by all ranks (mask, if no box respirator is available).

b) *Rouse* all men in trenches, dugouts and mine shafts, warn officers and artillery observation posts and all working men.

c) *Artillery support* to be called for by Company Commanders, by means of prearranged signals.

d) *Warn* Battalion H. Q. and troops in rear.

e) *All ranks stand to arms* in the front trenches and elsewhere where the tactical situation demands.

f) *Blanket curtains* at entrances to protected shelters to be let down, carefully fixed, and wet with water or chemical solutions.

g) *Movement* to cease except where necessary.

III. — Action to be taken in billets and back areas.

48. *a*) All men in cellars or houses to be roused.

b) The blanket curtains of protected cellars, etc., to be let down, fixed in position, and sprinkled.

c) Box respirators to be put on immediately the gas is apparent.

I. — ACTION DURING A CLOUD GAS ATTACK.

I. — Protective measures.

49. There should be as little moving about and talking as possible in the trenches. Men must be made to realize that with the gas now used by the enemy, observance of this may be essential for their safety.

When an attack is in progress, all bodies of troops or transport on the move should halt and all working parties cease work until the gas cloud has passed.

If a relief is going on, units should stand fast as far as possible until the gas cloud has passed.

Supports and parties bringing up bombs should only be moved up if the tactical situation demands it.

50. If troops in support or reserve lines of trenches remain in, or go into, dugouts, they must continue to wear their anti-gas appliances.

Officers and N. C. O.'s must on no account remove or open up the masks of the box respirators or raise their masks to give orders. The breathing tube may be removed from the mouth when it is necessary to speak, but it must be replaced before drawing breath.

51. Men must always be on the look-out to help each other in case a box respirator or mask is damaged by fire or accident. When a man is wounded, he must be watched to see that he does not remove his respirator or mask until he is safely inside a protected shelter; if necessary, his hands should be tied.

Men must be warned that if they are slightly gassed before adjusting their respirators or masks they must not remove them.

II. — Tactical measures.

52. From the point of view of protection against gas, nothing is gained by men remaining in unprotected dugouts or by moving to a flank or to the rear. It is, therefore, desirable that on tactical and disciplinary grounds all men in the front line of trenches should be forbidden to do these things. In support or reserve lines, where there are protected dugouts, it is advisable for men to stay in them unless the tactical situation makes it desirable for them to come out.

54. Nothing is gained by opening rapid rifle fire unless the enemy's infantry attacks. A slow rate of fire from rifles and occasional short bursts of fire from machine guns will lessen the chance of their jamming from the action of the gas and tends to occupy and steady the infantry.

55. It should be remembered that the enemy's infantry cannot attack while the gas discharge is in progress and is unlikely to do so for an appreciable time — at least 10 minutes — after it has ceased. It is, in fact, a common practice for the enemy infantry to retire to the second and third line of trench whilst gas is being discharged. There is, therefore, no object in opening an intense S.O.S. barrage of artillery on "No man 's land" during the actual gas cloud and it is advisable that the warning to the Artillery of a gas attack should be a signal differing from the ordinary S. O. S. signal, as the latter may have to be sent later if an infantry attack develops.

56. It must be remembered that smoke may be used by the enemy at the same time as, or alternately with, the gas and that under cover of a smoke cloud he may send out assaulting or raiding parties. A careful look-out must, therefore, be kept; hostile patrols or raiders may be frustrated by cross-fire of rifles and machine guns and should an assault develop the ordinary S.O.S. procedure should be carried out.

J. — PRECAUTIONS AGAINST GAS SHELLS.

57. When gas is smelt men may not realize its possibly dangerous character at once and so may delay putting on respirators or masks until too late. Men sleeping in dugouts may be seriously affected unless they are roused. The following points should therefore be attended to :

58. 1) All shells which explode with a small detonation or appear to be blind should be regarded with particular attention, though all shell should be suspected of carrying gas ; the respirator or mask should be put on at the first indication of gas, and blanket protection of shelters adjusted.

2) Arrangements must be made for giving a local alarm with klaxons, etc., in the event of a bombardment with poison gas shells, but **Strombos horns must on no account be used** to give warning of a gas shell bombardment.

3) All shelters in the vicinity of an area bombarded with poison gas shells must be visited and any sleeping men roused.

4) Box respirators or masks should continue to be worn throughout the area bombarded with poison gas shells until the order is given by the local unit Commander for their removal.

59. Lachrymatory or "tear" shells are frequently used by the enemy for the purpose of hindering the movements of troops, for preventing the bringing up of supports, or for interfering with the action of artillery.

Owing to the deadly nature of poison gas shells, however, the precautions given in par. 58 above must be taken for all shells, until certain no gas shells are being used.

K. — PRECAUTIONS TO BE TAKEN WITH REGARD TO OUR OWN USE OF GAS IN CYLINDERS, BOMBS, ETC.

60. Protection of troops is necessary during our own gas attacks. Adequate protective measures should always be possible, as arrangements can be made in advance and the element of surprise can be excluded. The following points should be noted :

I. — Handling gas cylinders.

61. Men engaged in carrying or digging-in gas cylinders should carry their box respirators in the "Alert" position.

II. — Action when gas cylinders are in position in trenches.

62. *a)* Box respirators should be carried in the "Alert" position by troops in front line trenches.

b) If a cylinder is burst by shell-fire, men should retire upwind for a short distance, if possible. Dugouts in the neighborhood of the burst must be evacuated at once.

III. — Action during our gas attacks.

63. *a)* It is advisable that all troops, except those whose presence is considered absolutely necessary, should be withdrawn from the front trench before gas is discharged. Any officer or man who has special orders to remain must *wear* his box respirator.

b) All troops in any part of the front line within half a mile of the nearest point where gas is being discharged must *wear* their box respirators.

c) If troops advance after a cloud gas attack has been made, it must be remembered that the gas may hang about for a considerable time in long grass, shell holes, and hollows, and for several hours in the enemy's dugouts and shelters. Raiding or reconnoitering parties after a gas discharge should carry their respirators in the Alert position. *Dugouts should not be occupied* until they have been thoroughly ventilated and the *absence of gas established.* This is equally necessary with regard to shelters which have been penetrated by gas from shells or bombs.

IV. — Gas bombs and grenades.

64. These may, if necessary, be stored with other ammunition. In the event of leakage they should be buried in the ground 3 1/2 feet deep. They should not be thrown into water. All rescue work and disposal of leaky shells should be carried out by men wearing box respirators and gloves.

L. — ACTION AFTER A CLOUD GAS ATTACK.

I. — General.

65. The most important measure to be taken after a cloud gas attack is to prepare for a further attack. The enemy frequently sends several successive waves of gas at intervals varying from a few minutes up to several hours, and it is therefore necessary to be on the alert to combat this procedure. The following measures should be adopted as soon as he gas cloud has passed :

a) Removal of respirators. — Anti-gas fans should be used to assist in clearing the trenches of gas, so as to admit of respirators being removed. Box respirators and masks must not be removed until permission has been given by the Company Commander, who will, when possible, ascertain from officers and N. C. O.'s who have been trained at a Gas School that it is safe to do so.

b) Return to the Alert position. — After removal of respirators in order to be ready for a subsequent attack, box respirators and masks must be put back in the Alert position.

A sharp look-out must be kept for a repetition of the gas attack, as long as the wind continues in a dangerous quarter.

II. — Movement.

66. Owing to the enemy gas sometimes causing bad after-effects, which are intensified by any exertion, the following points should be attended to :

a) No man suffering from the effects of gas, however slightly, should be allowed to walk to the dressing station.

b) The clearing of the trenches and dugouts should not be carried out by men who have been affected by the gas.

c) After a gas attack, troops in the front trenches should be relieved of all fatigue and carrying work for 24 hours by sending up working parties from companies in rear.

d) Horses which have been exposed to the gas should not be worked for 24 hours if it can be avoided.

III. — Clearing dugouts and other shelters.

67. It is essential that no dugout be entered after a gas attack, except with box respirators or masks adjusted, until it has been ascertained that it is free from gas. The only efficient method of clearing dugouts from gas is by thorough ventilation. The older method of spraying is not efficient.

An appreciable quantity of gas may be retained in the clothing of men exposed to gas attacks and also in bedding, coats, etc., left in shelters. Precautions should, therefore, be taken to air all clothing.

a) Ventilation.

68. Natural Ventilation. — Unless a shelter has been thoroughly ventilated by artificial means, as described below, it must not be slept in, or occupied without wearing respirators, until at least 12 hours have elapsed. It must not be entered at all without respirators on for at least 3 hours. The above refers to cloud gas attacks. In the case of gas shell bombardments the times cannot be definitely stated, as they depend on the nature of the gas used and the severity of the bombardment. With lachrymatory gases or mustard gas the times after which shelters can be used without discomfort may be much longer than those mentioned above.

69. Ventilation by Fire. — All kinds of shelters can be efficiently and rapidly cleared of gas by the use of fires. Shelters with two openings are the easiest to ventilate but most difficult to protect.

In dugouts provided with a single exit at the end of a short passage, the best results are obtained if the fire is placed in the centre of the floor of the dugout and at a height of about 6 inches.

In dugouts provided with a single exit at the end of a long and nearly-horizontal passage, the best results are obtained if the fire is placed in the dugout about one-third of the distance from the inner end of the passage.

In dugouts provided with two or more exits, the fire should be placed at the inner end of one of the exit passages away from the direction of the wind in order to give a good draft through the dugout.

70. In general, 1 lb., of dry wood per 100 cubic feet of air space is sufficient for clearance of any gas. The best fuel is split wood, but any fuel which does not smoulder or give off thick smoke can be used. The materials for the fire, e. g., the split wood, newspaper, and a small bottle of kerosene for lighting purposes. should be kept in a sandbag enclosed in a tin box provided with a lid. An improvised stove should be kept ready for use.

The fire must be kept burning for at least 15 minutes and the atmosphere in the shelter should be tested from time to time.

If mustard gas or a similar one with very high boiling point should burst so as to scatter liquid gas in the dugout, ventilation alone is not sufficient. In order to be safe under 2 to 3 days the liquid would have to be thoroughly treated with chloride of lime.

71. Ventilation by Fanning. — Dugouts can be ventilated by producing air currents in them by means of special anti-gas fans. A full description of the anti-gas fan and the method of using it to clear gas from trenches and shelters is given later (see par. 96-100).

If no anti-gas fans are available, ventilation can be assisted by flapping with improvised fans such as sandbags, blankets, etc.

b) Sprayers.

72. Vermorel sprayers will not clear gas from trenches. The solution has very little effect on phosgene, and even with the addition of other chemicals it cannot be relied upon to remove gas from the air. Vermorel sprayers are only for wetting blankets on doors of dugouts.

73. Rifles and machine guns must be cleaned after a gas attack and then re-oiled. Oil cleaning will prevent corrosion for 12 hours or more, but the first available opportunity must be taken to dismantle machine guns and clean all parts in boiling water containing a little soda. If this is not done, corrosion continues slowly even after oil cleaning and may ultimately put the gun out of action.

After a gas attack, small arms ammunition should be carefully examined. All rounds affected by gas must be replaced by new cartridges immediately and the old ones cleaned and expended as soon as possible.

74. All hand and rifle grenades exposed to the gas should have their safety-pins and working parts cleaned and re-oiled.

75. All bright parts of light trench mortars, together with all accessories and spare parts exposed to the gas, must be cleaned and wiped dry as soon as possible after the attack, and in any case within 24 hours, after which they should be thoroughly coated afresh with oil. The same applies to ammunition which may have been exposed to the gas.

Ammunition which, for any reason, had not been oiled, must be cleaned and oiled and fired as soon as possible.

For details regarding the cleaning of guns and artillery ammunition and signal equipment, see par. 109 and 116.

V. — Treatment of shell holes.

76. In the neighborhood of shelters or battery positions where gas from shell holes is causing annoyance, the holes and the ground round them should be covered with at least a foot of fresh earth or a quarter of an inch of chloride of lime. Shell holes covered with earth should not be disturbed, as the chemical is not thereby destroyed and only disappears slowly. This is particularly true of mustard gas.

III. — PROTECTIVE APPLIANCES.

A. — INDIVIDUAL PROTECTIVE APPARATUS.

I. — Box respirator.

a) *Description.*

77. The box respirator consists of a box packed with chemicals and connected by means of a flexible rubber tube to an impervious face piece or mask. The inspired air enters through a valve in the bottom of the box; the expired air is expelled through a valve just outside the face-piece. The wearer breathes in and out through a mouthpiece inside the mask, breathing through the nose being prevented by a nose-clip inserted in the face piece. The latter is made of gas-proof fabric and is arranged to fit the face closely, being held in position by two elastic bands. As it encloses the eyes, the mask is fitted with two eyepieces which allow a wide field of vision. These should be treated with anti-dimming composition, but if necessary they can be cleaned without removing the respirator, by means of folds in the material. The mouth-piece can be removed from the mouth to enable the wearer to speak without disturbing the fit of the mask. The complete respirator is carried in a special satchel which is divided into two compartments, one of which holds the box and the other the mask. The box rests on a metal saddle which raises it from the bottom of the satchel and allows the free access to air.

b) *Personal Fitting.*

78. It is necessary that each man should have a box respirator, the mask of which properly fits his face. For this reason the face pieces are made in six sizes, four of which are regular issues and the other two are obtained on special requisition. The various sizes will be needed probably in the following proportions :

No. 0. Extra small	0.1 %	(Special requisition)
No. 1. Very small	0.3 %	
No. 2. Small	3.0 %	
No. 3. Medium	75.0 %	
No. 4. Large	15.0 %	
No. 5. Extra large	2.0 %	

The fit of each man's mask must be inspected and then tested in a gas chamber. Almost any room which can be closed up tightly may be used for this purpose, but the most suitable arrangement is to have a double door or a door and a curtain, similar to the protected dugouts, so that as little of the gas as possible escapes into the outer air. A still better arrangement is to use two adjoining rooms, the inner of which is the actual gas chamber. A small quantity of lachrymatory liquid is sprayed into the room, and the man enters, wearing his box respirator. He must remain in the room five minutes and move about and talk. If the mask does not fit, lachrymation quickly ensues and the man retires. He should then be examined to see whether the lack of fit is due to bad adjustment or to his having a wrong size of mask. In the latter case, a different size must be issued and the test repeated.

The fitting and adjusting of masks cannot be too thoroughly carried out. Special attention must be paid to the fitting of the mask and nose-clip with men who wear spectacles.

c) *Method of Use.*

79. The satchel containing the box respirator is carried outside all other equipment. When away from the trenches, it may be worn slung over the right shoulder, but men in the trenches or proceeding thither must carry it slung on the chest in the "Alert" position. The flap of the satchel with the press buttons must always be towards the body, but the press buttons must be kept fastened, except during the actual "Gas alert". The method of wearing the box respirator and of putting it on from the "Alert" position are fully described in Appendix I. It is important that the methods therein described should be practised by all who are equipped with the box respirator, to ensure rapidity in adjustment and proper care in its use.

80. Men with perforated ear drums may be affected by the gas penetrating through the ear passages to the respiratory organs and causing irritation there. In these cases it is useful to plug the ears with wadding. C. O.'s should ascertain from the Medical Officers in charge of their units the names of those suffering from this disability in order that the above precaution may be taken.

81. It must be remembered that the box respirator can be worn in gas for many hours without losing its efficiency or causing any distress. It may be breathed through in drills for a period of an hour per week for 40 weeks when it should be turned in. This permits a drill period of at least an hour per week.

d) *Replacement. Record of Use.*

82. The correct keeping of records as to hours of use of the box respirator, by entries in the small book forming part of the repair outfit, is a matter of the greatest importance, as these records form the only guide as to whether the boxes should or should not be replaced. Decision as to replace ment should be made on the advice of the Chief Gas Officer of the Division. The approximate time of actually breathing through the box should be noted. These entries must always be made after drills and gas attacks, great care being taken that they are correct.

e) *Inspection.*

83. Box respirators must be normally inspected once a week and daily during "Gas Alert".
It is of the utmost importance that the inspection should be carried out regularly and with the greatest care. Any neglect in doing this may lead to loss of life.
The points to be attended to will be found in Appendix II.

f) *Anti-Dimming Composition.*

84. At the weekly inspection and after every time the respirator is worn, the composition provided for the purpose will be put on the eyepieces in the manner described in Appendix II.

g) *Local Repairs.*

85. A small repair outfit, consisting of pieces of adhesive plaster is included, with a record card, in each satchel.
Small perforations in the face-pieces can be made good by applying pieces of the adhesive plaster to the perforation, both inside and outside the mask. They should be large enough to overlap the hole all round. Box respirators so repaired should be exchanged as soon as possible. **The repair is only intended to make them safe until a new respirator can be obtained.**
No other local repairs are permitted and all defective respirators must be handed in and new ones obtained.
· **Box respirators which have fallen into water must be exchanged as soon as possible.**

II. — The mask.

a) *General.*

86. The mask is the reserve defence against a gas attack and great care must be taken by officers to insure that it is in good order and that men have been trained in its use.

b) *Sizes and proportion of each.*

The mask is made in 3 sizes and the proportion of each size which will be needed for issue to a command is approximately as follows.

Small . . . . 3 %.
Medium . . . . 87 %.
Large . . . . 10 %.

The main point to be impressed on the men is that the

chemically treated material of the mask acts as a filter and that all air breathed into the lungs must pass through the gauze.

The mask is therefore useless unless properly adjusted so that no air may pass in around the edges. During its passage through the material of the mask all poisonous gas is absorbed by the chemicals.

The mask must be preserved from wet and should be removed from its container only for inspection and drill.

Every man should shave at least once a day, as a heavy growth of beard may permit the entrance of sufficient gas to injure a man seriously. For the same reason the hair should be kept short enough to nowhere catch under the edges of the mask.

c) *Manner of Carrying*.

The mask should be worn over the left shoulder and should hang on the right side. It should be hung in position before the Box Respirator is hung on in order that the strap of the mask may not interfere with the ready adjustment of the respirator in the alert position.

d) *Drill*.

Mask drill should be carried out frequently by all ranks. It should aim at teaching the quick adjustment of masks under all conditions, accustoming the men to wear them for a long time and to exercise in them. Drill must be carried out both with and without overcoats and equipment, and by night as well as by day.

For details of drill, see Appendix I.

e) *Inspection of Masks*.

87. Masks should be inspected once a week and daily during "Gas Alert". It is of the utmost importance that this inspection should be carried out regularly and with the greatest care. Any neglect in doing this may lead to loss of life.

The points to be attended to will be found in Appendix II.

f) *Replacement*.

88. Masks will be withdrawn as follows :

1) After any gas cloud attack in which the mask was worn ;

2) After a total of 6 hours use for any purpose.

III. — Horse respirators.

89. A full description of the British type Horse Respirator and the method of using it is given in Appendix III.

226

B. — ANTI-GAS APPLIANCES FOR GENERAL USE.

I. — Strombos horns.

a) *General.*

90. The experience gained in recent gas attacks has shown that Strombos Horns are the most effective form of gas alarm appliance and are audible for very long distances.

b) *Description.*

91. Each horn is issued in a box containing one horn, two compressed-air cylinders, one length of rubber tubing with screw connections, one screwdriver, one gimlet and one adjustable spanner. One spare cylinder is issued with the horn, to be kept at the Division or Brigade H. Q. to replace used cylinders without delay. A reserve of charged cylinders is also kept at the Corps workshop.

c) *Method of Use.*

92. The horn should be mounted in a horizontal position by screwing to the outside of the case or to some other suitable support and must be protected as much as possible from rain or shell splinters. Should it be necessary to change its position, the horn should be fixed in the box by means of the butterfly nuts provided. Strombos horns must always be ready for use, the horn being connected to one of the compressed-air cylinders by the rubber tube. The union joints at both ends of the tube must be tight. The horn should be pointed toward the rear.

93. To sound the horn, unscrew the screwcap on the air cylinder two complete turns. The horn will sound for about one minute.

Immediately after use, couple up the horn to the second air cylinder and leave it ready for use in case of a second gas cloud. The used cylinder should be clearly marked **Empty** and replaced as soon as possible from the reserve.

d) *Replacement and Repair.*

94. The pressure of the cylinders will be tested under arrangements made by the Chief Gas Officer of the Division once every week, and defective ones returned for re-charging.

On no account is any adjustment of the horn to be attempted except by the Chief Gas Officer of the Division or trained N. C. O. 's. A horn will be thrown completely out of action by movement of any of its parts.

Damaged horns must be sent to the workshop for repairs.

II. — Other gas alarm devices.

95. No definite pattern has been adopted for secondary alarm devices suitable for installing at every sentry post. Bells, gongs (shell cases), suspended rails, and other appliances are all in use, but single bells and gongs are generally too weak, and all of these arrangements suffer from requiring the use of a man's hands.

A very suitable arrangement as an alarm is a triangle of light steel rail, mounted in such a way that it can be beaten by working a treadle. It can thus be sounded by a sentry while he is putting on his respirator or mask. Similar devices not requiring the use of the hands should be devised and installed where possible.

III. — Anti-gas fans.

96. The Anti-gas Fan consists of a sheet of canvas supported by braces of cane and reinforced in the middle. It is made with two transverse hinges and is fitted with a hickory handle. The flapping portion is roughly 15 inches square and the handle is 2 feet long.

Method of Use.

a) *Clearing Trenches.*

97. The fan blade is placed on the ground with the brace side downwards, the man using it being in a slightly crouching position with the left foot advanced, the right hand grasping the handle at the neck and the left hand near the butt end. The fan is brought up quickly over the right shoulder and then smartly flicked to the ground with a quick slapping stroke. This drives a current of air along the earth and, on the top strokes, throws the gas out of the trench as it were by a shovel.

It is essential that the part of the fan blade nearest the handle should touch the ground first, and this can be accomplished in all cases by ending the stroke with the whole length of the handle as close to the ground as possible.

98. In working round a traverse, etc., the fan should be flapped round the corner with the hinge on the corner and the lower edge of the fan as near the bottom of the trench as can be managed. The brace side of the fan is to be outwards and at the end of the stroke the whole length of the handle should be close up to the side of the trench.

If several fans are available, men should work in single file and with "out-of-step" strokes, i. e., one fan should be up while the next is down.

b) Clearing Shelters.

99. In the case of a dugout with a single entrance not exceeding 12 feet in length, the gas is first cleared from the neighborhood of the shelter as in 97, and then the corners worked round as in 98. The worker now advances to the inner end of the entrance, beating rather slowly on the ground to allow the gas time to get out of the tunnel and bringing the fan as near the roof as possible on the return stroke. This makes an overhead current outward with a floor current inward.

It may be desirable to have a second fan working just outside the dugout to throw the gas out of the trench as it comes out.

In the case of dugouts with two entrances or with one entrance and another opening, such as a chimney, it is only necessary to use the fan round the corner of one entrance in the manner described in 98. When the entrance is cleared, it is advisable to enter the shelter with a respirator on in order to beat up the gas from the floor boards, etc. This greatly facilitates the removal of the last traces of gas.

Special methods to be used after shelling with "Mustard gas" (Dichlorethylsulphide).

100. *a)* Mustard gas is very persistent and will render an area shelled with it dangerous for as long as two days.

b) Therefore, dugouts and shelters into which gas has penetrated or has been carried by clothing after a severe shelling with mustard gas should, if practicable, be temporarily evacuated, as it is very hard to clear the gas from dugouts. Those that remain in the shelled areas or dugouts must wear their respirators continuously.

c) Occupants of entire dugouts have been gassed from two or three men, who, having been exposed to the gas, had entered the dugouts.

d) Doctors have been gassed while attending gassed cases. For these reasons, it is imperative to remove entirely the clothing of gassed cases. The patient must, however, be at once reclothed with warm clothing or covered well with unaffected blankets, as chilling of the patient must be avoided by all means. Clothing must be washed in pure water for at least an hour then dried in the open. Temperature of the water should not exceed 80° C.

e) Chloride of lime freely spread on the ground destroys the gas. If not enough is used, the gas near the surface is destroyed but that which soaked in is not, hence ground so treated should not be again dug up. Men have been gassed from digging around "mustard" areas without wearing masks. Mustard gas shells should only be handled by men wearing masks and gloves.

f) Fresh earth may be used to cover up shell holes and areas affected by liquid mustard gas, but the respirator must be worn by the workmen while doing so.

IV. — Vermorel Sprayers.

101. Vermorel sprayers are withdrawn from general use for clearing out gas after an attack, but a certain number are retained for moistening the blankets of protected shelters and for use in medical dugouts. They should be kept for this purpose only, and on no account relied on for clearing trenches or shelters of gas.

102. Company Vermorel Sprayers. — Sprayers on the basis of two per Company are retained for moistening blankets in the blanket protected dugouts. They should be kept by Company Gas N.C.O.'s with other anti-gas trench stores, and should be kept one-third full of water. The solution must be kept in corked jars or other closed receptacles close to each sprayer. The liquid should not be kept in the sprayers owing to its corrosive nature. It is made up as follows :

Water, 3 gallons (one large bucket).
Sodium Thiosulphate (hypo.), 1 1/2 lbs.
Sodium Carbonate (washing soda), 3 lbs.

The necessity for keeping corked the receptacles holding the solution must be impressed on the personnel responsible for it.

When no solution is obtainable, water may be used for spraying the blankets.

V. — Gas sampling apparatus.

103. It is desirable that samples be obtained of the enemy gas used in attacks, especially cloud gas attacks. For this purpose two kinds of appliances are kept in the trenches, viz., Vacuum Bulbs and Gas-Testing Tubes. These should be looked after by the Company Gas N.C.O.'s whose duty it is to take the samples, but officers should take all possible steps to ensure that samples of the gas are actually taken, as the information obtained may be of the greatest importance.

Full details of the methods of taking samples are laid down in "Instructions for taking Gas Samples, etc." (Appendix VI).

IV. -- CONSIDERATIONS AFFECTING SPECIAL ARMS.

104. The foregoing notes apply to all arms and are complete as regards considerations of gas defense affecting troops in trenches generally. Additional information for the guidance of other arms on anti-gas measures which affect them specially is given below.

A. — CAVALRY.

105. It is unlikely that Cavalry, when mounted, will encounter high concentrations of gas from a gas cloud, or even from gas shells. It will probably be found, therefore, that, when acting as mounted troops, the mask will be adequate protection, besides being less cumbersome than the respirator.

106. On the other hand, Cavalry used to supplement Infantry in the line, or employed as working parties in or near the trenches, must be equipped for gas defense in the same way as the infantry.

B. — ARTILLERY.

I. — General.

107. Artillery are as liable if not more so than anyone else to bombardment with gas shells, both poisonous and lachrymatory. Owing to the suddenness of shell attacks and the long period that the neighborhood of a battery may be affected by lachrymators or mustard gas, it is essential that the following points be noted :

a) Where, owing to circumstances, box respirators are not actually worn on the men, they must be hung separately and within easy reach of the owners. If this course has to be adopted, the respirators should be ready prepared with the haversack sling shortened by means of the tab and stud and the slack of the sling tucked under the mask as in the "Alert" position. The satchel flap should be unbuttoned, but kept in position. (Respirators should not, if possible, be hung in the actual gun emplacements, owing to the concussion being liable to displace the chemicals in the box.)

Men must be thoroughly practiced in getting their respirators on in the shortest possible time when they are stored in this manner.

The mask will, in any case, always be carried on the man for use in case of emergency.

b) Men must be well practiced in wearing their box respirators for long periods and in serving their guns while wearing respirators or masks.

II. — Forward observing parties.

108. Forward observing parties must take all the precautions previously laid down for Infantry.

III. — Preservation of guns and ammunition.

109. The following precautions apply to medium and heavy trench mortars as well as to guns and howitzers :

a) *Protection*.

Batteries which are in constant danger of gas attacks, whether from gas clouds or gas shells, should keep all bright parts of their guns or mortars, carriages, mountings, and accessories well coated with oil.

Sights and all instruments should also be smeared with oil and protected with covers when not in actual use, care being taken that the oil does not come in contact with any glass or find its way into the interior of the instrument.

Cartridge cases of ammunition stored with the Battery and all uncapped fuses, or fuses which have been removed from their cylinders, should be wiped over with oil as soon as possible and protected with a cover.

b) *Cleaning*.

All bright parts of guns and trench mortars, together with all accessories and spare parts exposed to the gas, must be cleaned and wiped dry as soon as possible after the attack, and in any case within 24 hours, after which they should be thoroughly coated afresh with oil.

The same applies to the whole of the ammunition still in the Battery position. Ammunition which, for any reason, had not been oiled, must be cleaned and oiled. It is desirable to expend it as soon as possible.

IV. — Aiming points and aiming posts.

110. Aiming points and aiming posts are liable to be obscured by the gas cloud and arrangements should, therefore, be made in every Battery to meet this eventuality by providing gun-pits with means to check the line of fire if necessary, without depending on the use of aiming posts.

V. — Tactical measures during a gas attack.

111. Enemy gas attacks may be executed for purposes

other than the preparation of a subsequent infantry attack. During the gas discharge a heavy artillery fire on the actual trenches whence the gas is issuing is the best way of dealing with the situation. Also it is essential that the gas discharge should be interfered with as early as possible, as the opening periods of the discharge are the most effective.

112. To ensure an effective and immediate artillery fire the following points require attention :

a) Certain howitzer Batteries should be detailed to open a rapid fire for a short time as an anti-gas measure.

b) Only certain portions of the enemy's front trenches can be used for gas discharge in any given wind and these can easily be indicated on any accurate trench map. Each Battery charged with the task of hampering an enemy gas attack should be provided with a map and a table, showing from what portions of the enemy's lines (within the Battery's zone of action) gas can be discharged in any given wind.

113. Nothing in the foregoing paragraphs in any way affects the responsibility of artillery for dealing with any infantry attack, or for the execution of counter-battery work.

C. — TUNNELLING COMPANIES.

114. I) Tunnelling companies are again reminded that neither the box respirator nor the mask affords protection against mine or explosion gases. Oxygen breathing sets have been used with good results.

II) Owing to the difficulty in clearing gas, especially lachrymatory gas, from mine-shafts and galleries, the entrances to mine-shafts should be protected from gas by blanket curtains in the manner already described for dugouts.

III) The enemy has occasionally attempted to render galleries untenable by the use of gas bombs in conjunction with the explosion of a charge. If this is done, the box respirator must be worn if work has to be continued.

D. — SIGNAL SERVICE AND TELEPHONE OPERATORS.

I. — General.

115. It is essential that telephone and other signal operators should be able to work as much as possible during a gas attack without wearing respirators or masks. Signal dugouts must, therefore, be particularly well protected against gas, so as to allow this to be done.

II) Telephone and other signal operators must be specially trained in using their instruments when wearing box respirators, masks, or such other gas masks as may be furnished them. It may be necessary to rely on the fuller-phone or buzzer when gas equipment is being worn on account of the difficulty of speaking with the mask on. Special telephone transmitters are being designed, which will overcome this difficulty.

III) Linemen and signal men in general must receive plenty of practice in carrying on their work, both by day and by night, while wearing respirators and masks.

II. — Preservation of signal equipment.

a) *Protection of Instruments and Apparatus.*

116. The only effective method of preventing corrosion of electrical and other apparatus during a gas attack is to prevent the gas reaching it, and the best way of doing this is to have Signal Shelters and Offices thoroughly protected against gas. As the corrosive effect is very much greater on instruments if they are damp, the shelters should be kept as dry as possible. Instruments and apparatus which have to be used in the open will be less affected if kept perfectly dry.

The cases and covers of all instruments and apparatus must be made as nearly gastight as possible. The varnish and paint protection applied to the metal parts and coils must be carefully preserved. All apparatus, such as telephones, test boards, connecting frames, spare instruments, etc., which it is not essential to have uncovered should be well covered up with cloths, blankets, or spare clothing. A heavy mineral oil such as Cosmic may be used on metal parts and, in fact, on all articles which will not be injured by the oil, though great care must be taken to keep it off electrical contacts. Unless actually required for use, signal lamps must be closed and preferably packed, with accessories, in the carrying cases. Fireworks are, in general, little affected by gas if the moistureproof varnish has not been cracked or broken.

b) *Cleaning Instruments after a Gas Attack.*

117. After a gas attack, electrical apparatus that has been exposed to gas should be treated as follows :

The ends of all leading in wires should be removed from terminals and cleaned by being scraped with a knife, wiped with a damp cloth, and then carefully dried. Terminals, exchange plugs and all exposed metal work, especially the grounds and connecting wires of the Earth Telegraph sets and Radio sets should be cleaned first with a damp and then with a dry cloth. This process should be

234

repeated after 12 hours have elapsed. In general, the processes prescribed for cleaning arms and ammunition (pars. 3o to 34, incl.) may be followed for the cases and non-electrical parts and for nonelectrical apparatus.

The internal portions of the instruments should not be interfered with. If an instrument has been kept closed or covered up, it is very unlikely that internal portions will have suffered; but if these portions show signs of corrosion, the instruments should be sent back to Division or Corps Headquarters to be dealt with by an Instrument Repairer.

III. — Protection of carrier pigeons.

118. When the gas alarm is sounded, all baskets containing pigeons should be placed in the special Anti-Gas Bags provided for this purpose, or placed in gas-proof shelters. If for any reason the birds cannot be protected from the gas, they should be liberated at once. Anti-gas bags should always be kept near baskets containing birds, and should be regularly inspected.

Pigeons can be utilized during a gas attack. Experience has proved that they will fly through any gas cloud, but it is imperative that the bird should be exposed to the gas for as short a time as possible. The message and carrier should, therefore, be prepared and if possible, fastened to the pigeon's leg, before the bird is exposed to the gas. Twenty seconds should suffice to fix a carrier and liberate a bird.

APPENDIX I.

RESPIRATOR AND MASK DRILLS.

The following drills are designed to teach officers and men to adjust quickly their respirators and masks. The drills must be so thoroughly mastered that one will protect himself instantly upon hearing the gas alarm.

The breath must be held from the instant of alarm until the respirator or mask is completely adjusted.

Drills with box respirators.

Drills in defensive measures against gas will be conducted in each division in accordance with the programs of training furnished from these headquarters. After the training period and while not in the trenches, drills "A", "B", and "C" will be practiced twice weekly. While in the trenches or stationed within five miles of the front line, drill "B" will be practiced daily; the actual time during which the box is breathed through being as short as possible.

Drills "D", "G", and "H" will be practiced as frequently as possible, having regard to the amount of time during which the box may be breathed through, the respirator being good for 40 hours breathing.

In the initial training, drills must be so arranged that every man wears the respirator for one full period of an hour without removing the mask or nose clip.

Drill "A".

To bring the Box Respirator to the "Alert" position.

At the command "Gas Alert", hang the box respirator round the neck with the flap next the body. With the right hand seize the satchel by the leather tab, with the left hand seize the sling by the brass button and clip this into the leather tab. Then unfasten the press buttons which close the flap.

The heavy string attached to the top of the satchel will then be withdrawn from the right-hand compartment, passed through the ring on the lower right side of the satchel and carried around the waist to the ring on the left, where it is fastened. The press buttons closing the flap will be left unfastened, but the flap will be pushed into position to keep the respirator from getting wet.

Drill "B".

Drill "by numbers" to obtain complete and accurate adjustment of the box respirator from the "Alert" position.

This drill will be alternated with one without the numbers to insure as quick an adjustment as possible. The drill must be practiced until complete adjustment is obtained by all ranks in six seconds.

Before starting the drill. the respirator should be in the "Alert" position with flap down but not buttoned.

1) At the command "one", hold the breath, press down both thumbs between the satchel and the body and open the satchel. Immediately seize the face-piece with the right hand so that the metal elbow tube just outside the face-piece will be in the palm of the hand. At the same time knock off the steel helmet from behind with the left hand.

2) At the command "two", bring the face-piece quickly out of the satchel and hold it in both hands with all the fingers outside along the binding and the two thumbs inside, pointing inwards and upwards under the elastic. At the same time throw the chin well forward ready to enter the face-piece opposite the nose clip.

3) At the command "three", bring the face-piece forward, digging the chin into it and with the same motion bringing the elastic bands back over the crown of the head to the full extent of the retaining tape, using the thumbs.

4) At the command "four", seize the metal elbow tube outside the face-piece, thumb up on the right, fingers on the left — all pointing towards the face. Push the rubber mouth-piece well into the mouth and pull it forward until the rim of the mouth-piece lies between the teeth and the lips and the two rubber grips are held by the teeth.

5) At the command "five", adjust the nose clip to the nose, using the thumb and first three fingers of the right hand. Run the fingers round the face-piece on either side of the face to make sure that the edges are not folded over. Correct any faults in adjustment. Come quickly to attention.

Drill "C".

To adjust Box respirators when carried over the shoulder but not in the "Alert position".

Pull the satchel around until it hangs in front of the body. Unfasten the flap and adjust the face-piece as in practice "B", allowing the satchel to hang by the rubber tube.

After the nose clip is put on, at once proceed to adjust the satchel in the Alert position, as in practice "A".

Drill "D".

Drill to teach cleaning of eyepieces.

At the command "Clean eyepieces" the right eyepiece will be gripped between the thumb and first finger of the left hand. The first finger of the right hand will then be pushed gently into the fold of the face-piece behind the right eyepiece which will be cleaned with a gentle circular motion. The left eyepiece will be cleaned in a similar way.

Drill "E".

Drill to teach method of giving orders.

The squad is first cautioned that the nose clip must not be removed to talk and that before each sentence is spoken a long breath must be taken and the mouthpiece removed sideways from the mouth by turning the metal tube outside the face-piece on one side. After speaking and before drawing a breath, the mouthpiece is replaced.

The squad should then call off, intervals extended to four paces, and orders passed down the line.

Officers and N. C. O.'s should receive special practice in Drill "E".

Drill "F".

Drill to teach method of clearing face-piece from gas which may have leaked in.

Press the face-piece close to the face, forcing out foul air around the sides, then fill with air from the lungs by blowing out round the mouthpiece, and end by pressing the face-piece close to the face. Repeat at about 10 minute intervals as long as the face-piece is worn.

Drill "G".

Drill to teach method of testing whether trench or dugout is free from gas.

With the right hand pull the face-piece slightly away from the right cheek, loosen the nose clip on the nose and sniff gently (do not take a breath). If gas is smelled, the nose clip and face-piece are readjusted. Then clear face-piece of gas as in " F ".

Drill " H ".

Ordinary infantry drill will be carried out while wearing the mask. This will include double time for at least 200 yards at one time. This drill will be in heavy marching order. Musketry and bombing instructions and the training of specialists (including artillery, machine gunners, Medical Corps, signallers) will also be carried out while wearing the respirator.

Drill "I".

Drill to teach changing from the box respirator to the mask.

At the command "Change" hold the breath, get out the mask, and grip in the left hand. Knock off the steel helmet with the right hand. Take off respirator as in Note b) following. Put on the mask according to the method described under "Mask Drill". Protection must be obtained in ten seconds or less.

Note. — a) If after being worn for a long time, the pressure of the nose clip becomes unbearable, it may be relieved for a few moments by easing up the pressure, being careful not to remove the clip from the nose.

b) **Removing respirators.** — Care must be taken to remove the respirator without stretching the face-piece or elastic. At the command "Take off respirators" release nose clip, insert the fingers of the right hand under the face-piece of the chin, bend the head forward and open the mouth, at the same time removing the face-piece with an upward motion of the right hand.

c) **Folding face-pieces.** — The face-piece should be folded flat (no part tucked inward) and the elastic bands should be folded against the outside of the face-piece on one side.

d) After all drills the respirator must be wiped dry, folded correctly, and put away in such a way that the rubber valve is not bent.

Freezing or sticking of valve.

In cold weather the saliva on the expiratory rubber valve will freeze. This can be prevented by two drops of glycerine or heavy thick oil. However, as both tend to injure the rubber they should be used only in very cold weather.

The expiratory valve frequently sticks from the saliva drying on it. To prevent this, as well as freezing, always put the respirator away dry. If the respirator is put on and difficulty is experienced in respiration, take the expiratory valve between the thumb and fingers and rub it briskly with a rolling motion; do not remove respirator while doing this, but breathe out through the mouth around mouth piece.

Mask drill.

1. To obtain correct and quick adjustment of the mask the following drill will be carried out "by numbers". As soon as the movements are perfectly understood the number drill will be carried out alternately with "judging the time" drill. That is, as quickly as possible. The breath must be held while adjusting the mask because one breath of the poisonous gases now used may cause death or serious injury.

Remove the mask from the cloth satchel and hang it on the chest by the long tape, with the oiled canvas facing out. This is the "Alert position".

1) At the command "one", grasp the elastic with both hands in the following manner : the 3d, 4th and 5th fingers between the front elastic and the mask; the index fingers

between the two elastics, and the thumbs behind both elastics.

2) At the command "two", pull the hands apart so that the elastics are completely stretched.

3) At the command "three", push the chin well forward, at the same time carrying the hands upward so that the lower edge of the mask catches well under the chin.

4) At the command "four", carry the hands with a circular motion backwards and then downwards, letting go off the first elastic when the tape fastening the elastics together becomes tight and then carrying the posterior elastic as far down the back of the neck as it will go.

5) At the command "five", adjust the edges of the mask with both hands, being particularly careful to see that no hair lies under the edge of the mask and that there are no wrinkles.

6) At the command "six", pass the right hand back of the neck and grasp the elastic hanging down on the left side and carry it back of the neck and fasten it into the hook on the right-hand lower corner of the mask; the forefinger of the left hand will help guide the eye over the hook. Come to attention.

The mask is taken off by unhooking the elastic around the neck and then grasping the bottom of the mask with the right hand; pull down and outward until the mask is free of the chin, then with an upward and backward swing remove the mask from the head.

NOTE. — The elastic that goes behind the neck must be adjusted to the individual when the mask is issued so that it will fit his neck snugly. At the same time the median tape should be shortened by means of the safety pin supplied with it so that it will be taut when the mask is properly applied.

Care should be taken of the eyepieces as they are very fragile. They should never be wiped when moist as it spoils them. Extra eyepieces are provided to replace those in the mask when they become cracked or broken. To remove old ones, bend outward the little metal fasteners of the protecting rim on the front of the mask when the eyepiece frame slips out of the rubber socket. The new eyepiece is put in place from the inside of the mask by introducing one edge of the rim into the rubber groove and stretching the remainder of the rubber groove over the eyepiece. Care should be taken not to press on the transparent part of the eyepiece. Replace the metal rim and press the fasteners back into place.

Men must use their own masks for drill purposes.

Men must be warned that during a gas attack the smell of the chemical on the mask becomes stronger and may cause very slight irritation of the eyes, nose, and throat. This will disappear in a few minutes, and does not indicate that gas is coming through the mask.

Masks will be worn in the "Alert position" only when men are not provided with the Box Respirator.

General points on training with anti-gas appliances.

When training men in the use of anti-gas appliances the following points are of importance. They apply equally to box respirators and masks.

a) Practice with simple movements with box respirators or masks. Ordinary infantry drill should be combined with physical drill, including arm and leg exercises, leap-frog, and double time. The time of practice should not exceed 15 minutes at first in the case of the mask, but should be gradually extended.

b) Practice in bombing, rapid loading and aiming, judging distance and rifle firing, should be carried out while men are wearing box respirators or masks.

c) Men must swallow their saliva and not allow it to drain out over the lips or through the valve.

d) Officers and N. C. O.'s will receive the same training as the men, and, in addition, will be practiced in giving orders while wearing their respirators or masks.

Practice and drill in the use of anti-gas appliances should be carried out continuously. This applies especially to troops which return to trench warfare after having been in districts where more open fighting may have led (*a*) to a temporary lapse in this training, (*b*) to the subsequent incorporation of drafts only partially trained in anti-gas measures.

APPENDIX II.

INSPECTION OF PERSONAL
ANTI-GAS EQUIPMENT.

A. — Box respirators.

Box respirators must normally be inspected once a week and daily during "Gas Alert." Attention will be paid to the following points :

a) Boxes, facepiece, mouthpiece, noseclip, eyepieces, and elastic must be in good order. If the box is rusted through, the respirator must be condemned.

b) Facepiece must be firmly attached to the mouthpiece and to the elbow tube.

c) The metal tube inside the mouthpiece must be about 1/8th in. back from the opening of the latter.

d) The rubber tube must be intact and firmly attached to the box and elbow tube.

e) The expiratory valve should be tested by removing the box from the satchel and either closing the cap at the bottom with the hand, or pinching the rubber tube so as to prevent inlet of air at the same time attempting to draw in air through the mouthpiece. It should not be possible to draw in any air. This also proves the absence of leaks in the tube or box. It must be possible to breathe out easily through the valve. If the latter has stuck because of saliva drying in it, this must be remedied by rubbing the valve between the fingers.

f) See that the inlet valve is opening properly and that air can be drawn freely through the box.

g) See that the cord for tying around the body is present and not knotted.

h) Any small perforations in the facepiece should be temporarily repaired by applying pieces of adhesive plaster from the repair outfit to the perforation, both inside and outside the mask. The adhesive plaster should be large enough to overlap the hole all round.

Respirators so repaired must be exchanged as soon as possible.

i) Replace the box in the satchel so that the facepiece comes to the face without twist on the tube. Fold facepiece carefully and replace in the satchel so that the expiratory valve is not likely to crumple.

B. — Masks.

Masks must be inspected once a week, or daily during the "Gas Alert". Attention must be paid to the following points :

a) See that the carrying case is in good condition.

b) See that the eyepieces are not cracked or loose.

c) See that there is no evidence that the mask has been wet (mould); any mask which has been wet should be condemned.

d) See that elastics and tapes are in good condition.

APPENDIX III.

INSTRUCTIONS FOR THE USE
OF BRITISH ANTI-GAS HORSE RESPIRATOR.

I. — Description.

The respirator consists of a flannelette bag with a canvas mouthpiece which goes into the horse's mouth and saves the flannelette from being bitten through. The bag is provided with an elastic band which passes round the opening so as to draw the respirator close to the face when in use. The upper side of the mouth of the flannelette bag is furnished with a small unbleached calico patch by which the respirator is attached to the nose-band of the head collar when in the "Alert position", and while in use. Inside the bag and attached to the canvas mouthpiece there is a canvas frame which is stitched on to the bag in such a way as to prevent the material drawing into the nostrils when the respirator is in use. The whole is folded and carried in a canvas case provided with a flap, secured by three press buttons, and having two straps at the back by means of which the case is attached to the head collar.

II. — Method of use.

Horses can stand a higher concentration of gas than human beings without material damage, and it is not therefore necessary to protect them against cloud gas attacks when they are a considerable distance back from the trenches. Nor is it necessary to protect their eyes. The respirator is primarily intended for use on transport animals when they are sent to the vicinity of the trenches with supplies and ammunition. In the case of gas shell attacks, horses should be protected wherever the shelling is heavy.

1) *Carrying when not immediately required.*

When not required for immediate use the respirator can be conveniently carried on the supporting strap of the breast harness as shown in Fig. 5, or if a zinc wither pad is worn, still more conveniently inside this pad. If a collar is used in place of the breast-strap, it can be carried in the channel of the collar where drivers often carry a sponge However carried, the case is steadied by being strapped on either side to the metal ring on the supporting strap, and its flap should be passed under this strap, between it and the nunnah wither pad, and buttoned as in the "Alert position".

2) *Alert Position.*

When horses are being sent up to the trenches, the transport or other officer responsible should have the respirators adjusted in the "Alert position" before moving off, as follows :

a) The flap of the respirator case is unbuttoned and slipped under the nose-band of the head collar from below upwards.

b) The two straps at the back are also passed under the nose-band and secured to the cheek pieces of the head collar, above the metal D on each side.

c) The small unbleached calico patch on the upper side of the mouth of the respirator is buttoned on to the nose-band of the head collar so that the respirator is ready to be slipped on immediately in the event of a gas attack.

d) The cover of the case is then closed over the nose-band, and the respirator is thus protected from rain, and held in position on the nose-band. Fig. 6 shows a respirator in its case carried in the "Alert position".

3) *Wearing in Gas.*

The respirator being carried in the "Alert position" is adjusted for use as follows :

a) The flap of the case is unbuttoned and the respirator removed, leaving the case attached to the cheek pieces of the head collar and lying flat on the face.

b) The mouth of the bag is drawn down over the upper lip and upper teeth with one hand on each side of the mouthpiece. slipped into the mouth, and drawn well up to the angle of the lips.

c) The elastic band is seized on either side close to the mouthpiece, and pulled outwards so as to draw the mouth of the bag tight around the upper jaw, above the nostrils, and is then slipped over the poll.

The respirator is then in position and the animal may be worked in it without difficulty or undue distress. The bit and reins are not interfered with in any way. This is shown in Fig. 7.

4) *Replacement in Case.*

In folding the respirator and replacing it in the case ready for use the following points should be observed :

a) The canvas mouthpiece should be wiped as clean as possible.

b) The flannelette bag should be held with the canvas mouthpiece underneath and the elastic band placed over the top of the bag in such a way that when the canvas patch is buttoned on to the nose band the elastic band has simply to be passed straight up over the face and over the poll. The bottom end of the respirator should then be tucked in and rolled up over the elastic band to make a neat roll for insertion in the canvas case.

Fig. 5.

Fig. 6.

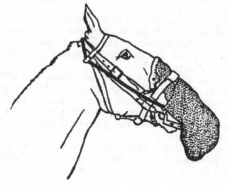

Fig. 7.

APPENDIX IV.

TYPICAL STANDING ORDERS
FOR COMPANY GAS N. C. O.'s.

1) They will assist officers at the inspection of box respirators and masks, and in making such local repairs as are possible. They will assist in training men in the use of anti-gas appliances.

2) Under the Company Commander they will have charge of all anti-gas trench stores as follows :

a) *Strombos Horns and Other Gas Alarm Devices.* — Inspect daily and see that sentries posted at them know how they should be used.

b) *Gas-proof Shelters.* — See that the blanket doorways fit and are kept in good order.

c) *Anti-gas Fans.* — See that they are in their proper position and in serviceable condition.

d) *Stores of fuel* for clearing shelters. — Insure sufficient supply for clearing all dug-outs, to be maintained under company arrangements.

e) *Vermorel Sprayers.* — Maintain in working order and see that supply of solution is available.

f) *Gas Sampling Apparatus.* — Have charge of the vacuum bulbs and gas-testing tubes. Keep a stock of corked bottles and small tins with well-fitting lids for collecting samples of earth and water after a gas shell attack.

3) On relief they will assist the Company Commander in taking over all anti-gas trench stores. The Company Gas N.C.O.'s should accompany the advance party and take over anti-gas trench stores (by daylight if possible).

4) They will make wind observations every three hours or more frequently if the wind is in or nearing a dangerous quarter, and will report any change of wind to the Company Commander.

5) During a gas cloud attack they will take gas samples by means of the vacuum bulbs and gas-testing tubes.

6) During or after the attack the N.C.O. must note down in writing as much information regarding the attack as possible. (See Appendix VI.)

7) As soon as possible after the conclusion of a gas shell bombardment, the Gas N.C.O. must fill his bottles and tins (2, f) and take samples of water, mud, or earth from those parts of the line which are smelling most strongly of shell gases. He should note the position of any blind shells. (See Appendix VI.)

8) As soon as possible after a gas attack, all samples and notes will be handed in to the Company Commander for transmission to the Division Gas Officer.

6

ARTILLERY IN OFFENSIVE OPERATIONS

This manual's full title is SS139/4 *Artillery Notes No. 4 Artillery in Offensive Operations* and was issued in February 1917. Like Part 5's gas manual, this handbook had been issued earlier in the war but new technology and tactics necessitated a revised version. It gives an excellent overview of the role of artillery in trench warfare and provides some interesting details on what different guns can achieve, such as 60-pounders, light trench mortars, 9.2-inch howitzers and the 12-inch 'heavy guns'.

I. ORGANIZATION AND COMMAND.

1. Artillery has so developed both in power and quantity during the past two years that it has become a much stronger weapon of offense than heretofore. To obtain the full value from this arm, which plays so great a part in battle, it is essential that its action should be so efficiently controlled as to insure that its maximum force is utilized. Every detail regarding the employment of artillery must be thought out beforehand. The efficient execution of its allotted tasks will largely depend on the early issue of clear orders and on the methodical supervision of its subsequent work.

2. A commander directs and supervises the action of his artillery through the medium of his artillery commander, who must be equipped with the authority, information, and technical knowledge essential to his position.

The artillery commander attached to the staff of an army or a corps may, within the discretion of his chief, command the whole of the artillery of the formation, in order that the commander's plan may, as far as the artillery is concerned, be translated into orders and be carried out in the most effective manner and with the least delay. The rapid transmission of orders to batteries is a matter of vital importance.

3. The army deals with the distribution and employment of the artillery allotted to it and with the details of artillery cooperation with armies on either flank. It provides for cooperation between the various corps and decides, within the limitations imposed by the commander-in-chief, the nature and duration of the preliminary bombardment.

The army is also concerned with the general direction of the preparatory arrangements, lays down the general principles to be followed as regards the employment of antiaircraft guns, counter battery work, night fire, enfilade fire, and concentrations of fire, and indicates the most effective methods to employ in the attack.

4. A corps commander disposes of every nature of artillery essential to the preparation and execution of an offensive operation. There can therefore be but one commander for all the

artillery of the corps, both field and heavy, if the energy of the whole is to be systematically and uniformly directed. At the same time the army commander may decide to retain certain units of heavy artillery under army control, and in many cases will at least lay down the special objectives to be engaged by the long-range big guns (6-inch, 9.2-inch, and 12-inch).

5. A table showing the details of organization of artillery commands is given in Appendix I.

This new organization recognizes the great importance of reconnaissance work on the part of the artillery, and each artillery staff is provided with an officer charged with the execution of such work. The study and collation of information derived from air photographs and maps, as far as it affects the artillery, form an important feature of the officer's duties.

The organization of the staff of the corps heavy artillery commander is designed to meet the double task that falls on his shoulders. Broadly speaking, destruction of defenses and of communications, combined with barrage work, comprise the one branch of heavy artillery work; counter battery work the other. It is, however, essential that no hard and fast line shall be drawn between these two main subdivisions of the heavy artillery commander's duties. Organization must be so supple as to insure that at all times it shall be a simple matter to devote any proportion of the heavy artillery to either task, according to the needs of the tactical situation, without delay and without confusion. Arrangements must be made to insure that heavy artillery groups engaged on trench bombardment are in a position to cooperate closely with the divisions interested in the hostile trenches in question.

6. Army field artillery brigades have been formed to provide a means whereby a mass of field artillery may be concentrated for any special purpose. Such brigades can be allotted to armies, corps, and divisions, as circumstances may require.

Despite this new organization, a division in the early stages of an offensive operation will often require for its support more field artillery than is afforded by its own divisional artillery, even though reenforced by such army field artillery brigades as may be allotted to it. In this event, two or even three divisional artilleries may be found supporting the operations of a single division. In such cases all this field artillery will normally be grouped under the C. R. A. of the attacking division.

7. The composition of heavy artillery groups may, as explained in "Artillery Notes, No. 3" (counter battery work), con-

sist of both gun and howitzer batteries, or of either nature separately, so long as the action of all the batteries devoted to any one area is controlled by one authority. One point, however, must always be borne in mind, and that is that the composition of heavy artillery groups must envisage the demands of an early advance. Mixed groups of medium and heavy weapons present the obvious disadvantage that in the event of a rapid advance either the medium batteries (which will be the first to advance) must break loose from their groups or fresh groups must be automatically formed to control the advancing batteries.

8. The relations between the artillery and the royal flying corps must be of the closest if these two arms are to work together effectively to the common good.

This particularly applies to the case of counter battery work, as is impressed in the " Artillery Notes, No. 3," dealing with that subject.

G. O.'s C., R. A., of armies (or corps) deal direct with the commanders of corps and balloon wings (or squadron and balloon companies) in all matters relating to their combined work, and should do all in their power to impress upon their subordinates the value resulting from mutual confidence based upon mutual understanding. The corps and balloon wing commanders are, however; the executive commanders of the corps squadrons and balloon companies, respectively, and as such act as the technical advisers of G. O.'s C., R. A., of corps, with whom they should be in the closest touch.

II. ARTILLERY IN THE GENERAL PLAN OF ATTACK.

1. THE RÔLE OF THE ARTILLERY.

The rupture of the enemy's front, generally strongly defended and organized in depth, is the first phase of an offensive battle.

This entails the destruction of the obstacles to the infantry's advance and of the means of defense that support those obstacles, the moral and physical reduction of the defenders, and lastly a rapid and combined advance of all arms acting in close cooperation.

Thereafter successive phases may comprise a modified form of the first, namely, the attack of improvised lines of defense with but little time for deliberate preparation, leading to a final phase of open warfare.

11683°—17——2

Experience has proved that effective artillery preparation is indispensable to success, the extent and nature of the preparation depending on the scope of the intended operation. In each subsequent phase the artillery must aim at maintaining the closest touch with and affording the greatest support to the infantry. The measure of ultimate advantage will largely depend on the momentum of the first blow and the rapid exploitation of early successes before the enemy has time to recover from the shock.

2. SELECTION OF THE FRONT OF ATTACK.

Granted the vital importance of effective artillery action in the offensive, it follows that the general plan of attack must be such as to admit of a full development of artillery fire and of complete cooperation between the artillery and the infantry.

For this it is not enough that the requirements in guns and ammunition should have been carefully estimated and adequately provided. The first and most essential element of success is that the front selected for attack should be of a nature to admit of this full development and cooperation. Conditions are most favorable when the ground allows of artillery commanders—

(i) seeing clearly the enemy's defenses, and also following the movements of the attacking infantry.

(ii) controlling the fire of their guns rapidly and effectively. For, however carefully thought out the arrangements for the control of both artillery fire and infantry movement may be, they are always liable to be thrown out of gear by some unexpected development.

It is, then, the first duty of the artillery commander to place before the general officer commanding the force full particulars as to the manner in which the ground affects the efficiency of the artillery preparation and support, so that the latter may give due weight to such considerations in selecting the front of attack. "An objective which may appear at first sight easy of access to the infantry may prove in the end costly to attack if it does not lend itself to the judicious application of artillery fire, and vice versa, localities which present difficulties to the infantry alone may, if it is possible to bring the converging fire of artillery to bear on them, be carried with comparatively little loss."

3. ESTIMATE OF GUNS AND AMMUNITION REQUIRED.

The general plan of attack having been settled, it is the next duty of the artillery commander to prepare an estimate of the amount of artillery and of ammunition required for the operation. The first point to remember is that the ammunition required depends upon the work to be done more than on the number of guns available. The latter is, however, the governing factor as regards the time which will be required for the preparation and has therefore an important bearing on the general plan of attack. If surprise forms any part of this plan, it is essential that sufficient fire units should be available to allow the different portions of the enemy's defenses to be bombarded simultaneously. The number of hostile batteries to be dealt with is another consideration directly affecting the amount of artillery that will be necessary.

The nature of guns required depends, like the ammunition, on the character of the work to be performed. Every type of gun or howitzer is particularly adapted for certain tasks, and the proportion of each type demanded should be based on such considerations.

An estimate of the guns and ammunition needed can, therefore, only be made after thorough reconnaissance of the enemy's system of defense, including his trenches, machine-gun emplacements, observing stations, communication trenches, rear lines, strong points, wire, etc. This reconnaissance must include not only the examination of the ground from all possible points of view, but also the reports of air observers and a very careful study of maps, air photographs, and of all information available in the intelligence section. This section should indicate the roads used by the enemy in bringing up reinforcements and supplies of ammunition and food, the places where they can best be blocked by artillery fire, and the forming-up places likely to be used for counter attack. The number and nature of the guns which may be brought into play by the enemy is also an important factor, as it governs the requirements for counter-battery work.[1]

It is important that the artillery commander should make this reconnaissance in company with the general staff of the formation and that the fullest information regarding not only

---

[1] Counter-battery work has been dealt with in a separate note (No. 3 of this series).

the enemy's defenses but also his habits should be obtained from both the artillery and the infantry holding the front.

III. THE ARTILLERY PLAN.[1]

1. SCOPE OF THE ARTILLERY PLAN.

In all offensive operations it is the duty of the artillery commander of the force engaged to prepare an artillery plan based on and supplementary to the general plan of attack.

To enable him to do this he should be informed as early as possible of the minimum resources of guns and ammunition that will be available.

The plan should consist of a clear and complete statement of the objects to be attained by the artillery and the methods to be employed. It will lay down the allotment, grouping and organization of the artillery (including medium and heavy trench mortars) for the attack, the tasks and zones of the various commands, and the arrangements for observation, communication, and the cooperation of aeroplanes and balloons. It will deal with the establishment of artillery command posts, the expenditure and supply of ammunition, arrangements for liaison with the infantry, the forward movement of batteries, and any other points regarding the action of the artillery which it is necessary to include. The measures to insure cooperation between subordinate formations and the possibility of bringing a heavy concentration of fire on to particular areas, if required, must be thought out and clearly defined. The preparation of this plan will thus involve a comprehensive consideration of all the tasks which the artillery will or may be called upon to perform during the preparation and execution of the attack.

The plan must embrace each phase of the battle, and careful arrangements must be made to insure that one phase shall follow another without any unintended break in the action of the artillery.

The lower the formation concerned, the more detailed will be both its artillery plan and the study and reconnaissance upon which that plan is constructed.

As soon as the broad outline of the artillery plan has been worked out and approved, it is advantageous to issue it to sub-

[1] See Appendix A, paragraph 2, of "Instructions for the Training of Divisions for Offensive Action."

ordinate commanders concerned, or at least to make it known to them at a conference, in order that they may have the earliest opportunity of studying and solving their individual problems. Even if circumstances ultimately entail modifications in the suballotment of artillery and in the apportionment of tasks, the inconvenience arising from minor changes in subordinate plans is far outweighed by the advantage gained by the increased time thus rendered available for consideration of the general tasks demanded and for reconnaissance. To complete the manifold arrangements essential to the successful execution of an artillery plan is necessarily a lengthy process. The early publication of the plan, even if not in all its details, will greatly assist the work of subordinate artillery commanders.

2. ALLOTMENT OF ARTILLERY.

The number and variety of the tasks which the artillery is called upon to perform necessitate very careful arrangement, if the different natures are to be employed to the fullest advantage. These tasks depend upon, and must therefore vary with the nature of the enemy's defenses and the strength of his artillery. The following principles, however, will generally apply:

RÔLES OF VARIOUS NATURES OF ARTILLERY.

Field guns (18-pounder) are primarily employed in barrage fire, repelling attacks in the open, raking communications and wire cutting. They may also be employed for neutralizing fire against batteries within their reach, and to assist in the destruction of such enemy defenses as are vulnerable to the H. E. shell of field guns, e. g., breastworks and barriers. They will also be required for the purpose of preventing the enemy from repairing damage to his defenses, where this work is beyond the power of the infantry.

Medium guns (60-pounders) are employed in counter-battery work, especially for neutralization; for raking communications, and forming barrages beyond the range of field guns.

Heavy guns (6-inch, 9.2-inch, and 12-inch) are used against villages, camps, dumps, railway stations, etc., beyond the range of other artillery. Also against observing stations, such as chimneys and church towers, and occasionally for long-range counter-battery work.

Six-inch guns are also used against balloons and for enfilading distant trenches.

Field howitzers (4.5-inch) are employed for the bombardment of the weaker defenses; enfilading communication trenches and against troops that are badly intrenched; for destructive counter-battery work against ill-protected batteries and for neutralization with gas shells; for barrage work, especially by night; also (when No. 106 fuse is provided) for cutting wire which is beyond the wire-cutting range of field guns (3,200–3,400 yards), wire at short distances from our own trenches, in hollows, on iron standards, and of the " knife-rest " type.

Medium howitzers (6-inch) are used for destruction of defenses and against intrenched troops. They are very effective for neutralizing fire against hostile batteries, though not really powerful enough to destroy well-constructed emplacements. They are of great value for destructive work in an advance, when the enemy's guns are forced back into positions more or less hastily constructed, and can also be used with No. 106 fuse for barrage fire and for wire cutting.

Heavy howitzers (8-inch and 9.2-inch) ; the principal rôles of these weapons are counter-battery work against batteries provided with good cover and the destruction of strong defenses. They also may be employed for barrage work with No. 106 fuse.

Superheavy howitzers (12-inch and 15-inch) are required for the destruction of specially strong defenses, bridges, etc. The 12-inch howitzer is also used with great effect for counter-battery work.

Light trench mortars [1] may be used to harass the enemy in the final stage of the bombardment, for barrage work and for the close support of the infantry. They are not usually employed during the course of the preliminary bombardment.

Medium trench mortars [1] are employed to assist other artillery in wire cutting and in the preliminary bombardment. Owing to their liability to be destroyed by hostile artillery fire it may often be advisable to defer opening fire with these mortars till the last day of bombardment.

Heavy trench mortars [1] are of value for the destruction of dugouts and strong points within the limits of their range.

In allotting tasks to guns and howitzers for the preparation of an attack on a large scale, simplicity must be the keynote of the scheme. Heavy howitzers' tasks should preferably be arranged in " lanes " in the same way as are those of field guns. Enfilade

[1] The handling of trench mortars as a whole is dealt with in Artillery Notes No. 6.—Trench Mortars.

fire against the enemy's main system of defense, in the case of all heavy artillery,[1] should, as a general rule, only be employed for special reasons (e. g., in the case of a limited offensive or of a marked salient). Guns and howitzers placed for enfilade can usually only play a very limited part in the actual attack, and the greater the success the earlier will they have to change to an entirely new arc of fire. Moreover, signal communications are greatly complicated under conditions of enfilade.

3. AIR OBSERVATION.

A great deal of artillery work, especially counter-battery work, must depend upon the cooperation of the royal flying corps. It is the duty of the artillery commander, in consultation with the royal flying corps commander concerned, to consider the most suitable allotment of the aeroplanes available and to include in his artillery plan the arrangements decided upon. A factor which must always be borne in mind is the jambing of wireless. This limits the number of machines which can work on any particular front at the same time. One machine to every thousand yards may be taken as a maximum.

Pilots and observers allotted to artillery work should, in principle, work with the same units throughout both the preparation and the battle itself and should be changed as seldom as possible. Close personal touch between pilots and observers and the battery commanders for whom they work is of the first importance.

Balloon companies are allotted to corps for artillery work and must work in close touch with the corps squadron. The selection of suitable targets for the aeroplanes and balloons is the duty of the artillery commander, who should make a point of seeing his corps squadron and balloon company commander together every evening to decide the allotment for the ensuing day. An intimate knowledge of the country is the chief essential of successful balloon observation. Balloons should, therefore, be changed from one area to another as seldom as possible.

The principles governing the work of aeroplanes and balloons for the artillery are explained fully in "Cooperation of Aircraft with Artillery" issued by the general staff, December, 1916 (S. S. 131).

---

[1] Enfilade fire from field artillery will often offer great advantages (see par. 12, Sec. VI).

IV. THE PRELIMINARY ARRANGEMENTS.

1. RECONNAISSANCE.

Through reconnaissance of the enemy's defenses and dispositions and also of the ground available is the first step in the work of preparation. With this object it is of the greatest importance that the various artillery commanders should get into touch as soon as possible with the commanders of the infantry whose attacks they are to support. Equally must they establish an early understanding with the R. E., signals and R. F. C. officers on whose assistance they rely.

Maps or diagrams require to be prepared showing the artillery tasks in detail, wire to be cut, defenses to be demolished, routes to be employed by artillery in movement, signal communications, allotment of O. P.'s charts of visibility from O. P.'s, and arcs of fire or other means of showing the quantity and nature of fire that can be brought to bear on any given point.

Many of the necessary reconnaissances must be made in conjunction with the infantry or other officers directly concerned with each particular problem; so that time may be saved by all arms and branches working in close cooperation from the first. Infantry officers should examine the ground from artillery observing stations, artillery officers from the trenches and from balloons and aeroplanes, while combined reconnaissances from the ground or from the air must be completed by joint study of aeroplane photographs and maps.

By these means not only should no point for consideration be overlooked but each arm will learn to appreciate the capabilities and limitations of the others.

2. DISTRIBUTION OF WORK.

A thorough understanding of the work to be done and of the time at which it is to be done, is essential to the success of the artillery preparation and subsequent action. The work must first be divided amongst the subordinate artillery commands, e. g., in the case of a corps between the different divisional artilleries and the heavy artillery. Subordinate commanders then allot tasks and zones to their brigades and groups and the commanders of these to their batteries.

Positions will have to be found for the large number of extra guns, howitzers, and trench mortars which will be required for an offensive operation of any size, as well as probably for several of those already in action whose original positions were selected with a view to defense.

The artillery must aim at extending its destructive action over as deep a zone as possible and at being able to engage the enemy's most distant batteries.

These considerations and the importance of reducing movements of guns to a minimum during the earlier stages of a battle demand that a large proportion of the attacking artillery shall be placed well forward.

What this proportion should actually be will depend chiefly on the range to the various objectives, the ground, the facilities for ammunition supply and the characteristics of the matériel. It is a mistake to mass a great number of batteries within too confined an area (particularly a valley), where they may all be neutralized at the same time by a comparatively few hostile guns or by a gas attack.

It may sometimes be necessary for corps and divisions to place their batteries outside their own area. Whenever this is the case the necessary arrangements should be made by the next higher formation; but it is to be remembered that the placing of a battery outside the area of its own formation nearly always entails certain difficulties as regards signal communications, ammunition supply, and subsequent advance. This procedure, therefore, is not to be recommended unless distinct tactical advantage is thereby gained.

4. PROTECTION OF POSITIONS.

The procedure of withdrawing the detachments from a battery which is being shelled is incompatible with the preparation and support of an infantry attack, when the guns must be fought regardless of the enemy's fire. In principle, therefore, every field and medium battery should, as far as possible, be provided with cover strong enough to resist bombardment by the enemy's heavy field howitzers (5.9-inch).

Considerations of labor and matériels may, however, prove to be limiting factors, and in this case a careful system of con-

11683°—17——3

cealment (camouflage) must be adopted for such batteries as are not otherwise protected. Even so, it is essential that shell-proof cover should be provided for the detachments close to the guns. The battery command post must always be strongly protected. Large reenforcements of artillery will usually arrive within a week or two of the opening of the preliminary bombardment, and their actual positions, telephone communications, approaches, and ammunition dumps must be well on the way toward readiness, as these matters are essential to control, direction, and delivery of fire. In order that on arrival these batteries may waste no time in preparing their positions, large dumps of R. E. matériel should be made at convenient points at an early date. Tables should be prepared showing the average amount of matériel required to dig in a battery of each caliber so that indenting may be simplified and a battery be able to draw its matériels and to begin work without delay. When batteries move forward there will be a great demand for protective matériel, and this fact must be borne in mind when allotting resources.

Apart from the question of the strength of the cover provided, the concealment of emplacements should always be studied during their actual construction. As soon as work starts, either camouflaged screens or rabbit netting threaded with grass, etc., can be erected on short stakes over the area to be excavated, while the personnel work underneath. In this connection it must be remembered that during the preparation for an offensive on a large scale the difficulty of concealing guns and tracks leading to them will be greatly lessened by the fact that the ground within about 3 miles of the trenches will be broken up in every direction by numerous other constructional works.

Guns concealed in the neighborhood of ruined villages, rubble heaps, brick stacks, and so on, are particularly difficult of location from the air.

Field artillery ammunition should always be strongly protected against hostile artillery fire; while the cartridges of heavier natures should be similarly treated, even if it is not possible to do the same for the shells.

5. OBSERVING STATIONS.

The provision of a sufficient number of strongly constructed observing stations and of covered approaches to them is a matter of vital importance. To risk the interruption at critical moments of the whole system of directing artillery fire for want of energy in this matter is inexcusable. Telephonists' dugouts and exchanges must be made practically impervious to artillery fire. All work of this nature must be treated as a matter for continuous attention, and must never be left to the eve of an offensive. Corps must arrange for considerable assistance by royal engineers in this work which can not be effectively executed by gunners alone. Every part of the hostile lines should be visible from at least one O. P.

The allotment of O. P.'s is a matter calling for the direct intervention of corps artillery commanders. All artillery headquarters, from corps downward, should possess a chart showing what can be seen of the enemy's defenses and territory from each O. P. under their control, and also a photograph of the view from each. Armed with this information it is the duty of the corps artillery commander to allot observing stations to the artillery of the corps so that the best value is obtained from them. O. P.'s will usually be allotted to certain batteries, at least as regards maintenance and control; but it will often occur with large concentrations of artillery that any one O. P. may have to serve two or even more batteries.

The establishment of special artillery observing stations for watching the progress of the infantry and reporting it to corps artillery headquarters has proved to be of great value. The probable future positions of similar stations on the far side of the hostile trenches should be studied and be made known to the infantry before the assault so that they may be available for the transmission of information in general.

6. ARTILLERY COMMAND POSTS.

The selection of artillery command posts (including brigade and group headquarters) is another important matter which must be done by general and R. A. staffs of corps in consultation. These command posts should not be changed until the time to advance arrives, when they should be moved to equally permanent positions. They must be so sited that they are likely to be out of constant shell fire, as once communication between artillery commanders and their batteries becomes impossible or even difficult, organized operations cease.

7. COMMUNICATIONS.

Previous to an offensive operation it will be necessary to provide the requisite communications for a much larger force of artillery than will normally be engaged in holding the line, and this requires very careful organization. The actual communications to be established in each case must depend upon the organization of the artillery. They will include, in addition to the ordinary framework in the way of command posts and observing stations, the communications required by the higher artillery commanders. These latter will be laid by the signal service, but it is essential that such circuits should be kept quite distinct from the general system.

In order to save labor, and at the same time to obtain real efficiency in telephonic communications, the whole of the artillery communications in the corps should be worked out as one plan by the corps signals, who must take executive control of all artillery lines. Corps signal schemes must be coordinated by army signals. An organized system of trunk lines and exchanges in the forward area, supervised by experts, is best calculated to attain the end in view at minimum expenditure of resources. Large infantry working parties for digging in wires will be required both in the preparatory stages and after an advance. This must be taken into consideration when labor requirements are being calculated. It is impossible to take too many precautions to avoid the interruption of communication.

In addition to protecting the telephone wires, as far as this is possible, preparations must be made for the rapid opening of alternative means of communication. Visual signaling is the most important of these, and stations should be selected and established. Possible points in the enemy's line should also be selected beforehand, so that, after the attack has succeeded, intermediate observers may know where to look for signals. The establishment of central stations from which messages can be sent on by telephone will prove of great assistance. Short-range wireless sets have been successfully used (up to 7,000 yards) where visual signaling is impossible; but in such cases reliance will often have to be placed on orderlies, either on foot or on bicycle. Here, again, arrangements must be made in advance so that everyone may know what to do when the time comes.

8. CONTROL AND DIRECTION OF FIRE.

Accuracy of fire is a matter of the utmost importance. It demands studious attention to calibration of guns, calculations for atmospheric and other errors, and to the selection and thorough registration of a few well-chosen datum points which must be daily used for checking ranges.

Artillery boards, carefully prepared and kept up to date, are an essential to this system which, particularly in the case of heavy howitzers, is more satisfactory, more economical in ammunition, and less likely to disclose the amount of artillery present than was the old system of indiscriminate registration of innumerable points. The latter has proved to be neither necessary nor desirable.

In order, however, to insure that newly arrived batteries shall be able to register their datum points with absolute thoroughness, and that all batteries shall be able to check their ranges two or three times a day on these points (a matter of the utmost importance during the bombardment, and even more so on the day of attack), it is essential that corps artillery commanders shall make detailed arrangements for this work to be carried out, so that confusion of observation shall be avoided.

As already explained, the simpler the artillery fire plan is the greater the hope of its successful execution. If the ground to be bombarded be divided up into lanes and clearly defined areas, both checking ranges on datum points and observation during bombardment will be immensely facilitated. Lanes or areas [1] must be distributed on a time-table issued daily by the corps, so that every hour is fully occupied. Unless every battery commander follows a clear system based on these lines, great confusion will inevitably result and the efficacy of the artillery fire will be correspondingly diminished.

9. TRENCH BRIDGES.

The preparation and transport by artillery of portable trench bridges has not been found to be universally necessary. Trenches are crossed more easily and more quickly by the simple process of filling them in. Good, strong bridges are, however, required in large numbers for constructing ammunition routes across captured trenches in the event of wet weather, as under such conditions the filled-in places over which guns may have crossed will soon become soft and impassable.

10. AMMUNITION SUPPLY.

During the preparatory period the preliminary arrangements in connection with the supply of ammunition are amongst the first matters to be taken in hand, for the commander's power

---

[1] Areas should be about 500 yards square, each containing a definite target, such as a line of trench, running approximately across the center.

of maneuver is largely dependent on the supply of ammunition. To insure the smooth working of this supply, careful plans must be made from the commencement.

The construction of railways, light railways, and roads for the conveyance of ammunition must be started a long time before operations commence. Roads without railways can ill stand the strain of ammunition traffic. Wherever possible, special roads should be reserved for the use of ammunition lorries and wagons, so that their own movements and the movements of troops may not be blocked. Matériel for the extension of the light railways should be dumped near their termini, in order that they may be carried forward as soon as the advance takes place. It has often been found that the state of the ground after a bombardment makes it impossible to supply ammunition, except by pack transport, to those batteries that have advanced. Arrangements must be made beforehand to deal with these conditions if there is any possibility that they will arise.

In order to meet any possible breakdown in the railway or other unforeseen emergency an army reserve of ammunition should be made in a central position before the commencement of operations. In excess of their echelons, which must be full, corps should dump sufficient ammunition for the preliminary bombardment and for expenditure on the day of attack and the day after the attack. At least 20 per cent of the ammunition so dumped should be held in corps reserve. In addition, each battery should dump at its position sufficient ammunition for its own requirements, plus a small reserve, and not according to a fixed scale. All the ammunition should be close to the guns in order to save labor during the strenuous periods of the preliminary bombardment and the day of attack.

11. ANTIAIRCRAFT GUNS.

Antiaircraft artillery must be disposed during the preparatory period so as to prevent hostile aircraft from reconnoitering and from bombing ammunition dumps, railways, etc.

As a general guide, units forming the front line barrage are best sited at about 4,000 yards apart and at an average distance of 3,000 yards behind the front-line trenches. Units required for the second-line barrage will generally amount to about half the number of those required for the front line and should be placed at a distance of about 5,000 yards from them. Antiaircraft gun positions, once definitely located by the enemy, are unlikely to remain tenable for long. Units should, therefore, change their positions frequently, and this entails the selection and preparation of an adequate number of sites, each of which must be linked up to the army antiaircraft telephone system.

V. THE PRELIMINARY BOMBARDMENT.[1]

1. OBJECT OF THE PRELIMINARY BOMBARDMENT.

The task of the artillery in an offensive battle is to prepare the way for the infantry and to support and protect the infantry throughout its progress. The preparation of the way is achieved by the preliminary bombardment, which aims at—

(a) The overpowering of the hostile artillery.

(b) The physical and moral reduction of the enemy's infantry.

(c) The destruction of matériel obstacles to the advance of the attacking infantry and of other defenses.

Action against the hostile artillery, a matter of the greatest importance in all operations, is dealt with in detail in G.H.Q. Artillery Notes No. 3.—Counter battery Work, and will only be referred to in this paper in general terms.

2. FIRE TO EFFECT PHYSICAL AND MORAL DAMAGE.

The enemy will suffer a certain degree of physical and moral loss both from action against his artillery and from the destructive fire directed against his defenses. But his power of resistance must be reduced by further special measures. Fire must be directed with the object of denying to the enemy the arrival of reliefs, reinforcements, ammunition, and supplies of all kinds. Communications, places of assembly, bivouacs, billets, dumps, railway stations, headquarters, etc., must all be attacked by artillery on a considered and clearly ordered scheme. The share of field artillery in this work consists by day chiefly in searching communication trenches (especially trench junctions) between the points bombarded by heavier natures and other approaches that are hidden from view, while by night it will fire on communication trenches, tracks, roads, cooking places, and so on in the forward zone. The heavy artillery should fire

---

[1] See Section III, paragraph 3, of " Instructions for the Training of Divisions for Offensive Action."

by day and by night on roads, railways, billets, and other targets beyond the reach of field artillery. The damage to roads effected by the general bombardment has proved to be a serious obstacle to the subsequent advance. This point must be borne in mind when ordering the fire of heavy howitzers on or in the neighborhood of main roads. The use of instantaneous fuses in these circumstances may minimize the damage done.

In selecting batteries for these tasks due regard should be paid to the obvious advantage of enfilade fire against communications of all kinds.

Gas shell, if used in sufficient quantity, may give good results against such objectives as ravines and woods; especially at night, when fear of them will compel the enemy to wear gas helmets.

The guiding principle of all artillery fire against communications, etc., is to employ short, sharp bursts of fire at irregular intervals of time. By day these tasks will not call for the special employment of a large number of pieces. On the contrary, batteries of suitable caliber and selected with regard to their position should be detailed to carry out this work in addition to other duties. By night, however, fire of this nature must be much more vigorously conducted in order that the enemy's efforts to relieve or supply his forward troops may only be possible at the cost of heavy casualties and that the morale of his garrisons may derive no benefit from a comparative lull in the artillery fire; indeed, a searching shrapnel fire on approaches must be almost continuous. To achieve this without imposing on the artillery too great a burden it is necessary to reserve a certain number of field batteries (gun and howitzer) and of sections of heavy artillery, especially for night-fire tasks, or else to organize a system of reliefs of personnel within batteries. Otherwise the artillery will either be tired out before the assault, or the night fire will not be conducted with the vigor and care that are so essential. Infantry can cooperate with the artillery against near objectives by means of direct and indirect machine-gun fire.

A sound fire scheme of this nature can only be prepared after a detailed study of maps and air photographs, assisted by information gleaned from prisoners. During the bombardment itself, if of any considerable duration, the plan should be constantly reconsidered and modifications introduced, so as to keep the enemy in a state of uncertainty as to our intentions and therefore exposed to loss. This phase of the artillery action is highly important and must never be allowed to become a mere matter of routine. Every round expended on a definite plan, right back to extreme range, is well spent.

3. DESTRUCTION OF OBSTACLES—WIRE CUTTING.

The principal obstacle that has usually to be destroyed is the enemy's wire.

Wire cutting has been in the past chiefly the "task of the 18-pounders and medium trench mortars, and is carried out in each divisional zone by the field artillery allotted to that zone, any assistance required from neighboring field artillery units being arranged by the G. O. C. R. A. Corps." The provision of instantaneous and nondelay fuses for howitzers introduces an entirely new factor into the wire-cutting problem, which it may become possible to solve far more easily and in much less time than has hitherto been the case.

"Wire cutting demands the closest cooperation between the artillery and infantry. Commanders of assaulting battalions should visit the O. P.'s of the batteries cutting the wire on their front to watch the progress of the work, and should inform the battery commanders when they consider that the wire has been properly cut. In addition, patrols should be sent out nightly during wire cutting to examine and report on the progress made during the day."

"Once gaps have been made it is the duty of divisional commanders to employ all means at their disposal to keep these gaps open during the hours of darkness throughout the period of the preparatory bombardment. These means include the use of rifle and machine-gun fire, rifle grenades, etc. Much artillery ammunition can thus be saved, and so can be used for strengthening the fire on communication trenches and other approaches." [1] The amount of artillery fire that is generally available in any offensive battle is now so great that wire as a factor of defense tends to lose much of its old importance.

4. DESTRUCTION OF DEFENSES AND THEIR ACCESSORIES.

The objectives that are to be destroyed during the preliminary bombardment are stated in the corps' artillery plan, after the ground, maps, air photographs, and all other sources of informa-

---

[1] See Section III, paragraph 3, of "Instructions for the Training of Divisions for Offensive Action."

11683°—17——4

tion have been thoroughly studied. To attempt complete destruction of the enemy's trenches is impracticable, except in the case of enfilade fire, and it is unnecessary. The artillery's task being to open the way for the infantry, its fire must be directed toward breaking down, firstly, the enemy's material powers of resistance, and, secondly, his means of directing his defense, incidentally thus increasing his demoralization by causing casualties and inducing confusion. The enemy's matériel powers of resistance include such targets as machine-gun emplacements, strong points, important trench junctions, selected dugouts, and other shelters. His signal communications, command posts, observing stations, water-pipe systems, etc., must be shelled with the object of disorganizing his defense. As a general principle, it is best, particularly in the case of a long bombardment, to destroy first those objectives which are most dangerous or will give the enemy the most trouble to repair.

The extent of the ground to be bombarded will naturally depend upon the objective assigned to the attack. In all cases the enemy's defenses for several hundred yards to either flank, the distance depending upon the lie of the ground and the trace of the works, must be dealt with as severely as the front of attack itself; while all salients within 1,200 yards of the front attacked, from which flanking fire could be brought to bear, must receive drastic treatment.

The enemy's system of communication (telephone and telegraph) should be broken down at the outset; fire being directed with this object in accordance with the information gleaned from prisoners and air photographs. The object will naturally be best obtained by shelling battle headquarters and telephone exchanges where many wires meet.

Important trench junctions must be destroyed so that reliefs and ration parties, etc., may be compelled to expose themselves to shrapnel fire.

Deep dugouts present an almost invulnerable target, even to the heaviest artillery; the best result that can be expected is the blowing in of some of the entrances. But such dugouts, though they afford good protection, should not prove an ultimate salvation to the enemy's infantry, who will be unable to emerge from them in time to meet the assault, if the barrage and the infantry's advance are properly coordinated and exactly executed.

Machine guns still remain a formidable asset to the defense. A certain number are housed in concrete emplacements, and these must be destroyed before the assault takes place. The best method of dealing with machine guns which are maintained in deep dugouts and brought up to the parapet to repel an assault is considered in the paragraphs dealing with the field artillery barrage. Another method frequently employed by the enemy has been to place machine guns in shell holes and other ill-defined positions outside the actual trenches. These, though more commonly met with in the later stages of the battle, may be successfully countered by searching all the ground in front of and behind the immediate objective with shrapnel every day, a procedure calculated to make any shallow position untenable. The "creeping barrage" should finally account for any machine gunners that survive.

The destruction of observing stations is dealt with in "Counter-Battery Notes;" they must not be everlooked.

The destruction of trenches and strong points is primarily the task of trench mortars and howitzers of all descriptions, other than the field howitzer which, in future, will have nothing but instantaneous fuses and so be chiefly a man-killing weapon. "Guns can, however, be employed with advantage against breastworks, trenches taken in enfilade, barricades, houses, and other vertical targets."

"The extent to which the enemy's trenches and works should be destroyed has become a matter for serious consideration."[1] If they are more or less completely demolished, little or no cover will be left for our infantry. This, though of no moment in the preliminary bombardment of the enemy's front-line system of defense before the launching of an attack on a large scale, has been found to prove a grave disadvantage when the trenches gained have to be held; a case that will arise in a limited offensive or in the later stages of a battle aimed at gradually wearing out the enemy's power of resistance.

The bombardment of woods and villages should not consist of an indiscriminate shelling of the whole area. The portions that require bombardment, whether because they are to be captured or because they flank the advance, must be definitely determined.

In all cases it is necessary to arrange to prevent by fire the repair of destroyed or damaged defenses. In this, as with cut wire, infantry can assist to a considerable degree.

---

[1] See Section III, paragraph 3, of "Instructions for the Training of Divisions for Offensive Action."

5. FLEETING TARGETS.

During the course of the preliminary bombardment, opportunities will occasionally be presented of causing loss to fleeting targets (reinforcements, reliefs, working parties, or troops driven from shelter by artillery fire). Certain batteries should, therefore, be held available on the "zone-call" system to engage any such targets located from the air. Arrangements should also be made to extend this system to ground-observing stations, so that any observer, seeing a favorable target, can pass information quickly to a selected and suitable battery. There is no reason to retain such batteries solely for this purpose; they can carry out other tasks as well.

6. ACCURACY OF FIRE.

The necessity for destroying definite points in the enemy's organized system of defense demands the greatest accuracy of artillery fire, particularly when the opposing lines are but a short distance apart. The importance of accuracy can not be overestimated, and must be constantly insured by means of definite orders, rigorous fire control, and constant supervision. To this end it is essential to arrange for periodical pauses in the bombardment of each section of the bombarded area; in order that fire may be checked on datum points, the detachments rested, the equipment carefully inspected, and minor repairs effected. During these pauses every endeavor should be made to take air photographs of the hostile area, for these will disclose beyond argument the accuracy of the fire brought to bear and will enable commanders to repeat or to modify their bombardment program accordingly.

Cases will occur where effect on the enemy's front trenches can only be insured at the cost of an occasional round into our own trenches. This is a matter of pure ballistics, beyond human influence, and must be recognized as such by infantry commanders. The advisability of withdrawing infantry from their trenches during a bombardment must depend on the local conditions. If the trenches are good and the men keep down, they may be safer in the front trenches than they would be if crowded in support trenches, which may be heavily shelled at times by the hostile artillery. If the distance between the opposing trenches is such that some rounds are likely to fall in or short of our trenches, then the trenches must be cleared for the requisite time. The only alternative is to place the "mean point of impact" of the artillery fire beyond the target. This is unsound, as it entails a much reduced chance of achieving the destruction required at a greatly increased cost of ammunition. In view of the consideration that a few of our own heavy shells dropped in a crowded trench, especially just prior to the assault, may prove disastrous to the morale of the attacking troops, it will almost always be advisable to clear our trenches for the sake of an effective fire. The enemy is not likely to rush them in any strength at such a time. It is the duty of the artillery commander to make these points clear to the general officer commanding; it is the latter's duty to decide. If trenches are to be cleared, it is important that ample notice should be given to the infantry, in order that they may have time to make the necessary arrangements for temporary evacuation and for denying to the enemy any opportunity of coming forward out of his trenches to avoid the effects of artillery fire.

7. FORWARD GUNS.

In some cases guns dug in, actually in or close to the front-line trenches, may prove of great value for special purposes, such as for making a breach in the hostile parapets or for knocking out machine guns. Provided time is available, experience shows that field guns can be got into almost any position, and that their fire at such short ranges produces a very marked effect. The secret of success lies in the most careful attention to detail. Unless every possible precaution is taken, the gun and detachment may both be put out of action before they have effected their purpose. Although there is no doubt that their presence has a great moral effect, their use must not be overdone, and they should not open fire just before the assault.

8. ADVANCED BATTERIES.

Batteries placed right forward to open fire at or after the time of assault are considered in paragraph 18, Section VI.

9. CHARACTER OF THE BOMBARDMENT.

The program of bombardment must be so arranged as to keep the enemy in a state of uncertainty as to the time when the infantry attack will be launched. The approximate hour of assault should be settled early and not changed. It will then be possible to insure that, as far as the artillery is concerned, the actual assault shall come as a surprise. The German is peculiarly accustomed to order and regularity, and so it is advantageous to accustom him daily at the proposed hour of assault to a regular routine to which he must conform under pain of suffering casualties. Then, when the real hour comes, there will be a very good chance of letting the infantry into the enemy's trenches by making some slight alteration in that routine.

False ("Chinese") attacks are generally carried out during the bombardment with the object of inducing the enemy to man his parapets and then subjecting him to an intense man-killing fire. The infantry, trench mortars, etc., should participate in these feints so as to give the greatest impression of reality.

The lifts for the attack should be practiced during the bombardment. Officers must be detailed to watch all such shoots so that thin places in the barrage or inaccurate shooting may be rectified in time. For the former purpose balloon observations may also be employed with great advantage. Further, the results can be corroborated by means of air photographs, and arrangements should be made to photograph each practice barrage. Besides watching our own barrages, steps should be taken to observe and record those put down by the enemy, as much valuable information may be gleaned from this source.

10. THE BOMBARDMENT OF REARWARD LINES.

As already stated, a vigorous and systematic artillery fire must be maintained over the enemy's back areas up to the limits of gun range, with the immediate objects of inflicting casualties, arresting movement, and generally disorganizing his supply and other services. This will entail the deliberate destruction of many selected points in the enemy's rearward lines of defense, but does not constitute a regular bombardment.

The extent to which rearward lines must be bombarded depends on several factors. The ultimate object of the first day's attack, the range to the rearward lines, the number of guns available and the duration of the bombardment all directly affect this question. It will rarely be possible to effect any extensive damage to the enemy's third line, where such exists, owing to the factor of range which limits the number of guns that can reach the objective.

If the attack is to go through to as great a depth as possible, and if time allows, then certain points in the enemy's second line should be selected for destruction on the same principles as govern the artillery attack of the front system of defense. If, on the other hand, the attack has a limited objective, or if the attack of successive objectives, spread over several days, is contemplated, then there can be but little value in any extensive bombardment of the second line. It is not unusual to find that before the assault considerable anxiety is expressed as to the destruction done to the wire and trenches of the second line. The fighting subsequent to the assault, particularly the various barrages, will do much toward opening a way through the second line of defense. It is easy to exaggerate the resisting power of rearward defenses and to press for its reduction. But the first essential is to insure the infantry's passage over the enemy's front-line system of defense, and to take any chances in this respect in favor of more distant systems is manifestly indefensible.

11. DURATION OF THE BOMBARDMENT.

No definite guide can be laid down as to the ideal length of an artillery bombardment. The underlying factors are numerous and the daily results achieved carry great weight. Hitherto the moral effect of the enemy's wire has involved organized wire cutting, which in reality means a prolonged bombardment. It is possible, as explained in paragraph 3, Section V, that wire cutting in the future will be carried out much more rapidly. The time theoretically required to destroy definite objectives depends on their nature and extent, upon the number of fire units available, and on the facilities for observation. If fire is to be conducted deliberately and with careful observation, this period can be calculated with considerable accuracy. Shortening the period may increase the chances of surprise and may so give the enemy no opportunity of bringing up additional artillery. A long bombardment is calculated to reduce the enemy's morale by its insistence, a short one by its intensity. In all cases it is the duty of the artillery commander to watch closely the progress of the artillery preparation, making such modifications in the allotment of guns and ammunition as he may consider necessary.

The evidence of photographs, corroborated by the reports of patrols and special observers, is the surest guide to the extent of matériel damage effected. The effect of the fire should be continuously observed by selected artillery officers and aeroplane observers. "Photographs showing the progress of the work of demolition are taken daily when conditions are favorable, and issued to all divisional commanders concerned, as well as to the corps commander. Divisional commanders must satisfy themselves that all danger points in their zones are adequately dealt with, and they should bring to the notice of the corps commander any points which, in their opinion, require further treatment. In considering the state of the enemy's defenses, as disclosed by photographs, it must be remembered that considerable further effect will be achieved by the bombardment which remains to be carried out between the time that the last photograph is taken and zero hour on the day of attack, and also by the howitzer bombardment which lifts forward from trench to trench from zero hour onward." [1]

VI.—THE SUPPORT OF THE ATTACK.

1. THE GENERAL MISSION OF THE ARTILLERY.

Adequate artillery preparation will not alone insure the success of an attack. The support of the infantry during the attack is at least as important, and in this phase the general mission of the artillery consists of—

(a) Beating down all resistance to the advance from either front or flanks.

(b) Preventing the assembly and approach of counter attacks of all sizes.

In a word, the artillery must aim at overcoming the enemy's batteries, riflemen, and machine guns that have not been destroyed during the preliminary bombardment.

2. IMPORTANCE OF CONCEALING THE HOUR OF THE ASSAULT.

Every precaution must be taken to insure that the actual assault should come as a surprise. It will probably be impossible to conceal from the enemy the intention of an attack on a large scale. If any indication of the actual hour of assault is afforded (as by an obvious change in the intensity or nature of artillery fire, bayonets showing over the trenches, advancing "tanks," etc.), the enemy's infantry will be in instant

---

[1] See Section III, paragraph 3, of "Instructions for Training of Divisions for Offensive Action."

readiness to man the parapets, the hostile artillery barrage may come down, and the assault may possibly never start.[1]

If, on the other hand, no notice is given to the enemy, he will not know until too late exactly where his barrage is required.

3. BARRAGES.

The barrage system has been lately developed. It must be remembered that, while the following notes deal with the procedure that has recently been the most successful, it is only to be expected that the enemy will devise new methods to defeat our barrage fire. New methods on his part will call for immediate modifications in our artillery tactics.

4. OBJECT OF THE BARRAGE.

The object of the artillery barrage is to prevent the enemy from manning his parapets and installing his machine guns in time to arrest the advance of our infantry. It has already been explained that permanent concrete emplacements for machine guns must be destroyed during the preliminary bombardment and that a daily searching of the ground with shrapnel fire is a helpful method of dealing with machine guns sited in shell holes and shallow positions in front of or behind the immediate objective. Machine guns kept in deep dugouts, or even in deep shell holes if undercut, can not be destroyed by these means, but, on the other hand, a certain period of time is required to bring up and mount such guns. Though this period is not long, it is quite sufficient to enable the attacking infantry to deal with the situation if they are close up under the barrage. The barrage must, therefore, be sufficiently heavy to keep the enemy in his dugouts and shelters as long as possible, and sufficiently accurate to allow the infantry to get so close to the trench attacked that when the barrage lifts they can cover the remaining distance before the enemy can prepare to receive them.

5. THE FIELD ARTILLERY BARRAGE.

To deal with the enemy's infantry and his variously sited machine guns the field artillery barrage may consist of "creeping," "back," and "standing" barrages applied separately or simultaneously.

---

[1] See Section V of "Instructions for the Training of Divisions for Offensive Action."

The "standing" barrage opens on each objective when it is to be assaulted, with the object of forcing the enemy to take cover and of preventing him manning his defenses before the infantry reach the position.

The "back" barrage meanwhile searches and sweeps all the ground in rear of the objective whence rifle or machine-gun fire might be directed against the advancing infantry.

Whether in addition to these two barrages a "creeping" barrage will also be required depends on the distance to be traversed by the infantry from their "jumping off" place to their objective. If this distance is such that the infantry is not sufficiently protected by the fire of the "standing" barrage against any machine guns or riflemen that may still lurk in shell holes, then a "creeping" barrage should precede the advancing infantry, with its mean point of impact at a distance of 200 yards or so in front of them, and move forward till it joins the "standing" barrage, when both barrages lift off together. It must, however, be remembered that the simultaneous employment of three barrages is to be avoided on principle, as it entails a maximum dispersion of effort on the part of the artillery available.

In the first assault, a "creeping" barrage will usually be unnecessary, as the distance between the opposing trenches will, as a rule, be such that the "standing" barrage will be all that is possible or necessary.

In later stages, when the enemy has been forced back into hastily dug trenches, the "standing" barrage may sometimes be dispensed with in favor of the "creeping" barrage which can fill the dual rôle by dwelling for a certain time on each objective to be assaulted. In this case the object of the barrage is to allow the infantry to "follow close up to the barrage from the instant it commences, and then taking advantage of this 'dwell,' work up as close as possible to the objective, ready to rush it at the moment that the barrage lifts." In either case the one essential is that the infantry shall be able to move as close up to the barrage as is possible, so that "the time which elapses between the barrage lifting and the infantry entering the trench may be less than that required by the enemy to man their parapets" and install their machine guns. Success or failure is a matter of a few seconds.[1]

----

[1] See Section III, paragraph 4, of "Instructions for the Training of Divisions for Offensive Action."

The barrage will meanwhile approach the next objective, picking up the back barrage en route and being organized on a similar system to that arranged for the first objective.

The following figures may be taken as a general guide to the relative strengths of field artillery barrages.

One 18-pounder gun per 15 yards should provide adequate barrages of all natures.

An 18-pounder " back " barrage does not require a large number of guns; about one-eighth of the total available should suffice.[1]

7. THE ORGANIZATION OF THE BARRAGE.

The barrage lines throughout the corps must be arranged by the G. O. C. R. A. corps, in accordance with the corps commander's directions, after consultation with divisional commanders, and are best communicated to subordinate commanders in the form of a map showing all the lifts. No changes should be permitted once the barrages have been worked out and issued, except on a change of the general plan of attack.

It is laid down ("Instructions for the Training of Divisions for Offensive Action")—issued by the general staff, December, 1916—section 135, p. 62, par. 3 (i), that the front or jumping-off trench must be as nearly parallel as possible to the enemy's front line so that the leading waves may jump off square to their objective. This is of great importance to the placing of the barrage, as the first objective (the enemy's front trench) can thus be subjected to a barrage from the heavy artillery along its whole length, and then to an 18-pounder barrage followed by a simultaneous assult by the infantry. Against subsequent objectives, however, it will often follow that the infantry can not jump off from a parallel line, and in this case the barrage should swing so that it is parallel to the objective along its whole length before it finally lifts on to the objective. Occasionally it may be difficult to execute this " swing " of the barrage; in such cases the alternative method is to arrange for each small sec-

---

[1] Where both " creeping " and " standing " barrages have been employed it has been found that the latter has usually consisted of about one-third of the available guns, the " creeping " barrage of the rest, but the proportion must depend on the ground and on the dispositions of the enemy.

tion of the barrage, as it reaches the trench line, to stop there until gradually the whole length of the barrage has been built up. In both cases the barrage ultimately lifts off simultaneously; the fact that certain portions of the assaulting lines are kept waiting while the barrage either swings or is built up does not matter. A barrage that remains parallel to the jumping off the line does not keep the troops waiting in the open; but the infantry's arrival on the objective is not simultaneous and, wherever the trench bends, there is an open space between the barrage and the part of the trench occupied by our troops. This may contain the entrance to a dug-out and it is quite possible that the enemy's machine gunners may receive warning and get their guns mounted in time (see Appendix II).

8. PACE OF THE BARRAGE.[1]

"(i) The secret of a successful assault rests upon the assumption that the infantry conform their movements exactly to the timing of the barrage. The importance of this timing, therefore, can not be overestimated. If the lifts are too quick, the pace will be too fast and the infantry will fail to keep up with the barrage. Once this happens the whole advantage of the barrage will be lost, as the enemy will have time to man his parapet before the infantry reach it. The advance will then be brought to a standstill under close-range enemy rifle and machine-gun fire, while the barrage moves farther and farther away in accordance with the time table.

" If there is too long a pause between each lift, the pace will be too slow, and the rear waves will push on too fast and become mixed up with the leading waves, thereby forming a thicker line and increasing casualties, besides losing the driving power which a series of waves gives to the attack.

"(ii) It is impossible to lay down any definite ruling as to the best pace; it must be regulated entirely by local conditions." The great thing is not to go too fast. The pace must be such that the slowest man can easily keep close up under the barrage. One hundred yards in 3 minutes is a good average pace over dry ground pitted with shell holes.

" The state of the weather, the extent to which the ground is cut up by shell fire, the length of the advance, the number of

---

[1] See Section III, paragraphs 5, 6, and 7, of " Instructions for the Training of Divisions for Offensive Action."

enemy trenches to be crossed, all affect the pace at which the infantry, and consequently the barrage, can move. In actual practice, the pace has varied from 75 yards a minute, when conditions were very favorable, to 15 yards a minute when they were very unfavorable.

"(iii) A uniform pace throughout the advance is unsound; at the commencement the pace of the barrage should be quicker, gradually slowing down toward the finish as the men become exhausted, in order to give them time to get close up to the barrage and to pull themselves together for the final rush.

" In the case of a long advance, it is advisable to keep the barrage on the objective for a double period, in order to make quite certain that the men are closed up and ready to rush the trench.

"Above all, it is essential that in the attack of a more or less intact system of defense the infantry should cross ' No man's land ' as quickly as possible. To achieve this, it is of vital importance that the infantry should start off at zero time with absolute punctuality, for any delay at this moment may be disastrous."

9. TIME TABLES.

" The timing of the barrage is fixed, as part of the corps artillery plan, by the corps commander after consultation with divisional commanders, particular attention being paid to the points of junction between divisions to insure that the barrages on each divisional front overlap properly.

" The timings worked out are then embodied in a program or time table and issued to all concerned.

" The duration of the barrage depends on the number of objectives to be gained.

" Where there is only one objective, the barrage, after lifting off the objective, will continue to creep forward till it reaches a line about 300 yards beyond the objective. This distance is necessary to give room for outposts to be pushed out to cover the consolidation.

" The barrage then becomes stationary and gradually dies down, ceasing altogether as soon as the infantry report that they have secured the objective.

" When there is another objective there will be a certain pause, previously arranged and laid down, to enable the troops detailed for the assault of the next objective to get into position;

the barrage will then commence moving forward again in accordance with the time table."

10. CONTROL OF THE BARRAGE.[1]

"(i) The control of the barrage remains in the hands of the corps commander throughout the assault, but, in order that divisional commanders may be able to deal promptly with any situation which may arise on their front, they will be given a call on a certain number of batteries (18-pounder, 4.5-inch and 6-inch howitzer) from the commencement of the assault.

"All batteries thus detailed will have tasks allotted to them in accordance with corps orders and will carry them out, unless and until their assistance is demanded by the divisional commander concerned.

"The divisional commander will demand the assistance of these batteries through the commander of all the field artillery supporting his division. The latter officer will have his headquarters at divisional headquarters, if possible, and will be in drect communication with all the field artillery groups under him and also with the G. O. C., R. A. corps.

"(ii) To enable commanders of assaulting brigades to take immediate action in any situation which may arise, the divisonal commander may delegate to the brigadiers concerned the power to call direct on some of the batteries placed at his disposal.

"The brigadier will call on these batteries through the commander of the field artillery directly supporting his brigade. This latter officer will, whenever possible, establish his headquarters in the immediate vicinity of the infantry brigade headquarters, but where this is not possible he will maintain the closest touch with the infantry brigadier by means of a senior artillery liaison officer.

"The governing factor as to which of these two methods should be followed is to a great extent a question of communications. Unforeseen situations will always arise necessitating the passage of orders and information between a divisional C. R. A. and his group commanders. If the headquarters of an infantry brigade is so placed that communication between an

---

[1] See Section III, paragraphs 5, 6, and 7, of "Instructions for the Training of Divisions for Offensive Action."

279

artillery group commander at or near those headquarters and his divisional C. R. A. has a reasonable prospect of remaining continuously open, such is the best solution. If not, then the artillery group commander is better represented by a responsible liaison officer.

"(iii) Except when minor operations by single battalions are being carried out, it will usually be unnecessary to give officers commanding assaulting battalions the power to call on batteries, and consequently these officers will not require artillery liaison officers."

11. RATE OF FIRE AND DEPTH OF LIFTS.

The rate of fire of 18-pounders should never exceed 4 rounds per gun per minute and this rate should only be maintained for short periods. The equipment will not stand more.

Field artillery lifts should be approximately 100 yards at a time. Intermediate lifts must be arranged so that any trenches or works in front of the objective are included in one of the lifts, and so that the final lift brings the fire right on to the objective. Except in these cases lifts of less than 100 yards are disadvantageous, as time is lost in adjusting the sights, and experience both in the field and on the range shows that at average ranges a 100-yard lift every three minutes completely searches the whole ground.

12. ENFILADE FIRE.

Enfilade fire is of value in the support of an infantry assault not only on account of its great effect, but also because of the accuracy with which it can be used. If the guns placed in position for this purpose are anchored and carefully registered for line on the enemy's front trench when at extreme traverse, the fire can be moved forward slowly as the infantry assault; but their utility comes to an end as soon as the other limit of traverse is reached. Guns so placed can also be used to form a "cross-barrage," i. e., one formed by guns firing at right angles to one another, which will insure some fire from a flank on any route which is attempted through the barrage. Care must be taken in using enfilade fire in support of an attack that there shall be no risk of hitting any bodies of our own infantry on the flank of or beyond those which the guns are immediately supporting.

13. AMMUNITION FOR THE FIELD ARTILLERY BARRAGE.

The barrage has two main properties:
- (a) It is a man-killing agent.
- (b) It acts as a screen to cover the movements of the infantry from view.

Therefore shrapnel (with long corrector) presents distinct advantages for use in a "creeping" barrage under which the infantry has to advance, owing to the high proportion of possible man-killing missiles released by the burst of the shell and to the smoke cloud given off. If a large proportion of H. E. shell is employed, the covering screen will be too thin and the enemy will be able to bring aimed machine-gun fire to bear through the barrage from positions in rear. H. E. shell may, however, prove very valuable to cover attacks on woods and villages.

It is possible that the future may bring about considerable modifications in the method of carrying out barrages in view of the introduction of smoke shell. The use of H. E. shell for the "creeping" barrage may, be capable of increase if preceded by a smoke barrage to form the necessary screen; or a mixed shrapnel and smoke barrage may conceivably be found useful, either of these methods releasing 18-pounders for the back barrage. H. E. and smoke shell, again, may prove of great use in this latter form of barrage. The employment of smoke shell is, however, still in its infancy, and the above possibilities are only to be regarded as indications of the direction in which artillery thought may ultimately turn.

14. THE HOWITZER BOMBARDMENT.[1]

At the moment of assault the enemy's artillery is a target of vital importance, and an adequate number of batteries must be employed to reduce the enemy's guns to comparative impotence. All howitzers not engaged in counter battery work should begin an intense bombardment of the enemy's trenches, working up lanes in the same manner as the field artillery barrage. It depends upon the ground whether this bombardment moves forward just in front of the field artillery barrage or whether it dwells on commanding points in rear within machine-gun range, thus increasing the strength of the back barrage.

---

[1] See Section III, paragraph 4 (ii) of "Instructions for the Training of Divisions for Offensive Action."

The moral effect of the former procedure is very great.[1] In either case this bombardment ultimately "works forward well beyond the objective and then remains stationary on trenches, hollow roads, woods, villages, etc., where the enemy might assemble for a counter attack. The effect of this bombardment can be increased if indirect machine-gun fire is brought to bear simultaneously on the areas which are being bombarded, with a view to dealing with any of the enemy who attempt to escape the bombardment by leaving their trenches, etc."

15. CONSOLIDATION AND COUNTER ATTACKS.

The artillery plan must include arrangements necessary to insure the protection of the infantry after their ultimate objectives have been gained.

At every pause of any considerable length care must be taken that trenches, works, and approaches on the immediate flanks of the general infantry line, as well as areas suitable for the assembly of counter attacking troops, are kept under fire. The extreme flanks, where they bend back to the original line of departure, present an opportunity to the enemy unless they are rendered unapproachable by fire.

A final or "protective" barrage must be maintained beyond the ultimate objective as long as it is required by the infantry (see par. 9).

The rate of fire can gradually slacken, and medium and heavy howitzers need not ordinarily be used after the first hour unless called for; but any attempt to economize ammunition at this period may lead to the undoing of the whole attack. The principles of crushing hostile counter attacks must be thoroughly understood. It is a critical period for the infantry when they first become exposed to the hostile artillery fire in preparation of the main counter attack, which will not, of course, ordinarily develop for some hours. The artillery, however good the counter-battery work, can not prevent the infantry being shelled at this period when distant or even new hostile batteries will probably have come into action and when every hostile gun that can fire will do so, regardless of losses. But the artillery, working in conjunction with the air service, should be able to prevent the

---

[1] A mixed barrage—that is, a barrage of field and heavy artillery combined—has been found very efficacious as covering fire in the attack of a wood.

enemy from assembling for a counter attack. That must be the chief aim of the artillery. If, however, the enemy does manage to launch a counter attack, then the guns must bring it to a stop.

Directly the enemy's artillery preparation begins our artillery must fire in counter preparation. The enemy's batteries must be engaged; a destructive fire directed on his foremost trenches, works, and likely places of assembly; and all approaches and roads, as well as billets, dumps, etc., must be shelled.

Fire in counter preparation must be conducted with an energy and intensity superior to that of the enemy and last for as long a time. At the first sign of an infantry attack a strong protective barrage must be at once placed close in front of the infantry throughout the length of the line attacked.

16. ZONE CALLS.

(See "Cooperation of Aircraft with Artillery," 1916, pars. 22–25.)

The zone-call system has proved its value in battle. Batteries should be specially detailed to answer zone calls and deliver an overwhelming fire on every target notified by this means. The material results are often great, but the moral effect is greater still. The hostile infantry feel that if they are seen moving even in a trench by an airman, a heavy fire is quickly brought to bear on them and their morale suffers accordingly.

Zone calls from the air have proved particularly useful while the infantry are consolidating under cover of the protective barrage. Targets presented by bombing parties preparing to attack our "stops," local reserves leaving their dugouts and larger bodies farther to the rear, forming up for counter attack can be quickly and effectively engaged by this means. It is for these reasons that, when arranging barrages, some batteries should always be earmarked to receive and act upon these calls, most particularly at that period when the final objective has been gained.

17. INFORMATION AND COMMUNICATION.[1]

The chief trouble of the artillery is lack of information during the first hours of the battle, for infantry find it extremely difficult to report their exact positions in a shelled country whence all landmarks have disappeared.

---

[1] See Section III, paragraph 8, of "Instructions for the Training of Divisions for Offensive Action."

Reliable communications and constant touch between artillery and infantry commanders are essential to successful cooperation; but difficult to achieve in the actual course of a battle. Every possible means must be considered and utilized where suitable; telephone, signaling apparatus, wireless sets, rockets, flares, light pistols, carrier pigeons, messenger dogs, and, above all, runners. For the first hour or so after the assault, until communications can be well established, the difficulty of maintaining communication between the two arms is felt, and this difficulty increases when the artillery make their first advance.

Lights.—During these periods communication will generally be restricted by force of circumstances to calls for barrage fire by means of light signal rockets or light pistols. All such signals from the front line must be repeated back by intermediate stations, if necessary as far as the batteries themselves.

Visual signaling often proves a valuable adjunct for maintaining communication in difficult positions and can be used in combination with telephones and runners. The following system has been found useful:

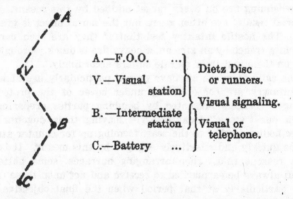

A.—F.O.O. ... ⎱
                 ⎰ Dietz Disc
V.—Visual   or runners.
      station ⎰
                 ⎱ Visual signaling.
B.—Intermediate
      station ⎰
                 ⎱ Visual or
C.—Battery ...   telephone.

" *Colored flags,* carried by one or two men in each platoon, can be used to indicate to the artillery the line gained by the leading infantry. These flags must not be stuck in the ground and will mean nothing unless they are waved; the poles should be short and blunted at the end. A combination of black and yellow on a flag about 18 inches square is the easiest to observe."

" *Flares.*—The position of the leading infantry has been successfully indicated to aeroplane observers (and so transmitted to the artillery) by the lighting of flares at certain prearranged times or at an agreed signal from the aeroplane." [1]

Special artillery observing stations have already been mentioned as a means of great value for watching the progress of the infantry (see par. 5, Sec. IV).

Artillery command posts have also been discussed so far as regards their position (see par. 6, Sec. IV). The work of the heavy artillery is so intimately connected with that of the field artillery that direct communication should always be established between divisional artillery commanders and commanders of either corps heavy artillery or of heavy artillery groups, according to the artillery plan; so that in the stages subsequent to the assault no time may be lost in rapid intercommunication and consequent action when required.

Battery commanders must be where they can best see the general situation. Once the attack has been launched this changes so rapidly that there is often no time to receive orders from higher commanders, and battery commanders must be prepared to act instantaneously on their own initiative, of course informing their brigade or group commander of the action taken.

18. THE ARTILLERY ADVANCE.

Artillery on the move is for the time being useless and the advance, particularly that of heavy artillery, is a lengthy process unless it has been worked out in every detail.

Continuity of artillery in action can only be obtained if its advance is made by echelons and practically without interruption.

The next positions must be decided, at least approximately, for each brigade or group and the time when it will probably have to move must be considered.

In order to assist the necessary continuity of artillery fire it will often be advantageous to place certain batteries in action close to the front trenches, with the proviso that they do not open fire before the attack takes place. Such positions must be carefully concealed.

Additional positions in this area may be earmarked, or even prepared, for other artillery and should be capable of early occupation. Even if the emplacements can not be dug, it should be

---

[1] See Section III, paragraph 8, of "Instructions for the Training of Divisions for Offensive Action."

possible to do much toward preparing the artillery boards, communications, and approaches. Here again camouflage must be freely employed.

The provisional selection of positions between the trenches or beyond the enemy's front line must be based upon study of the map and air photographs, assisted by personal reconnaissance from observing stations.

For all positions that are not constructed before the attack (see Appendix III), the artillery commander and the general staff concerned must consider the provision of labor. The mass of artillery will have been at work almost unceasingly since the opening of the bombardment and, if their fire is to be reopened after movement with minimum delay, every endeavor should be made to assist the batteries with personnel for labor.

The amount of artillery that is called upon to advance early will of course vary directly as the measure of success is attained; but, whatever the number of batteries involved, support of the infantry remains the foremost consideration. As the infantry push well ahead, the first step in their distant support is assured by means of those batteries which have been placed right forward. The first batteries to move will be certain field batteries and a proportion of the more mobile heavy artillery units (60-pounders and 6-inch howitzers) which must have been earmarked for this duty. If it is possible to relieve these batteries of any participation in the first phases of the battle, their subsequent movement can be made at short notice. Their routes must have been ordered in advance and improved where necessary. Beyond this again it will naturally follow as a principle that the most retired batteries must be moved forward early, before the battle line progresses beyond the limits of their range and while the more advanced batteries have sufficient range left to cover their movement without unduly weakening the artillery support.

While field artillery is in motion, an increased responsibility will be thrown on the heavy artillery as regards the direct support of the infantry and this also must be arranged for.

Careful organization is necessary for the proper command of guns pushed forward battery by battery, particularly in the case of heavy batteries. These latter must either be attached to divisions or, if it is desired to retain them under Corps control, may be organized to form a special heavy artillery group under a selected commander.

APPENDIX I.

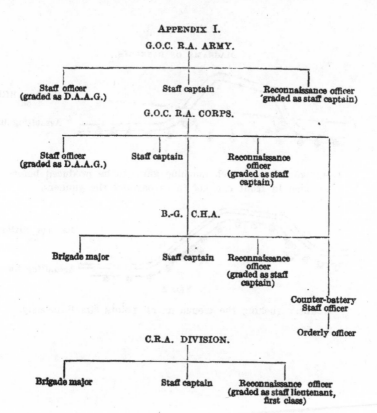

G.O.C. R.A. ARMY.

Staff officer (graded as D.A.A.G.) — Staff captain — Reconnaissance officer (graded as staff captain)

G.O.C. R.A. CORPS.

Staff officer (graded as D.A.A.G.) — Staff captain — Reconnaissance officer (graded as staff captain)

B.-G. C.H.A.

Brigade major — Staff captain — Reconnaissance officer (graded as staff captain)

Counter-battery Staff officer

Orderly officer

C.R.A. DIVISION.

Brigade major — Staff captain — Reconnaissance officer (graded as staff lieutenant, first class)

DIAGRAMS OF BARRAGES.

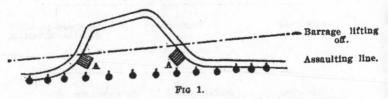

FIG 1.

A.—Dugout from which machine gun can be produced before men in front can get in to bayonet the gunners.

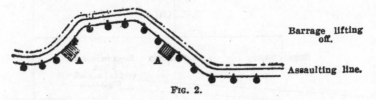

FIG. 2.

Infantry rushing the trench at all points simultaneously.

SCHEME OF WORK TO BE UNDERTAKEN BY A BATTERY TO OBTAIN
COVER WHEN IT HAS ADVANCED TO A NEW POSITION BEYOND OUR
OLD FRONT-LINE TRENCHES.

1. Dig a pit for each gun deep enough for the gun to fire at
the lowest angle of depression when just clearing the ground
level.

The pit should be as small as possible consistent with the
quick working of the gun and the maximum switch which may
be required. The exact measurements should be worked out
beforehand for varying angles of maximum switch. The excavated earth must be thrown to the sides and back of the pit,
making a parapet not more than 1 or 2 feet above ground level
around the pit, except at the front.

2. Camouflage the pit as far as possible; a tarpaulin over the
gun, stretched across the pit, is a good method for use when the
guns are not in action and wire netting stuffed with grass or
other means of camouflage are not available.

3. Connect up the gun pits by digging a zigzag trench 3 feet
wide at the bottom and 5 feet deep; when matériel is available
the trench should be camouflaged by roofing; a deep covering
of earth should not be allowed on the roof.

4. If matériel for cross strutting the top of the trench is
available, this trench should then be deepened in places to 7
feet, but if strutting matériel is not available the shallower
trench is the safer.

(A well-strutted trench, 7 feet deep, affords better cover than
hastily constructed dugouts.)

5. Construct ammunition recesses near the gun pits. In the
case of the heavier natures of artillery these can only be used
for cartridges.

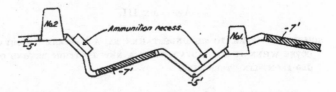

PLAN.

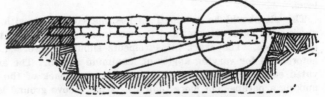

Sectional elevation through center of pit.

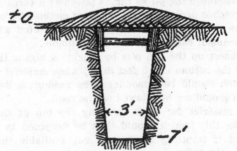

Sectional elevation of deep part of trench.

ESTIMATE OF THE AVERAGE AMOUNT OF AMMUNITION REQUIRED PER GUN OR HOWITZER, UNDER NORMAL CONDITIONS, FOR SEVEN DAYS' "ALL OUT" FIGHTING—TO BE PLACED AT THE GUNS OR WITHIN EASY REACH.

Estimate for an army.

Nature.	Rate per day.	Total for 7 days.
18-pounder	200	1,400
4.5-inch howitzer	150	1,050
60-pounder	150	1,050
6-inch gun	100	700
6-inch howitzer	150	1,050
8-inch howitzer	110	770
9.2-inch howitzer	110	770
12-inch howitzer	70	490
15-inch howitzer	25	175

N. B.—Individual batteries may require more ammunition according to their positions and tasks.

AMMUNITION IN RELATION TO TASKS.

The following figures may be taken as a rough guide to the amount of ammunition required for the tasks specified under normal conditions and for medium ranges:

Task.	Weapon.	No. of rounds.
1. Wire-cutting........	18-pdr............	7½ rounds (shrapnel) + 5 % H.E. per yard of front, for a depth of wire not exceeding the 50% zone of the gun at the range.
	2″ T.M..........	(Fuse percussion No. 107—Instantaneous) 1 round per 10 square yards of barbed wire. 1 round per 6 square yards of loose wire.
2. Trenches — frontal fire— (a) Destruction of selected points, averaging 30 yards apart.	2″ T.M..........	100 rounds per point, *i. e.*, 3½ rounds per yard run.
	6″ or 8″ How....	80 rounds per point, *i. e.*, 2¾ rounds per yard run.
	9.2″ How.......	60 rounds per point, *i. e.*, 2 rounds per yard run. This expenditure should entail a general measure of destruction of the trench between selected points.
(b) Total destruction	2″ T.M	5 rounds per yard.
	6″ or 8″ How....	4 rounds per yard.
	9.2″ How.......	3 rounds per yard.
3. Trenches — enfilade fire.	2″ T.M.......... 6″, 8″ and 9.2″ Hows.	Allow one-half of the above rates.
	18-pdr............	20 rounds (H.E.) per yard—for total destruction.
4. Machine gun emplacement (roof of 3 rows of pit-props); if stronger use 9.2″ Hows. or 9.45″ T.M. only.	2″ T.M..........	80 rounds (assuming top cover does not exceed 3′ earth).
	6″ or 8″ How...	65 rounds (assuming top cover does not exceed 3′ earth).
	9.2″ How.......	50 rounds (assuming top cover does not exceed 3′ earth).
	9.45″ T.M.......	50 rounds (assuming top cover does not exceed 3′ earth).

Task.	Weapon.	No. of Rounds.
5. Very strong points (concrete roofs or deep dugouts).	8″ How.........	130 rounds per point.
	9.2″ How.......	100 rounds per point.
	12″ How........	{ 75 rounds up to 9,500 yards. {100 rounds over 9,500 yards.
6. Cellars..............	9.2″ How.......	8 rounds }
	12″ How........	4 rounds } per 100 square yards of actual cellar area.
	15″ How........	4 rounds }
7. Houses..............	6″ How.........	12 rounds }
	8″ How.........	10 rounds } per 100 square yards of actual built-over area.
	9.2″ How.......	8 rounds }
8. To prevent repair of damaged defences.	18-pdr..........	250 rounds per 12 hours per 300 yards length of target.
9. Night firing on communications.	18-pdr..........	50 rounds per point per hour.
	4.5″ or 6″ How. or 60-pdr.	35 rounds per point per hour.
10. Smoke barrages ...	18-pdr..........	2 rounds per 10 yards per minute.
	4.5″ How.......	Groups of 8 shell at 200 yards interval per 2 minutes.
11. Gas shell	4.5″ How.......	See "Instructions on the Use of Lethal and Lachrymatory Shell"—O. B. 816.
	60-pdr..........	

7

INSTRUCTIONS FOR THE TRAINING OF PLATOONS FOR OFFENSIVE ACTION

SS 143, published in February 1917, was one of the most important British infantry manuals published during the war. It marked a revolution in tactics for the infantry, devised from the experience of combat during the Somme and the French army's own operations. Essentially it marked an end to lines of infantry soldiers attacking with a few separate 'specialist' sections (machine gunners, hand-grenade, rifle-grenade sections). Now the platoon had more specialists, fully integrated with the traditional riflemen which still made up the majority of the platoon as a combat unit. It represented a much more flexible, modern approach, made the most of new equipment, and was based on a better understanding of the organisation necessary to exploit this equipment in battle.

INSTRUCTIONS FOR THE TRAINING OF PLATOONS FOR OFFENSIVE ACTION, 1917.

PART I.—ORGANIZATION AND TACTICS.

1. Organization of a Platoon.

The platoon is the smallest unit in the field which comprises all the weapons with which the Infantry soldier is armed. It has a minimum strength, exclusive of its headquarters, of 28 O. R. and a maximum of 44 O. R. If the strength falls below the minimum, the platoon ceases to be workable, and the necessary numbers will be obtained by the temporary almalgamation of companies, platoons, or sections under battalion arrangements.

Taking an average strength in the sections of 36 O. R., a suitable organization would be as follows:

	Total O. R.
Headquarters—1 officer and 4 O. R.	4
1 section bombers—1 N. C. O. and 8 O. R. (includes 2 bayonet men and 2 throwers)	9
1 section Lewis gunners—1 N. C. O. and 8 O. R. (includes Nos. 1 and 2)	9
1 section riflemen—1 N. C. O. and 8 O. R. (picked shots, scouts, picked bayonet fighters)	9
1 section rifle bombers—1 N. C. O. and 8 O. R. (includes 4 bomb firers)	9
Total	36

Every N. C. O and man should carry a rifle and fix his bayonet for the assault, except Nos. 1 and 2 of Lewis gun and rifle bombers, if using a cup attachment.

2. Parade.

The platoon should parade in line, sections at two paces internal, or in column of sections; commanders should be two paces in front of their sections.

105280°—17——2

295

3. Ammunitiom, Bombs, etc., and how Carried.

In each section enough ammunition and bombs can be carried for immediate requirements.

In the trench-to-trench attack every man (except bombers, signalers, scouts, runners, and Lewis gunners who carry 50 rounds) carries at least 120 rounds S. A. A. and 2 or more bombs.

The Lewis gun section carries 30 drums (a good method is 2 haversacks joined with slings or braces, 1 on chest—2 drums; 1 on back—3 drums).

In bombing sections each thrower carries 5 bombs, and the remainder 10 or more each.

Every man in a rifle bomb section can carry at least 6 rifle bombs (a good method is a haversack carried on the back with six or more holes punched in the bottom to take the stick, canvas being attached to the haversack in shape of a bag to protect the sticks).

Flares must be distributed throughout sections.

Two P. bombs should be carried by each "mopper up" in addition to other descriptions.

Any further requirements in S.A.A. bombs, etc., must be met by carrying parties from other companies specially detailed.

In open warfare the number of bombs to be carried in the section of bombers and rifle bombs in rifle bomb sections may be regulated according to the objectives to be attacked.

4. Characteristics and Uses of the Various Weapons.

(*a*) The rifle and bayonet, being the most efficient offensive weapons of the soldier, are for assault, for repelling attack, or for obtaining superiority of fire. Every N.C.O. and man in the platoon must be proficient in their use.

(*b*) The bomb is the second weapon of every N.C.O. and man, and is used either for dislodging the enemy from behind cover or killing him below ground.

(*c*) The rifle bomb is the "howitzer" of the infantry and used to dislodge the enemy from behind cover and to obtain superiority of fire by driving him underground.

(*d*) The Lewis gun is the weapon of opportunity. Its chief uses are to kill the enemy above ground and to obtain superiority of fire. Its mobility and the small target it and its team present render it peculiarly suitable for working round an enemy's flank or for guarding one's own flank.

5. The Normal Formations for Platoons and Companies in the Attack.

A. Trench-to-Trench Attack.

The platoon.—Appendix I shows a platoon in 1st and 2nd waves. Appendix II shows a platoon in artillery formation of sections. These can move in fours, file or single file, according to the ground and other factors. Platoon H.Q. should move with that column best situated for purposes of command; this will usually be the rear section.

The company.—Appendix III shows the normal formation of a company in two waves, in which the formation of the platoon remains the same.

B. Open Warfare (Appendix IV).

The formation may conveniently be the same as the above when deployment first takes place. The first wave becomes the firing line, the second wave the supports.

" Moppers up " will not usually be required.

6. Working and Carrying Parties.

Working and carrying parties should be detailed by complete sections under their leaders, irrespective of the weapon with which they are armed. They should never be found by detailing a certain number of men from the platoon.

A platoon acting as a carrying party should move in file, the sergeant at the head with the guide, the platoon commander bringing up the rear. The pace at the head should be slow and section commanders must pass down word if they can not keep up.

When a platoon is detailed for a working party its commander, and no one else, is responsible for the quality and quantity of work performed; he can not take too much interest in this matter.

7. Tactics of a Platoon in Attack.

In either a trench-to-trench attack or in open warfare these resolve themselves in the majority of cases into the method of attack of tactical points.

A tactical point may be described as a locality, the possession of which is of first importance locally to either side. It may take the form of any of the following: A "strong point," the junction of a communication trench, a cross roads, a bank, a hedge, a house, or other locality of limited dimensions.

The tactics to be employed may be summarized as follows:

(i) Push on to the objective at all costs and get in with the bayonet.

(ii) If held up, obtain superiority of fire and envelop one or both flanks.

(iii) If reinforcing another platoon which is held up, help to obtain superiority of fire and envelop a flank.

(iv) Cooperate with platoons on either flank.

For purposes of instruction these may be considered under: A. Trench-to-trench attack; B. Attack in open warfare.

A. TRENCH-TO-TRENCH ATTACK (APPENDIXES VIII AND IX).

In regard to—

(i) No further comment is necessary, other than to lay stress on the point that waves must go direct above ground to their objective.

(ii) The action of the various sections and commanders should be as follows:

The section of riflemen should, without halting, gain a position on a flank from which to attack both with fire and with the bayonet.

The section of bombers should, without halting, gain a position on a flank and attack under cover of the bombardment of rifle bombs.

The section of rifle bombers should open a hurricane bombardment on the point of resistance from the nearest cover available.

The section of Lewis gunners should in the first instance open traversing fire on the point of resistance from the nearest cover available. At a later stage it may be desirable to work round a flank.

Section commanders control and lead their sections, keeping touch with the platoon commander.

The platoon commander controls and directs the sections and sends back information to the company commander.

(iii) One of the most important factors in the action of a platoon reinforcing another is that of its commander. He should make himself acquainted with the situation before he commits his platoon to any line of action. This is called the personal reconnaissance of the commander.

(iv) The means to be employed in cooperation depend so greatly upon the circumstances at the moment that it is impossible to lay down a definite line of action to adopt. Cooperation means help. If a neighboring platoon is held up, one of the surest ways of helping it is to push on. Touch must always be maintained; this can be effected by means of a patrol of two men, as well as by signal.

B. ATTACK IN OPEN WARFARE (APPENDIXES X TO XIII).

The line of action described above will usually be found suitable. Owing to the more extended field of action, however, the use of scouts and the personal reconnaissance of the platoon commander become of increased importance.

Great opportunities will also occur for mutual support from rifles or Lewis guns for the movement of neighboring sections and platoons.

8. THE TACTICS OF THE PLATOON IN DEFENSE.

In both trench and open warfare the action to be taken in the defense is practically the same, namely, to hold ground by occupying mutually supporting tactical points, so situated as to be screened from artillery fire, and to obtain—

(i) Observation.

(ii) Field of fire for all rifles.

(iii) Enfilade fire for the Lewis gun.

For these purposes the analogy between trench and open warfare is not far to seek. For instance, in occupying a captured position—

"Consolidation" in trench warfare corresponds to the occupation of an "outpost position" in open warfare.

"Observation posts" in trench warfare corresponds to "sentry groups" in open warfare.

"Strong points" in trench warfare corresponds to "picquets" in open warfare.

In both cases the necessity for visiting and reconnoitering patrols is equally important.

9. General Rules as to Tactics.

In regard to all tactical situations on the battlefield, the old principles are applicable both to trench warfare and to open warfare, and should become a second nature or subconscious habit. They may be summarized as follows:

(i) Aim at surprise, i. e., see without being seen. Do not let bayonets show over the parapet, and take care the assembly is not given away by perceptible movement.

(ii) Reconnoiter before movement; that is to say, work by "bounds," making ground good with scouts before advancing to it.

(iii) Protection. Never remain halted on the field of battle without a lookout. Sentries must be posted, no matter what troops are supposed to be in front.

(iv) The flanks. (a) Guard your own flanks and keep touch with neighboring units; (b) try and get the enemy's flank. For example: (a) In trench warfare booming and Lewis gun sections guard the outer flank and liaison is kept with neighboring units; in open warfare scouts must always be employed on an outer flank, one section, usually the Lewis gun section, must be told off to act in that direction if necessary, and touch must always be kept with troops on either flank. (b) Employ enveloping tactics.

(v) Send information back to your company commander. Negative information is as important as positive. You can not expect assistance from your superiors or from the artillery unless you tell them where you are and how you are situated.

(vi) Hold what you gain. Never withdraw from a position without being ordered to do so. If where you are is unhealthy and appears untenable owing to casualties, any attempt at withdrawal—anyhow in daylight—will end in increased casualties. Therefore, stay where you are and send back information.

PART II.—TRAINING.

1. To obtain uniformity of ideas and tactics it is necessary for the method to be followed in training platoons to be laid down on broad lines.

2. The requirements to be attained are:

(*a*) The offensive spirit. All ranks must be taught that their aim and object is to come to close quarters with the enemy as quickly as possible so as to be able to use the bayonet. This must become a second nature.

(*b*) Initiative. The matter of control by even company leaders on the battle field is now so difficult that the smaller formations—i. e., platoon and section commanders—must be trained to take the necessary action on their own initiative, without waiting for orders.

(*c*) Confidence in weapons, necessitating a high standard of skill at arms.

(*d*) Cooperation of weapons is essential on the battle field, and is the corollary of (*c*).

(*e*) Discipline is most necessary at all times, and particularly on the battle field.

(*f*) Morale must be heightened by every possible means; confidence in leaders and weapons goes a long way toward it.

(*g*) Esprit de corps. True soldierly spirit must be built up in sections and platoons. Each section should consider itself the best section in the platoon, and the platoon the best in the battalion.

3. The method of attaining these requirements is as follows:

(i) The platoon commander should divide the time allotted to him for training into two periods, the first being devoted to individual and section training and the second to collective or platoon training and tactical exercises.

(ii) Training should be progressive, beginning with section drill without arms, saluting, etc. working up to battle formations and tactical exercises.

15

(iii) A refresher course every evening for section leaders, in which the next day's work should be gone through, is essential : if they are shaky in it, they should practice it then and there.

(iv) A high standard of skill at arms can only be produced by both the platoon commander and platoon sergeant being proficient in the use of and able to impart instruction in all the weapons with which the platoon is armed.

(v) Soldierly spirit in the platoon and sections is obtained by encouraging section leaders to take a pride in their sections and in their work. The formation adopted in falling in on platoon parades tends to bring this about. Section leaders should inspect their sections before the platoon commander inspects the platoon, and they should report them correct or otherwise. At evening entertainments and lectures regimental history and accounts of skill at arms and feats of daring on the battle field should be given prominence.

All ranks must be trained in the following :

(vi) Steady drill and ceremonial are necessary to inculcate discipline, of which cleanliness, smartness, and steadiness are the bedrock.

(vii) Bayonet fighting produces lust for blood ; much may be accomplished in billets in wet weather, as well as out of doors on fine days.

(viii) Bomb throwing and duties of moppers-up require practice and careful study. Moppers-up should work in pairs under their own commander. They drop into their objective and work laterally outward. They kill any enemy met with in the trenches and guard the entrances to dugouts and side trenches. They must not penetrate down into the dugouts before the platoon for which they are mopping up arrives.

(ix) Musketry : Too much stress can not be laid on practicing the standard tests laid down in musketry regulations. These can be practiced in billets on wet days just as well as out of doors. Tripods and aim correctors are easily improvised. Good bolt manipulation, produced chiefly by the application of the standard tests in the barrack room on wet days, kept the enemy out of our trenches at the beginning of the war, when such luxuries as wire entanglements were not forthcoming. Ranges also are easily improvised.

(x) Physical fitness : Route marching, physical training, and recreational training, such as football, paper chases, etc. These latter are best carried out on Wednesday and Saturday afternoons, which, if training is progressing satisfactorily, may be half holidays.

(xi) Fire discipline.

(xii) Wiring.

(xiii) Field works and filing on tasks: The placing of frames for mined dugouts may suitably be included in platoon training.

(xiv) Work in the field: Tactical exercises in which the use of ground and choice of cover in both trench and open warfare must receive close attention are most necessary. An intelligent use of ground frequently enables forward movement to be made without loss. In choice of cover, as a general rule, anything marked on a map or very well defined should, if possible, be avoided to obviate casualties from shell fire. Such exercises can be carried out, as a rule, within a few hundred yards of billets; it is seldom necessary to waste time by going too far afield, except when route marching and march discipline is being practiced. Schemes should comprise the attack of tactical points in trench and open warfare, the action of a platoon, as vanguard to an advance guard, an outpost picket, etc. The platoon sergeant and section commanders can be usefully trained by this means when the men are otherwise employed; it enhances their powers of initiative.

(xv) Gas drill, including bombing, bayonet fighting, and musketry with masks or box respirators on.

Sections must be exercised in their particular weapon:

(xvi) The bombing section in bombing attack.

(xvii) The rifle bombing section in quickly forming a rifle bomb bombardment or barrage.

(xviii) The Lewis gun section in coming into action and opening fire quickly.

(xix) The rifle section. The training of this section is very important. Each man should be a marksman, first-class with bayonet and bomb, and a scout, in addition to being either a Lewis gunner or rifle bomber.

Training in certain other subjects is necessary for certain individuals:

(xx) Section commanders. Fire control and description of targets, map reading, observation, and information. Salient points in writing messages. Simple tactical exercises.

(xxi) Scouts and snipers. Map reading, observation, information, and salient points in writing messages and use of appliances. Each section should produce a pair.

(xxii) Runners and dispatch carriers. How to find an individual and how to deliver a message.

Certain training must be practiced by night as well as day, namely:

(xxiii) Bayonet fighting, bomb throwing, Lewis gun firing, musketry, wiring, running and dispatch carrying, and tactical exercises.

(xxiv) Live ammunition. No form of instruction with arms can be considered complete until it has been carried out with live ammunition under conditions as nearly as possible approaching those which would pertain on the battle field.

(xxv) Competitions. Each form of instruction should be made the subject of a competition, from saluting and clean turnout up to musketry, accuracy of rifle bombs, scouting, sniping, etc., etc. Prizes are seldom necessary for such competitions, if the result is published in battalion orders.

(xxvi) Thoroughness. As regards dress and arrangements generally, no part of the training should be perfunctory; that is to say, nothing should be left to the imagination; work must always be based on the actual ground and situation as they exist. The turnout should always be in fighting order, with haversacks properly packed and with the full complement of arms and ammunition which would be carried in battle.

PART III.—GENERAL REMARKS.

A platoon commander will have gone a long way toward having a well-trained platoon if he has gained the confidence of his noncommissioned officers and men and has established a high soldierly spirit in all ranks.

The confidence of his men can be gained by—

(a) Being the best man at arms in the platoon, or trying to be so.

(b) Being quick to act, taking real command on all occasions, issuing clear orders, and not forgetting to see them carried out.

(c) Example, being himself well turned out, punctual, and cheery even under adverse circumstances.

(d) Enforcing strict discipline at all times. This must be a willing discipline, not a sulky one. Be just, but do not be soft—men despise softness.

(e) Recognizing a good effort, even if it is not really successful. A word of praise when deserved produces better results than incessant faultfinding.

(f) Looking after his men's comfort before his own and never sparing himself.

(g) Demanding a high standard on all occasions, and never resting content with what he takes over, be it on the battle field or in billets. Everything is capable of improvement from information on the battle field down to latrines and washing places in billets.

(h) Being bloodthirsty, and forever thinking how to kill the enemy and helping his men to do so.

The platoon commander should be the proudest man in the Army. He is commander of the unit in the attack. He is the only commander who can know intimately the character and capabilities of each man under him. He can, if he is so disposed, establish an esprit de platoon which will be hard to equal in any other formation.

The Platoon, Taking an Average Strength of 36 and H.Q. 4—Formation for Trench-to-Trench Attack.

(Showing 2 platoons in 2 waves, with the right the outer flank.)

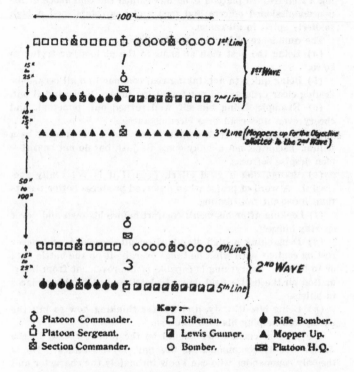

Key :—

○ Platoon Commander.	□ Rifleman.	● Rifle Bomber.
⊕ Platoon Sergeant.	◪ Lewis Gunner.	▲ Mopper Up.
⊠ Section Commander.	○ Bomber.	⊠ Platoon H.Q.

NOTES.

Two platoons are depicted, showing the different positions of leaders in first and second waves.

The platoon is the unit in the assault, moves in one wave of two lines, and has one definite objective.

Every man is a rifleman and a bomber, and in the assault, with the exception of the No. 1 and No. 2 of the Lewis gun, fixes his bayonet. Men in rifle sections must be trained either to the Lewis gun or rifle bomb.

Bombing and Lewis gun sections are on the outer flank of platoons.

In assembly, the distance between lines and waves may conveniently be reduced to lessen the danger of rear waves being caught in enemy barrage, the distance being increased when the advance takes place.

"Moppers up" follow the second line of a wave and precede the unit for which they are to mop up. If the numbers are large, they must be found from a different company or battalion. Small numbers are preferably found from the unit for which they are to mop up. They must carry a distinctive badge and have their own commander.

G.S.

O.B. No. 1919/T

APPENDIX II.

The Platoon in Artillery Formation with the Right the Outer Flank.

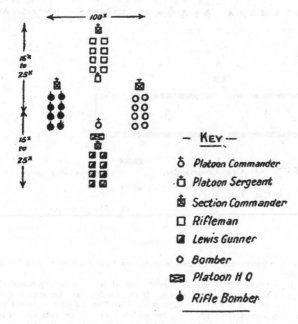

— KEY —

ठ *Platoon Commander*

ठ *Platoon Sergeant*

䨑 *Section Commander*

☐ *Rifleman*

◼ *Lewis Gunner*

○ *Bomber*

⬛ *Platoon H Q*

● *Rifle Bomber*

NOTES.

Sections move in fours, file, or single file, according to the ground and other factors of the case.

Platoon H.Q. moves with that column best suited for purposes of command.

The Company, Taking 4 Average Strength Platoons of 36 O.R. and Coy. H.Q. 14.—Formation for Trench-to-Trench Attack.

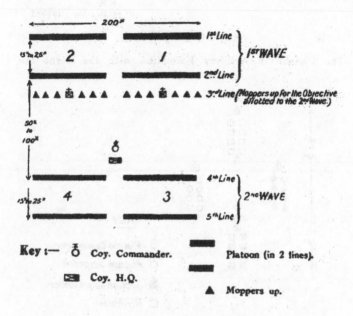

Key :—

ठ Coy. Commander.

Coy. H.Q.

▲ Moppers up.

Platoon (in 2 lines).

NOTES.

The company moves in two waves, has two objectives, and is distributed in depth.

"Moppers up" follow the second line of a wave and precede the unit for which they are to mop up. If the numbers are large they must be found from a different company or battalion. Small numbers are preferably found from the unit for which they are to mop up. They must carry a distinctive badge and have their own commander.

G.S.
O.B. No. 1919/T

The Platoon, Taking an Average Strength of 36 and H.Q. 4.— Formation for Attack in Open Warfare.

(Showing two platoons in two lines, with the right the outer flanks.)

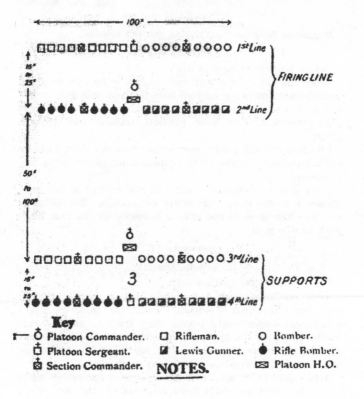

Key

Ŏ Platoon Commander.	□ Rifleman.	O Bomber.
Ḃ Platoon Sergeant.	◪ Lewis Gunner.	● Rifle Bomber.
⊠ Section Commander.		⊠ Platoon H.O.

NOTES.

NOTES.

Two platoons are depicted showing the different positions of leaders in firing line and supports.

The platoon is the unit, has one definite objective, and can move in two lines, as above, or form one line as circumstances dictate. Two lines are most easily obtained from artillery formation.

Every man is a rifleman and a bomber, and in the assault, with the exception of the No. 1 of Lewis gun, fixes his bayonet. Men in rifle sections must be trained either to the Lewis gun or rifle bomb.

Bombing and Lewis-gun sections are on the outer flank of platoons.

The number of bombs and rifle grenades to be carried will be decided by the nature of the objective distance to be traversed and other considerations.

G.S.
O.B. No. 1919/T

APPENDIX V.

Suggested daily program during summer months:

FIRST PERIOD.

Before breakfast: Section drill.

After breakfast: One hour each section in its own weapons, the rifle sections being allotted half to the Lewis gun section and half to the rifle bomb section. One hour the whole platoon bomb throwing. One hour physical training and bayonet fighting.

Finish the morning with ceremonial; that is to say, form up and march past the platoon or company commander on the way to dinner.

After dinner: Communicating drill and control of fire drill. Musketry on the range alternately by sections. Recreation at 4 p. m. Noncommissioned officers refreshed in the next day's work at 6.30 p. m.

APPENDIX VI.

SECOND PERIOD.

Before breakfast: Platoon drill.

After breakfast: Half hour whole platoon bomb throwing. One hour instruction in wiring, digging, and filing on tasks; scouts and snipers—information, map reading, and message writing; runners and dispatch carriers; moppers up. One hour physical and bayonet training. Last half hour fire control and fire discipline. Ceremonial on the way to dinner.

After dinner: Simple tactical schemes. Recreation at 4 p. m. Noncommissioned officers refreshed in the next day's work at 6.30 p. m. Simple tactical schemes.

NOTE TO SUGGESTED PROGRAM.

For examples of exercises in the field both in trench-to-trench attack and in open warfare see Appendixes VII to XIII.

If training is progressing satisfactorily, half-holidays should be allowed on Wednesdays and Saturdays.

Men who prove themselves efficient should be excused certain parades. Individual keenness is easily promoted and easily rewarded.

During winter months work should not begin till after breakfasts, e. g., at 8.30 a. m. The half-holidays are of greater importance than during the summer, because on other days there is not sufficient light after 4 p. m. for games.

Smoking concerts and lectures should be given on Wednesday and Saturday evenings.

Appendix VII.

EXAMPLES OF USEFUL EXERCISES IN OPEN WARFARE.

1. *Advance or flank-guard schemes.*—The platoon finding the advance parties is held up by a tactical point, necessitating a fight. (See Appendixes X and XII.)

Points to be watched:

(i) The use of ground and scouts.

(ii) The correct use of weapons.

(iii) The plan should be that of enveloping tactics.

2. *Outpost schemes.*—This should involve the placing of each individual on the actual ground. For instance, sentry groups, the sentry over the picket, reliefs for visiting and reconnoitering patrols, deciding what points are to be held, and how they are to be held in event of attack, the placing of the Lewis gun.

3. A tactical point is encountered with a machine gun. Tactics of the supporting platoon. Particular attention should be paid to the personal reconnaissance of the commander to the use of ground and weapons, and to the plan, which should be of the nature of enveloping tactics. (See Appendixes VIII, IX, X, and XII.)

4. *Village fighting.*—In this the Lewis gun can be employed to keep down the enemy's rifle fire, while bayonet men and bombers bound down the right-hand side of the street, clearing house by house. It is always better, if possible, to enter a house from the back rather than the front.

5. *Wood fighting.*—A line of skirmishers who fire while advancing (v. par. 8 of S. S. 135, Instructions for the Training of Divisions for Offensive Action), followed by sections in small columns, has been found a convenient formation. Much attention to keeping direction is necessary.

APPENDIX VIII.

Trench-to-Trench Attack—Platoon in First Wave Meeting a Point of Resistance.

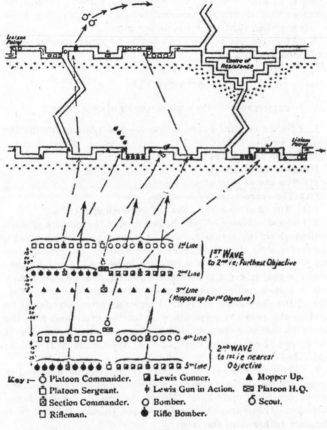

Key :—
Ǒ Platoon Commander.   ◪ Lewis Gunner.   ▲ Mopper Up.
◻ Platoon Sergeant.   ⚲ Lewis Gun in Action.   ⊠ Platoon H.Q.
◙ Section Commander.   ○ Bomber.   Ǒ Scout.
◻ Rifleman.   ● Rifle Bomber.

NOTE.

The position of the commander.

The rifle bombs and Lewis gun fire and rifle fire are obtaining superiority over the enemey's fire.

The bombers and riflemen have gone straight above ground to their objective, where they are turning the flank of the center of resistance.

The use of scouts and liaison patrols.

The "moppers up" are guarding the entrances to dugouts and communication trenches.

Trench-to-Trench Attack—Platoon in Second Wave Meeting a Point of Resistance.

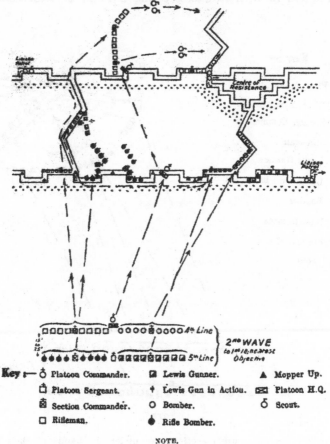

Key :—
Ȯ Platoon Commander.
☐̇ Platoon Sergeant.
☒ Section Commander.
☐ Rifleman.

☒ Lewis Gunner.
✚ Lewis Gun in Action.
○ Bomber.
⬤ Rifle Bomber.

▲ Mopper Up.
▭ Platoon H.Q.
Ȯ Scout.

NOTE.

The commander of the second wave gets in touch with the situation on reaching his objective through the commander of his moppers up and the commander of the first wave. He then decides to help the first wave, the commander of which goes on to his own objective.

Note, especially in the action of the various sections, the attack above ground.

Attack in Open Warfare—Correct Method of Action of a Platoon in Firing Line, Meeting a Point of Resistance.

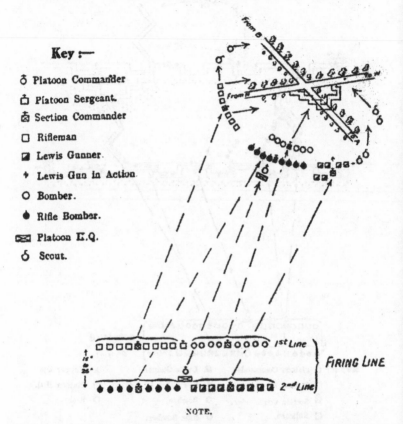

Key :—

⚇ Platoon Commander

⚇ Platoon Sergeant.

⚇ Section Commander

☐ Rifleman

▨ Lewis Gunner.

✚ Lewis Gun in Action.

○ Bomber.

● Rifle Bomber.

▧ Platoon H.Q.

⚇ Scout.

1st Line

2nd Line

FIRING LINE

NOTE.

Correct use of scouts. Sections are under the hands of their commanders. A firing line has been built up, rifle, bombs, Lewis gun fire, and rifle fire are being used to obtain superiority over enemy fire. A flank is being turned.

APPENDIX XI.

Attack in Open Warfare—Incorrect Method of a Platoon in Firing Line, Meeting a Point of Resistance.

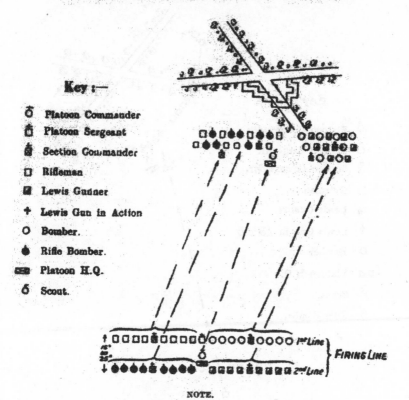

Key :—

⚲ Platoon Commander
⚲ Platoon Sergeant
⚲ Section Commander
◻ Rifleman
◼ Lewis Gunner
✚ Lewis Gun in Action
○ Bomber.
● Rifle Bomber.
▭ Platoon H.Q.
δ Scout.

NOTE.

No scouts are employed. Sections are mixed up and not under the hands of their commanders. No firing line has been built up. No attempt at enveloping tactics is being made.

APPENDIX XII.

Open Warfare—Correct Method of Action of a Platoon in Support.

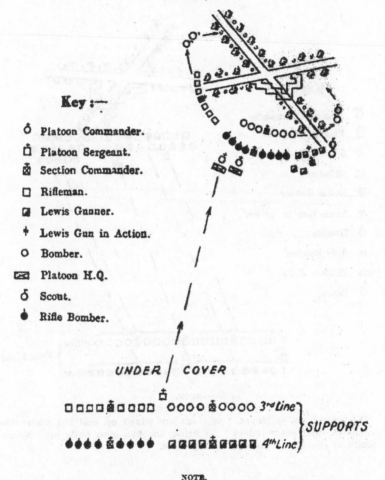

Key :—

○̇ Platoon Commander.

☐̇ Platoon Sergeant.

⊠̆ Section Commander.

☐ Rifleman.

◪ Lewis Gunner.

✝ Lewis Gun in Action.

○ Bomber.

▱ Platoon H.Q.

○̇ Scout.

● Rifle Bomber.

UNDER | COVER

☐☐☐☐⊠○☐☐☐   ○○○○⊠○○○○ *3ʳᵈ Line* }

} *SUPPORTS*

●●●●⊠●●●●   ◪◪◪◪⊠◪◪◪◪ *4ᵗʰ Line* }

NOTE.

The platoon commander is seen making his personal reconnaissance some hundred yards ahead, with the platoon waiting under cover under platoon sergeant. On result of this reconnaissance he can act on either flank, dependent on the ground and the situation.

Open Warfare—Incorrect Method of Action of a Platoon in Support.

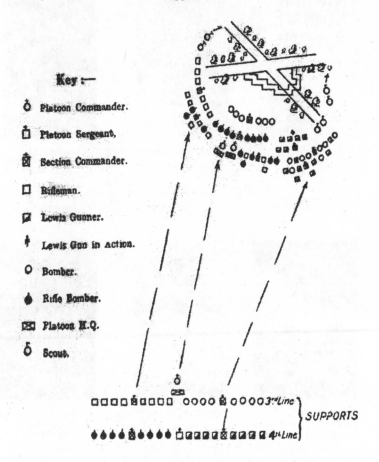

Key :—

ȏ Platoon Commander.

Ȋ Platoon Sergeant,

☒ Section Commander.

☐ Rifleman.

◪ Lewis Gunner.

☥ Lewis Gun in action.

O Bomber.

● Rifle Bomber.

▨ Platoon H.Q.

ȏ Scout.

SUPPORTS

3rd Line

4th Line

NOTE.

The platoon commander of the supports is shown as having led his platoon right up to the platoon already engaged, where it arrives in confusion. He has made no personal reconnaissance and is committed to one flank only. This line of action could only be adopted where good cover exists immediately in rear of platoon engaged, in which case even, the platoon commander should have gone ahead and finished his personal reconnaissance by the time his platoon arrives.

O

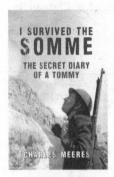

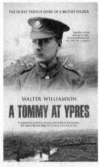

First World War Books from Amberley

VERDUN
William F. Buckingham
£20 HB
978-1-4456-4108-9
320 pages, 40 illustrations

THE TOMMIES MANUAL 1916
Hannah Holman
£9.99 PB
978-1-4456-3822-5
320 pages, 80 illustrations

THE GREAT WAR COOK BOOK
May Byron
£9.99 PB
978-1-4456-3388-6
240 pages, 20 illustrations

FIRST WORLD WAR IN THE AIR
Phil Carradice
£14.99 PB
978-1-4456-0512-8
192 pages, 100 illustrations

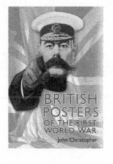

BRITISH POSTERS OF THE FIRST WORLD WAR
John Christopher
£20 HB
978-1-4456-3316-9
192 pages, 259 illustrations

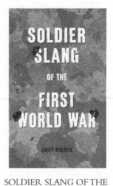

SOLDIER SLANG OF THE FIRST WORLD WAR
Emily Brewer
£12.99 PB
978-1-4456-3783-9
224 pages

ALSO AVAILABLE AS EBOOKS
Available from all good bookshops or to order direct
Please call **01453-847-800**
www.amberleybooks.com